Television at the Movies

Television at the Movies

Cinematic and Critical Approaches
to American Broadcasting

Jon Nelson Wagner
and
Tracy Biga MacLean

continuum

NEW YORK • LONDON

2008

The Continuum International Publishing Group Inc
80 Maiden Lane, New York, NY 10038

The Continuum International Publishing Group Ltd
The Tower Building, 11 York Road, London SE1 7NX

www.continuumbooks.com

Printed in the United States of America

Library of Congress Cataloging-in-Publication Data

Wagner, Jon Nelson.
  Television at the movies : cinematic and critical approaches to American
broadcasting / Jon Nelson Wagner and Tracy Biga MacLean.
      p. cm.
  Includes bibliographical references.
  ISBN-13: 978-0-8264-2962-9 (hardcover : alk. paper)
  ISBN-10: 0-8264-2962-9 (hardcover : alk. paper)
  ISBN-13: 978-0-8264-2963-6 (pbk. : alk. paper)
  ISBN-10: 0-8264-2963-7 (pbk. : alk. paper)
  1. Motion pictures and television.
  2. Television in motion pictures. I. MacLean, Tracy Biga. II. Title.

PN1992.63.W34 2008
791.4509—dc22

                                                      2008000798

Table of Contents

Acknowledgments

We would like to acknowledge the inspiration of our late teacher Beverle Houston, and the continuing support of our advisor Marsha Kinder. In addition, we would like to thank our colleagues at the California Institute of Arts and the Claremont Colleges, including Alexandra Juhasz, James Morrison, Lauri Mullens, and Dwayne Moser, as well as our many fine students. Steve Erickson was essential in his encouragement and perspective, and we received valuable help from our close friends Chris Lippard and Gregg Daskalogrigorakis. We also thank our families—our wonderful mothers, Pauline Wagner and Janice Biga; Tracy's husband, Duncan MacLean; and constant companion to our endeavors, Rabbit.

This book had its origins in a friendship that began at the University of Southern California School of Cinematic Arts. We would like to thank all of our teachers, colleagues, and students in that great program.

1

Introduction

It is as impossible to discuss television without a qualification of terms, as it would be to discuss cinema in its entirety or, for that matter, novels or poetry as a whole. Nevertheless, television has been addressed as a monolithic presence in its cultural setting far more frequently than have cinematic or literary forms. By unpacking the major themes of how one prominent art form of the twentieth century represents another aesthetic, in what we call the "cinema of television," we seek to accomplish multiple goals: first, to think of television as made up of distinct modes—some historically sequential, some simultaneous; second, to engage with what has been called "intermedia studies" and to develop a close and critical reading of how an established medium engages with a newer, but related, one[1]; and finally, to trace how cinematic attitudes and critical models are duplicated in television scholarship and criticism. To accomplish these goals, we utilize a double, often parallel, canon, that of films and critical writing about television; we also utilize a less-developed canon, that of the televisual text.

The films we select for close analysis, though not comprehensive as a group, have been chosen for several reasons. They all, in various ways, represent widespread attitudes about television. Their expressions are clear and pointed, even when these are expressions of confusion. Equally important is to note that the films we discuss in depth extend beyond our specific concerns and carry multiple resonances. Many have won both popular and critical acclaim. For practical reasons, the films we have selected are available on videotape and/or DVD. In the interest of focus (and reflecting, no doubt, our personal preferences), we discuss primarily American films. Their dates of production range from Elia Kazan's *A Face in the Crowd* (1957) to Warren Beatty's *Bulworth* (1998), with subordinate consideration of films as recent as European auteur

1

Michael Haneke's *Caché* (2006). While the films are mainly auteurist and post–studio system, they function largely within the values of classical Hollywood cinema and are often committed to a concept of cinematic purity, if not elitism.

Many of the issues discussed here could also be identified in foreign films such as Michelangelo Antonioni's *Professione: Reporter* (1975, Italy); Bertrand Tavernier's *La Mort en direct* (1980, France/Germany); Federico Fellini's *Ginger e Fred* (1986, Italy); Maurizio Nichetti's *Ladri di Saponette* (1989, Italy); Benoit Poelvoorde's *C'est arrivé près de chez vous* (1991, Belgium); or Michel Poulette's *Louis 19th, le roi des ondes* (1994, Canada/France); or in films produced before 1957, such as Marcel L'Herbier's *L'Inhumaine* (1924, France); Clifford Sanforth's *Murder by Television* (1935); or Donald Siegel's *Invasion of the Body Snatchers* (1956). Nor has the impulse that inspired these films been exhausted in the United States, as can be seen by the continuing production of films about television, some significant examples being Barry Levinson's *Wag the Dog* (1997); Gary Ross's *Pleasantville* (1998); Peter Weir's *The Truman Show* (1998); Ron Howard's *EDtv* (1999); Spike Lee's *Bamboozled* (2000); Daniel Minahan's *Series 7: The Contenders* (2001); Gore Verbinski's *The Ring* (2002); and Jake Kasdan's *The TV Set* (2006).

In addition to many films about television, there is a growing critical discussion of the interrelationship between the two media. Paul Young's survey of how the cinematic institution represents other media forms, including television, focuses on the fantasies, realized and unrealized, of their emergence. In *Cinema Dreams Its Rivals*, Young doesn't locate what he calls the rivalry between cinema and electronic modes of media as a simple economic competition, but as a more fundamental problem, "the maintenance of the Hollywood cinema as an *institution* that is and will remain distinct from competing media institutions."[2] While fascinating, this approach often valorizes primitive forms and offers "fantasies" of the road not taken: what the telegraph, telephone, radio, television, and the like might have become.[3] Our interest here is in a television fully realized, depicted by a cinema that knows it intimately.

Within a context of examining British and U.S. television "techno-genesis" through cinema, Jane Stokes's *On-Screen Rivals* discusses many films about television and suggests that cinema's hostility to television is not universal and can at least partially be attributed to film studio exclusion from television ownership, if not production.[4] Stokes's discussion gives a greater account of genre than we do here, and is deliberately not engaged with television theory. Her strategy leads to some enlightening observations about the relationship of cinema and television and how the subject of television has been represented in films across an extended time period. As her study demonstrates, media criticism often takes the form of a critique of representation. While that is an aspect of our purpose here, the goal is to consider the nature of the media or the "mediality" of television.[5]

The distinction between a critique of representation and a critique of the nature of the media has been demonstrated in several films about television. An example can be seen in one of the earliest films to explicitly depict electronic, audiovisual transmissions. In *Murder by Television*, the "tube" is invented by a brain researcher. It is capable of marshaling interstellar frequencies, transforming the device into a death ray, as well as transforming one television viewer—Bela Lugosi, in the "evil twin" half of a double role—into an agent of foreign governments. Control of the media and its influences is at stake. The actual content to be broadcast on the proposed device is innocuous, pleasant, and familiar: a series of images shows China and other faraway places, and the inventor's daughter trills a bit of light opera. The variety-show content of the transmissions reflects the familiar qualities of the film's plot. The exciting new technology is in the service of a travelogue and a musical program; after the new device kills its inventor, the film becomes a poorly executed version of a country-house murder mystery.[6]

Both Paul Thomas Anderson's *Boogie Nights* (1997) and Paul Schrader's *Auto Focus* (2002) implicate electronic representation in pornography, depravity, and destroyed lives, in contrast to cinematic representation. The first half of *Boogie Nights* presents the film-based San Fernando Valley porn industry as a prosperous, family-oriented party presided over by impresario Jack Horner (Burt Reynolds). As the porn producers are reluctantly forced by economic reality to switch to videotape, the sex workers fall prey to violence, crime, and drug addiction. Although AIDS is never mentioned, its specter hangs over the film as the narrative moves into the 80s. The industry changes dramatically as old-style theatrical distribution is replaced by isolated home viewing of videotapes. *Auto Focus* similarly indicts the use of electronic pornographic representation, telling the real life story of *Hogan's Heroes* actor Bob Crane. Crane is an "early adopter" of video equipment and this technology propels his initial interest in photographic porn into a dangerous obsession. The combination of new video technology, public sex, and the threat of homosexuality—seen as almost inextricable in both films—is depicted as career-, soul-, and life-destroying.

Yet if we acknowledge a particular mediality of television, or even a televisuality, with profound implications for agency and subjectivity, we are reluctant to perpetuate the practice, common in texts—no less in popular discussion—of using only one term and one concept to reference all of the material that might be viewed on a television set as *television*. An interesting example can be found in Anna McCarthy's *Ambient Television*.[7] We take no issue with McCarthy's analysis—an important look at how audiovisual material is and has been situated and viewed on monitors in a variety of nondomestic spaces—but we question the implications of grouping an assortment of uses together as site-specific television: regular broadcast material shown on monitors in public spaces such as video arcades and sports bars; specialized content, such as CNN's airport network; and nonentertainment uses such as surveillance cameras. McCarthy's portmanteau approach, when extended beyond her specific project (as it has been), limits what can be said or studied about specific moments in television history and aesthetics.

In the present study, *television* means, in particular, American, network-based or broadcast-dominant television—what is known in Britain as "terrestrial television," and what, following other critics, we shall call *classic network television*.[8] The term implies more than a collection of texts or even a specific historical period; it represents a popular idea of a phenomenon, a dominant myth, a pattern or paradigm. It possesses several features that are often automatically implied by the word *television* although they hardly characterize everything that can be seen and heard on a television set. These include: serial form and syndication; "liveness"; an economic model with advertising as the dominant form of payment; an implied mass audience; a broadcast delivery system with local and national elements; a combination of private and public support; a high degree of government regulation; and an industry organized within national boundaries. Just as classical Hollywood cinema is a persisting idea of film, incorporating notions of individuality, self-development, linearity, and closure, classic network television is a persisting idea of television—one that represents fundamentally different values from those of film and, indeed, a fundamentally different notion of subjectivity. At this point we should acknowledge our reliance on apparatus theory and its theorists such as Jean-Louis Baudry, Daniel Dayan, Jean-Louis Comolli, Christian Metz, and Laura Mulvey, and its heritage in structuralist and post-structuralist discourses of subject, gender, and spectatorial construction.[9] Still, we just as often implicate grand theory in the blindness of a critical insight that would reconstruct ideological and technological determinism.

The period of classic network television began with the post–World War II diffusion of television sets, continued through the extension of broadcast networks and the development of radio programming practices, and ends when network dominance begins to erode. We place this erosion in the mid-1980s, around the time of the last episode of the TV series *M*A*S*H* in 1983, which had a viewing audience estimated at more than 100 million households that will probably never be equaled; or 1985, the first year that, according to James Lardner, one had to have a VCR.[10] This model of television still holds an important global currency and maintains a good deal of contemporary relevance for evaluating programming, from *I Dream of Jeannie* to *The Sopranos* to Star TV and Internet streaming video. Nevertheless, this model of U.S. television no longer exists in the same way. In practical terms, the model has been substantially eroded by social, artistic, economic, and technological changes, such as the growth of cable, twenty-four-hour news networks such as CNN and Fox News; satellite distribution; competing broadcasting networks such as Fox, the CW, and the Disney Channel; and new consumer technologies such as premium cable and pay-per-view movies and events, and digital advances such as the DVD or TiVo.[11]

Still, popular and critical perceptions of television's omnipresence have shifted less than television itself has. Just as television is often characterized by an attitude of nostalgia, as seen in the Nick at Night and TVLand channels, popular and critical attitudes toward television are also infused with nostalgia—in this case, nostalgia for a "bad" television that must be reevaluated. The evolution of new technologies hasn't entirely overthrown the essential myths and paradigms of television. Though it is certainly possible that "one-box" technology will be developed and integrated into the home, the nearly absolute penetration of daily life by electronic mediation has not appreciably diminished the traditional cultural paranoia about technological "advances." It has instead led to a myth of channel infinity—a belief on the one hand in a "westward ho" proliferation of channels and access and, on the other hand, a suspicion of ever-increasing fragmentation, disconnection, and confusion. An innovation is never simply invented; it must be adopted and employed. As Comolli reminds us, the machine is always ideological before it is aesthetic.[12] Or, as Brian Winston argues, there must be a "supervening social necessity."[13]

Television comes to represent an ever-flowing and absolute subversion of established cultural value, psychologically maintained by audiences and producers alike. Furthermore, its *absoluteness* is a crucial element of television's relationship with cinema. We rarely witness a television program that denigrates cinema; rather, cinema is held up as an artistic ideal to an extent that is almost masochistic. In a dynamic that recalls Gilles

Deleuze's "coldness and cruelty," television's masochism seems paradoxically "contracted" to guarantee its own mastery, to license its violation of cinema's dominant practices or laws in constant self-abnegation. This is mastery in the sense of G. W. F. Hegel's notion of the *absolute*—a continual dialectic of self-canceling or self-overcoming. Television's success vis à vis cinema represents the tyranny of the slave. The libidinal economy of cinema's dark superego requests of television acts of effrontery—even as it punishes them.

We observe this symbiotic relationship in the broadcast of film award shows such as the Golden Globes and the Academy Awards. Commentators often ask, Why do so many people watch and care about these shows when they honor films that few people have seen? This speculation ignores the important function of these awards in promoting ancillary markets (cable broadcasts, and DVD rental and purchase). It is easy to castigate the film industry by dismissing its dominant ticket buyers as fifteen-to-twenty-four-year-old men looking for car chases, explosions, and a place to take their dates. What these observations ignore is how few people actually ever go to the movies at all.[14] An illusion, which constructs television as a subordinate other, maintains that there is a real cinema and it takes place in urban movie theaters for Fellini-loving adults. Like grand opera or the symphony, "real" cinema, then, becomes so elite and rarified that "cinephilia," as it has come to be known, can hardly be enacted.[15]

Just as television contracts a notion of cinema to define itself, cinema's ossified attitudes toward television are crucial to its own self-definition. With television as its foil, cinema can maintain all its classical illusions. One of our goals is to interrogate some of the clichés about television perpetuated by cinema's overwhelming gestalt. A classic example can be found in Billy Wider's *Sunset Boulevard* (1950), when faded movie goddess Norma Desmond (Gloria Swanson) is told, "You used to be big." She responds, "I'm still big. It's the pictures that got small." Although she doesn't spell it out, Norma is talking about television, using a metaphor of diminished aesthetic value. Though today's movie studios may all be busily producing television shows, and even own their own cable networks, television still represents what it always has: a subordinate form. For better or for worse, broadcast-era television may be over or overcome, but the ideas and attitudes that it created persist, just as the network-honed conditions for economic success will never be entirely obsolete.[16] HBO may feel compelled to announce, "It's not TV; it's HBO," but it is the concept of classic network television that compels that announcement.

Classical cinema and classic network television have influenced the way everyone watches the screen, and many of the cinema of television's attitudes are echoed in television criticism: both discourses react to a particular historical movement and idea of television. In the present study, we concentrate on theoretical positions articulated by specific articles representative of significant interventions at particular historic moments. These have begun to form a canon in such anthologies as *Channels of Discourse, Reassembled*; *Logics of Television*, and *Television: The Critical View*.[17] Although we sometimes disagree with their premises or conclusions, the critics whose articles we discuss herein have made key contributions, establishing markers and a critical metaphysics for further speculation. The fact that this ground is itself imbued with the high theory of cinema is an aspect we remain cautious about when we consider how cinema itself reads television.

In "Turn Off TV Studies!" Toby Miller shares this caution about borrowing modes and "données" from high cinema theory, with its emphasis on post-structuralist discourses of psychoanalysis, spectatorship, and archival methodologies, although he concludes that the answer is to abandon a humanities-based approach in favor of one from the social sciences.[18] His highly polemical discussion is one of several articles on the place of current television studies compiled by William Boddy in a 2005 issue of the tellingly titled *Cinema Journal*. Miller's study, along with articles by John Hartley and Horace Newcomb, describe a crisis in the disciplinary place of television studies in the academy, but their conclusions raise questions about the relevance of humanities in general. When Miller asks questions about television that would never be asked of literature and Hartley argues that, unlike the "positive" criticisms of literature and cinema, television is built on a "negative," they foster a notion of television exceptionalism. The "study of television" as opposed to "television studies" is so exceptional, in this view, that it can become the institutional base for the transformation of students of television into commercially and politically enlightened consumers and citizens rather than effete theorists. While it is true that the field of television studies has entered the academy—not at its inauguration, as literature did, nor at a moment of U.S. expansion, as cinema did, but at a moment of little growth and attack from conservatives—this fact doesn't make scholarly approaches to television irrelevant. The academy may want to hide television in the rhetoric of new media, visual culture, or screen studies, or hide the fact that television has been neglected within those terms[19]; nevertheless, as we will argue throughout this book, there is room for multiple approaches to the study of our dominant medium.

How do we justify and negotiate the high-theory, low-example strategy of the present volume? For one thing, we don't want to be boxed into concepts that we are trying to challenge. As viewers—and, after all, we are all viewers—we need to recognize how we already look at television. We don't see television as a simplistic, mechanistic code that only requires decoding in one way, or possibly several ways, and—unlike British cultural studies theorists such as John Ellis, John Fiske, Stuart Hall, and Raymond Williams—we don't attempt to locate a text mainly for the purposes of resistance. Our strategy seeks a different way of challenging high theory than that of David Bordwell and the Madison school, whose wholesale critique of "SLAB" (Saussure, Lacan, Althusser, Barthes) theory tends to leave all theory behind in its return to formalism. Nevertheless, our use of high theory within the perceived banality of the medium does not occasion an apology from us, just as it does not from Paul Cantor in *Gilligan Unbound: Pop Culture in the Age of Globalization*.[20] Although Cantor notes the incongruity of applying serious political analysis or philosophers such as Plato, Jean-Jacques Rousseau, G. W. F. Hegel, and Friedrich Nietzsche to a television program like *Gilligan's Island* ("It is one thing to point to America's superior technology as the source of its global preeminence. It is another to point to Gilligan"[21]), he firmly defends a theoretical and philosophical approach to the medium.[22]

Television at the Movies proceeds in chapter 2 with an initial consideration of the melancholy passing of cinema's ascendancy in Peter Bogdanovich's *The Last Picture Show* (1971) and then, in chapter 3, investigates sources for cinematic paranoia toward television, focusing on Kazan's *A Face in the Crowd* (1957). Pandemic within this paranoia is the suspicion that television is seeding a new subjectivity, a posthuman new flesh, articulated in science fiction and horror films such as Siegel's *Invasion of the Body Snatchers* (1957), but receiving its fullest expression in David Cronenberg's *Videodrome* (1983). Chapter 4 begins a meditation on the sources and manifestations of this subjective shift within the context of other paradigm shifts, both apocalyptic and utopian. In chapter 5, ambivalence toward the televisual future forms the basis of our discussion of the "vidiot," a creature of assumed sociopolitical derangement in Jerzy Kosinski's novel *Being There*,[23] but one strangely reconciled to the dying of the old establishment in Hal Ashby's 1979 film adaptation.

A sustained paradox in cinema's regard of television is the simultaneous projection of apocalyptic and nostalgic attitudes. Unrestrained "mediality" leads to multiple and conflicting predictions: world-ending consequences accompanied by their recuperation in moral or nostalgic courage. Chapters 6 and 7 investigate this and other paradoxes inherent in television's "absolute" determination. We give special attention to the ethical hypocrisies played out in the futuristic films *Rollerball* (Norman Jewison, 1975) and *Max Headroom* (Annabel Jankel and Rocky Morton, 1985), and then relate these dilemmas to the revisionist version of television's golden age in Richard Benjamin's *My Favorite Year* (1982).

The necessity for "men of character" to defend their masculinity in the Medusa-like face of television's insidious alliance with femininity is the matrix around which we organize the three sections of chapter 8 that make manifest a latent cinematic assumption about most of the films we analyze in this volume. Nothing can exceed Faye Dunaway's Oscar-winning performance in Sidney Lumet's *Network* (1976) in the equivalency of evil, television, and women, discussed in the chapter's first section; the next two sections explore variations on the theme of femininity and television in Sydney Pollack's *Tootsie* (1982) and Ben Stiller's *The Cable Guy* (1996), and also introduce a more focused attention on television genres, such as the soap opera.

Chapter 9 uses Beatty's *Bulworth* to chart a curious shift in classic cinematic strategy: having abandoned white women to television, cinema seeks to recover its own recuperative dynamic in the TV-immune virtue of a good black woman. We note, however, that in films as diverse as *A Face in the Crowd*, *Being There*, and Martin Scorsese's *The King of Comedy* (1982) that this subtext of black authenticity continues a tradition of racial stereotyping in cinema and the media.

A fuller consideration of television's master mode, seriality, in chapter 10—which is devoted to *Henry, Portrait of a Serial Killer*—links the perplexities of negotiating television textuality with an expression of criminally damaged masculinity. Henry's melodramatic inscription in an oedipal nightmare repeats cinema's reliance on classic psychoanalytic determinations while at the same time reiterating cinema's paranoia over the "new flesh." In chapter 11 this oedipal hangover sounds a note of cinematic nostalgia in the otherwise ruthless portrayal of Rupert Pupkin as a sociopathic citizen of celebrity-obsessed culture in Scorsese's *The King of Comedy*. In some ways akin to *Being There*'s Chauncey Gardner (Peter Sellers), Rupert Pupkin (Robert De Niro) invites a broader deliberation on the relationship of audiences to television textuality and culture. We speculate, along with Charlotte Brunsdon,[24] whether the despair over television aesthetics should provoke an exclusive shift to demographic study. Recalling the "absolute" nature of televisual metaphysics to the continuing role of technology in overcoming those metaphysics, we caution readers throughout the book about predictions of the death of television as we know it. By observing the invasion of digital effects into cinema in such films as *The Matrix* (Andy and Larry Wachowski, 1999) and the power of auteurism in films such as *War of the Worlds* (Steven Spielberg, 2005), *Poltergeist* (Tobe Hooper, 1982), and *Signs* (M. Night Shyamalan, 2002), we reiterate the resilience of mainstream cinema in appropriating new media formats for traditional narrative and institutional purposes while insisting on the adaptability of television culture and its audiences to enact the fundamentally mediated nature of our lives.[25]

2

Elegy

It is interesting and possibly unique in civilization that the chief signifying device of a culture is also almost universally regarded as bad. Cinema, up until the 1950s, had itself been the chief signifying machine of the century, one that produced the most signs and pumped the most powerful content into the culture. In movies about television, the cinematic point of view clashes with a new industry. A mechanical device (cinema) collides with an electronic device (television), and a battle then rages.

How does the transition from cinema culture to broadcast culture create a film universe of paranoia, fear, and outrage? Even after the dominance of television could be said to have been accomplished, films such as Gus Van Sant's *To Die For* (1994), Ben Stiller's *The Cable Guy* (1996), or Jake Kasdan's *The TV Set* (2006) consistently present television as a carrier of pathology, brainwashing behavior, or creative enervation. The causalities of television in these films aren't only aesthetic, but embody the very ideals of our age, such as democracy, liberalism, and patriarchy.

For critic George Trow in *The Context of No Context*, "The work of television is to establish false contexts and to chronicle the unraveling of existing contexts; finally, to establish the context of no context and to chronicle it."[1] It isn't easy for Trow to describe precisely what, in the form of a context, has been lost, although he creates a powerful symbol out of his father's fedora. As a child, Trow writes, he had happily anticipated acquiring one of his own. But the world has changed; as he notes, "Irony has seeped into the felt of any fedora hat I have ever owned—not out of any wish of mine but out of necessity. A fedora hat worn by me without the necessary protective irony would eat through my head and kill me."[2] While it might be tempting, for those of us whose birthrights consist of hardhats, baseball

11

caps, or helmets, to belittle Trow's nostalgia for the fedora, we shouldn't lose sight of the great chasm in social life that his story reveals. Robert Redford's *Quiz Show* (1994), in which the white Anglo-Saxon Protestant son of a famous literary critic turns out to be just another cheater on a TV game show, charts the same terrain with the same regrets. Modernism collides with postmodernism; the mechanical collides with the electronic; and human beings unwittingly evolve through technological exposure. Now, at the beginning of a new century, it isn't so surprising that we might encounter a new psychological evolution or that it might have become associated with a new and pervasive medium. It isn't surprising that we may all need to wear new hats—or no hats at all.

Trow's book belongs to a canon of elegiac accounts of television's betrayal of culture. In response, we say, you can be as negative about television as you wish, but don't forget that nothing forces you to watch. It is inadequate to say, "Oh, it addicts us; we are all addicts," because that doesn't explain much.[3] Does it mean that we can all go to TV Anonymous and undertake the twelve steps to quit watching? The concept of television addiction turns what we can't understand into pathology, and sounds suspiciously like an excuse to offer ourselves to institutional cure. Capitalism may create the addiction, but it is capital that offers all the cures. For an addiction analogy to work we would have to imagine six billion people—our entire civilization—as junkies. It would be more accurate to just say that it's "bad." This is, in fact, how many critics do describe television. In the very first sentence of their preface, the authors of *Down the Tube: An Inside Account of the Failure of American Television* ask, "Why is television so bad?"[4] Trow concludes, "No good has come of it."[5] The critical canon on bad television includes Jerry Mander's *Four Arguments for the Elimination of Television*, Neil Postman's *Amusing Ourselves to Death*, Neal Gabler's *Life, The Movie*, David Marc's *Bonfire of the Humanities*, Todd Gitlin's *Media Unlimited*, and Pierre Bourdieu's *On Television*. George Ritzer's *The Globalization of Nothing* and *The McDonaldization of Society* extend this reactionary lament.[6] While these books acknowledge the power, potential, and failed promise of the media, their complaints seem as dated as the prewar Frankfurt school.

And it isn't just media insiders, critics, and sociologists who make these assessments. They can be found everywhere in popular discourse, as in this excerpt from Kurt Vonnegut's novel *Timequake*:

> When the bad sister was a young woman, she and the [lunatics in the garden of the asylum next door] worked up designs for television cameras and transmitters and receivers. Then she got money

from her very rich mom to manufacture and market these satanic devices, which made imaginations redundant. They were instantly popular because the shows were so attractive and no thinking was involved....

The bad sister's name was Nim-nim. When her parents named her that, they had no idea how unsweet she was going to be. And TV wasn't the half of it. She was as unpopular as ever because she was as boring as ever, so she invented automobiles and computers and barbed wire and flamethrowers and land mines and machine guns and so on. That's how pissed off she was.[7]

In *Uses of Television*, John Hartley adopts Vonnegut's term "blivit" to refer to the way in which television "mixes fact, fiction, faking and forecasting,"[8] or, as Vonnegut himself puts it, how it puts "two pounds of shit in a one-pound bag."[9]

For Gore Vidal, television offers a vision of Hell. In *Live from Golgotha: The Gospel According to Gore Vidal*, the novel's holy man, Timothy, is surprised when a television set is delivered: "For a week now, I've been unable to stop watching television. Like a madman, I switch from channel to channel. I cannot get enough of the astonishing electronic world of the future as glimpsed through that small black window. The sickening yellow and the atrocious pulsing reds are like a never-ending, always-changing yet ever-the-same nightmare. I can now say, in life, that I have gazed on Hell, and it is even busier than one had feared."[10]

For Kathleen Fitzpatrick, the "anxiety" of the novel in the wake of technological change is its increasing "obsolescence" as a medium. The chief factor in the novel's "seemingly tenuous position in contemporary US culture" is television. Through readings of Don DeLillo's and Thomas Pynchon's novels, Fitzpatrick demonstrates how "serious" literature employs a "cachet of marginality" as a bulwark against an increasingly female, increasingly nonwhite television audience and asks, Whose interests are served by this intermedia conflict?[11] Meanwhile, she notes, sales of books continue to rise. Television may have killed print culture, but print culture remains surprisingly robust as a consumer category.

Another strange-bedfellows version of the conflict between so-called high literature and television culture can be found in Joyce Maynard's memoir of her 1960s adolescence. In the sections of the book devoted to Maynard's relationship with J. D. Salinger, she doesn't confine herself to sexual gossip. She also exposes the famous recluse's surprising television watching habits:

The frame of reference we share is television—the one current medium where his otherwise withering critical sense seems suspended. "We're both watchers, you and I," he tells me—though I have already known this about myself for years, and recognized it in him too. We are not just talking about television either.

"The worse the television—the more American—the more I love it," he says. We reminisce about particular episodes of *The Andy Griffith Show*...."[12]

The scene plays out within the context of the older Salinger's relationship with the much younger, and decidedly disgruntled, Maynard. As such, it is yet another example of the writer's peculiarity rather than an open-minded appreciation of a beloved sitcom.

Denunciations of television are not confined to high literary culture. An old Neiman Marcus Christmas catalog includes a list of what it calls "The Things that Count." Along with "A photograph of your great-grandfather" and "An Italian silk tie," it includes, "An evening without television." How bad does a medium have to be for a glossy catalog— a compendium of advertisements!—to confidently assert moral superiority over it as part of the sales pitch?

What do people mean when they simply assume the negative nature of an entire medium? How is television bad, and how bad is it? The physical perils of television are seldom noted even though legislation has been proposed in the U.S. Congress to mandate anchoring devices to prevent television sets from tipping over and crushing small children, many of whom are injured or killed that way every year. But this very real physical risk is usually not what is meant by television's danger. Instead, the danger is presented as psychological and intellectual. The American Academy of Pediatrics advises that children under two watch no television and that older children's viewing be limited and supervised, offering various rationales, including threats to brain development and good nutrition, susceptibility to addictive substances, and imperiled family interactions.[13] Aside from these warnings, the danger that television represents has been difficult to precisely categorize or evaluate. Television is additionally said to distort reality, cause social disintegration, promote "meaningless" violence, zombify, enslave, and reject history.[14]

In other words, what critics mean by the term *bad* is multiple, shifting, and unspecific. There is no consistency of complaints or complainants, including those multifaceted complaints issuing from within television programming itself. Television functions as an ironic and negative critical agent that comments on and objectifies itself as well as the world. The particulars of the charges often depend on where the critic positions him- or herself on the political spectrum. From the Left, television is accused of halting critical thinking and acting as a rigid support of the capitalist status quo. From the Right, it is accused of undermining the nuclear family and providing validation for deviant liberal lifestyles.

It is clear from these various attacks that television doesn't know the difference between right and wrong, true and false, us and them, subject and object. Does evil emanate from the individual, or from society? Television doesn't say which is which—just that the difference doesn't matter, and there's no sense bothering about it. Television takes traumatic difference and reduces it to variety. Otherness is transformed into multiple brands and sales pitches, and it co-opts exactly those distinctions that in the past may have caused revolution. The label *bad* isn't good enough; it is both inadequate and irrelevant to television's dynamics and historical situation. In chapter 1 we introduced television as an "absolute" force of signification in our culture—a comprehensive and powerful self-negation in the process of its own realization. It thrives within the global success of an economy and an ideology variously called *consumer capitalism*, *late capitalism*, or *American popular culture*. Television, in fact, is the very instrument of this ideological triumph. Nothing is critical, nothing is crucial, nothing makes that much difference. This is the power and glory of television.

Like every chief signifying device before it, including print media and cinema, television works to justify its own ideology. As an agent of capitalist culture's imperial spread it accustoms citizens of the global economy to its own proliferation. Even with such a purpose, television appears to be an instrument of indifference: It insists that you remain indifferent to the particular ideology that you inhabit. One of the ways television does this is to ignore or banalize many of the trends of the late twentieth and early twenty-first centuries and especially to desensitize us to the fact that the twentieth century was the most violent century in history, haunted by the reality of genocide and the possibility of global annihilation. Television rehearses to the point of indifference the holocaustic capacity to vaporize cities, extinguish or incinerate the planet, and bring an end to the entire problem of existence. From the two world wars; through the apocalyptic civil conflicts of Korea, Vietnam, Kosovo, and Rwanda; and to various other bloody global conflicts and environmental degradation, the "century of hell"—as the poet Arthur Rimbaud previewed the twentieth century—has been one of historical catastrophe. For those who lived through it, the twentieth century was not a stable context but a shifting matrix, requiring constant monitoring. Positioned as we are at the beginning of a new century, we may look back and consider what attitude global citizens can possibly take toward the terror of the century just endured.

Some theorists, such as Jean-François Lyotard, believe that the current cultural trend of postmodernism defines itself through an attitude that says we've had enough of terror. But in a post-9/11 world, perhaps terror hasn't had enough of us. Even so, television adopts a posture of sensational indifference toward totalitarianisms, holocausts, gulags, and other key features of the twentieth and twenty-first centuries. The particular strategies with which television defuses the terror of our times create new problems, however. These strategies are too often steeped in images of the ultra-violent and the banality of that violence.

The goal of twentieth-century modernism had been to solve the epistemological problem of time and to recapture our centrality within it. "What is to be done?" asked Vladimir Lenin. What can happen and what can we do about it? How can we awaken and recover from this historical nightmare? The modern dilemma has been how to recuperate from tremendous losses, gigantic betrayals, and disinheriting violence as our only heritage. From the purity of abstraction and the abandonment of representation to totalitarian politics and ethics, modernism struggles to reach an aestheticized total vision. The condition that most demands alleviation is our seeming inability to inhabit the planet without working toward extinction. How can we cure the fact that our desire torments us, that what we really want from desire is the end of desire? How is it that an entire century has proved that what we want is the end of everything? The most chilling question of the century is, What is "the final solution"? History is over, Francis Fukuyama has told us, but what does that mean? Is it possible to recognize an ontological difference between history extant or history exterminated?

The indifference with which popular culture incessantly reduces the catastrophes of the twentieth and twenty-first centuries to banality is a persistent problem for academics and critics. The dominant critical impulse, at least since post-structuralism, has been to discover what is subversive, subtextual, radical, or resistant in the examined object. But this method becomes problematic when applied to the "bad" objectivity of television. Taken to inane lengths, the attempts to criticalize or radicalize banality can elevate figures such as Howard Stern and Madonna into antihegemonic gods and goddesses. Meaghan Morris calls these critical contortions "*criticism* that actively strives to achieve 'banality,' rather than investing it negatively in the object of study."[15] In a sense, this is criticism that improperly assumes the fixed place of the object while attempting to maintain a critical dynamic. Criticism becomes banal when it becomes rhetorical, eliding its responsibility to critique the banality of objects outside itself.

In a consideration of Jean Baudrillard's notion of banality, Morris locates it in a condition where nothing exceeds the conventional. How can something remain subversive when it happens every day, or when everything changes in order to stay the same? For Baudrillard, the continual banalization of the subversive produces within its spectators (or citizens) a "fatal banality." He pronounces as finished all attempts to overcome desire, resolve relationships with others, solve the dilemma of difference, or seduce the world into giving back some satisfaction and mastery. Banal fatality: that's what it means to be at the dead point of history. We no longer live in the hot world of seduction, but in the cold one of pornography and obsession. The only "charm" in this world is the fatal "force of the object." This approach to the world takes the form of a challenge: Is there anything out there adequate to my consumption or my critique? The answer is no, because we're always hyperconscious of the object's banality, its weakness and transience. This may be the charm of an obscenely dynamic nihilism. Nevertheless, Morris calls Baudrillard to task for his implicit elitism and his reversible pairing of "banality" with "fatality": "It's a very simple but, when well done, dizzying logico-semantic game which makes Baudrillard's books very easy to understand, but any one term most difficult to define."[16] What can it mean to resign the anxiety of subjectivity to insignificance while at the same time allowing the force of the object to enact our fate?

This active quest to criticalize banality and banalize criticism prompts Morris to suspect attempts to use "such a classically dismissive term as 'banality' ... to establish, yet again, a frame of reference for discussing popular culture."[17] Her interpretation of banality's etymology emphasizes its negative connotations of "coercive" leveling. Another reading could foreground its suggestions of mass dissemination and accessibility. After all, the word *banality* ultimately derives from the same Indo-European root as the word *fame*. We might also bear in mind Hannah Arendt's use of the term in her famous phrase "the banality of evil." Hers has been a controversial notion because it implies that the murder of millions can be attributed to the cowardice of clerks and button pushers rather than to the evil of a great Satan. Does this not diminish the stature of the victims, even as it makes the question of how to avoid this in the future so much more manageable? Nevertheless, whenever banality achieves the fatal notoriety of a subculture, a holocaust, or an end-time—or, vice versa, when the extraordinary is indistinguishable from the quotidian—then Morris is right to question criticism's agenda.

The infamous banality of television is not necessarily something wrong with television. It *is* television. To banalize and serialize the critical aspects of our existence is television's job, and it is there that its ideological power lies. Again, like contemporary criticism, television is both an object of critique and that critique in itself. We can watch the TV series *Kid Nation* while at the same time TiVo-ing its denunciation on another channel. By leveling and reversing vast differences that might otherwise lead to conflict, television transforms difference into mere variety—into hundreds of brands of bottled water. It produces an atmosphere in which shopping and purchasing, with the constant talk that accompanies those activities, can substitute for more radical solutions. Forget your agonized individuality, your heroic will. Go buy something. Talk about it on TV.

Television may have ruined culture, but it may also have saved the planet. Though tested in 1939, network broadcasting only gained its momentum in the immediate aftermath of the bombings of Hiroshima and Nagasaki. Its cultural force addresses the end of the world by substituting endless desire. In the mid-1980s an ABC billboard announced— as part of the network's so-called controversial "TV is Good" advertising campaign—"Before TV, two World Wars. After TV, Zero." If you can manage your chronic condition, you can abandon a cure. If you can't solve it, exploit it. Television doesn't partake of the beauty of purified, total systems, or of radical will. Television acts so insidiously that the discourse of cinema has perceived it as sneaky and creepy, an evil like Satan in the Garden of Eden. Or is it Lucifer in starlight? In cinema's founding myth of its rival, even a little exposure will compromise your identity or, alternatively, send you into idolatry.

Cinema, high modernist even in its mainstream form, prefers to deliver audiences to pleasure and resolution. By the time you leave the movie theater, you will have seen and understood all that you need to see and understand. Mainstream cinema is based on linear and logical delivery of narratives that move efficiently to an end. These narratives provide a unified experience; they travel a complete circuit of desire and comprehension. Television, in contrast, has no intention of ever closing any circle or resolving anything. Cinema can only sneer at television and at the people who inhabit its irresolute imaginary.

Television tutors us in acceptance rather than resolve. It simply isn't interested in resistance or recuperation, in apocalypse or utopia, but in the continual maintenance or flow of discontent. Unlike the films of Michelangelo Antonioni, Ingmar Bergman, or Federico Fellini, lack of closure in television never reaches the sublime.[18] Horace Newcomb was the first of many critics to use "flow" as a metaphor for the organization of television programming and how it positions viewers in relationship to their world; the key idea of flow in this context is that it doesn't include an endpoint. We may all believe of television that it is "bad," but that kind of frustration is merely the course of raw desire streaming without any hope of coming to an end. This is the engine of the capitalist machine, the main economy of which relies on endless consumption.

Television is so self-reflexive, such a parody of itself, so continually broadcasting its unseriousness and meaninglessness that this objective unseriousness must be seen as part of its critical power. As long as television remains stupid, it can go on wielding its incommensurable ideological power without interference. The unseriousness of television becomes a problem of how to study it. Despite the fact that we are writers of a book about television, and have therefore positioned it as an object of theoretical and critical study, we also harbor some contempt for it. The impulse to kill one's television set, which we admit to sharing at times, reflects, to some degree, cinema's *weltschmerz* about its fate in a televisual world. We want to keep watching television and still save cinema. Best exemplified by Susan Sontag in her 1996 essay "A Century of Cinema," this impulse sees the commercial cinema settling for "a policy of bloated, derivative film-making, a brazen recombinatory art.... Cinema, once heralded as the art of the twentieth century, seems now, as the century closes numerically, to be a decadent art."[19]

Television just doesn't seem good enough, important enough, or aesthetic enough for us to actually grasp it as an object of study and, as a critical force, it is itself in many ways responsible for this dismissive attitude. Television is seriously involved in decriticalizing itself, making sure that its meanings are considered worthless, that its pleasures are minor, that desire has no hope of actually being fulfilled—or at least not for very long. The unseriousness of television is its deadly seriousness. Its meaninglessness is its extraordinary and century-shaking significance.

One of the reasons we may find it difficult to study television seriously is that it doesn't possess many of the characteristics traditionally associated with serious art. First and most obviously, television isn't perceived to have an autonomous existence as art for art's sake because we are always aware of its fealty to another purpose: advertising. While we may be intellectually aware that all art exists within an economic framework, few forms so relentlessly foreground their commercial foundations.

Second, television can't be said to be author-centered. Sontag mourns the death of "cinephilia—the name of the very specific kind of love that cinema inspired" as largely the death of the author.[20] Few people waste time wondering about the auteurs of the TV series *Another World, Baywatch,* or *How I Met Your Mother.* To the extent that audiences and critics contemplate a television auteur it's typically a producer such as Stephen Bochco, David Kelly, or Norman Lear, or a host such as Bob Barker, Dick Clark, or Alex Trebek. Robert Thompson considers the "authorially ambiguous" nature of television by identifying various creative entities involved in the "quality" series *St. Elsewhere*: inspiration from an actual doctor's life, a novel, the series *Hill Street Blues,* its several writers and producers, the independent studio MTM led by Grant Tinker, and the network NBC as represented by programming chief Brandon Tartikoff and network president Fred Silverman.[21] Thompson emphasizes these complicated layers of influence and argues that "creation by committee and compromise ... isn't always a bad thing" (78), but he can't refrain from referring to the group as a "horde" (79); "all the ducks in the pond" (82); and "this mob of auteurs" (83).[22]

Much of what Thompson identifies as the marks of the auteur in this series are simply intertexual references to other programs and complicated in-jokes: "They [the jokes] announced that there *is* a television tradition and they helped position *St. Elsewhere* within that tradition" (88). In fact, many television programs are predominantly based on television intertextuality: *The Colbert Report, Saturday Night Live,* and *Second City Television,* to name only a few late-night examples. With this observation, Thompson calls attention to yet another way in which television differs from other arts: the nature of its canon. To give any meaning to the jokes and references, at least some viewers—the cognoscenti—have to be aware of the other programs to which the program alludes. An art form must establish a canon, but, to the extent that it possesses one, television's canon is subterranean and self-generating rather than established by outside authorities. Just as the author of television is irrelevant to us, there is also no accepted value hierarchy, no canon of the great works of Western television. Though you might find Marcel Proust's *Remembrance of Things Past* on television, monumentality in television (*The Simpsons, The Sopranos, Twin Peaks*) is always more cult than canonical.

Another difficulty about considering television as art is that its world is very often the same as the nontelevision world: it possesses a different sense of separation from the represented world than do other media. Its critical force draws on the rhythms of the everyday. Television is serious about the fact that the world of seriousness—the world that could produce something as beautiful and terrible as a mushroom cloud—has died. That extinction is the fact of television. We can't help noticing the sociopathic triviality and strident opportunism with which television performs its autopsy, and we're filled with loathing, irony, or a combined indifference of both.

Early television studies borrowed from communication or sociology models, primarily based on quantitative analysis. Before the advent of reception studies in the 1970s and 1980s, research gathered functional data on audiences, material geared to the needs of broadcasters and sponsors, with methodology borrowed from well-established, logic-based fields such as statistics.[23] Popular and fan-oriented material in the United States also emphasizes the assembly of facts, although this often consists of trivia. What planet do Tribbles come from? What is Calista Flockhart's astrological sign? Can Mulder and Scully cure the black cancer and save humanity? Yes, if they find the right serum. Attempts to interpret or assign fundamental meaning to televisual phenomena—such as charges brought by Christian conservatives that Teletubby Tinky Winky is gay or that Barney promotes secular humanism—are routinely ridiculed.

The shift to a qualitative approach, a shift away from calculating techniques and results toward understanding ideology and psychology, contains its own problems. These newer models rely on an older and more established critical approach to cinema and literature. But it's a mistake to imagine that television simply evolves from or represents a lesser form of cinema. In cinematic terms, television is an interloper rather than a genetic mistake. Cinema is far better at maintaining its boundaries and, therefore, its status as a legitimate object of criticism and as a critic of the world outside itself. As Marshall McLuhan has argued, the message of television is not distinct from its medium, and the message of self-criticalization is the medium of modern television culture. The televisual age is the televisual age precisely because it is always just threatening to arrive and to arrive outside the line of legitimate artistic succession.

The Last Picture Show, filmed in 1971 by Peter Bogdanovich in grief-stricken black and white, is drenched in nostalgia for a period of moviemaking before television. It invokes Howard Hawks's *Red River* (1948) and Anthony Mann's *Winchester '73* (1950) in the great cinematic gestures it makes. This is a movie that weeps with awareness that cinema has had its day. This is absolutely the last picture show, though other films of the same period, including Dennis Hopper's *The Last Movie* (1971) and Wim Wenders's *Der Stand der Dinge* (1982), compete for the cinematic twilight. The mythical town of Thalia—based on novelist Larry McMurty's hometown of Archer City, Texas—is disintegrating and its movie theater is closing. Its male inhabitants are passively self-destructing and its women are turning into desperate housewives.

Sam the Lion, the last noble man on earth (played with ponderous Academy Award–winning grace by Ben Johnson), stands as the last bastion of the old order. He fishes, rides horses, protects the weak, is loved by women, and is, significantly, the owner of the town's movie theater. But even he hasn't been able to keep the young men from leaving or the young and not so young women from their greed for money, sex, and amusements. When Sam dies, so does the town.

The town also has an idiot, a holy fool named Billy (Sam Bottoms) whose death enacts the slaughter of innocence not long after his exposure to too much knowledge of the world and its cruel ways. Almost every aspect of the film shows disintegration. The townspeople have lost any ability to carry on committed, communal relationships. They fail at all connections, whether they take place on the football field, where the town's team consistently loses, or in the ramshackle motel rooms, from which no character emerges satisfied. People are locked into cold and empty relationships of every configuration—father/son, mother/daughter, wife/husband, mentor/protégé, boss/employee, lover/friend.

Throughout, the film offers unsubtle contrasts of the proper and the perverse. The youthful affair between Sam and Lois Farrow (Ellen Burstyn) is described as having taken place out in the open air, as they swam in the "tank." But Lois lost faith long ago. Jacy, the daughter Lois had with a repressive local oilman, is excited to ditch her boyfriend Duane (Jeff Bridges) and attend an indoor pool party. Played by a teenage Cybill Shepard in her first film role, Jacy is a cold and ruthless pleasure seeker. She performs a striptease for her new crowd of friends with only the slightest hesitation. She hardly registers the damage done to her watch—a gift from Duane—caused by the pool water. Jacy is also responsible for perverse uses of the local landmarks. The boys, Sonny (Timothy Bottoms), Duane, Billy, and Lester (Randy Quaid), play pool at Sam's down-at-heels diner in a rite of male bonding and tenuous community feeling. Jacy uses the pool table as a trysting ground with one of her father's roustabouts, who is also one of her mother's lovers. (This scene was cut from the original theatrical release, but restored for the home video version.) The most positive union in the film is an adulterous affair between Sonny and the football coach's meek and infertile wife Ruth Popper (Cloris Leachman, who won the best supporting actress Oscar). Their first kiss happens next to some garbage cans behind the community center as they take out the trash.

By the film's conclusion, Sam is dead, the movie theater has closed down, and dust blows up the main street. Billy, the last oblivious believer, has been run over by a truck while he was sweeping. *The Last Picture*

Show is one of the most elegiac, funereal movies you'll ever see about the coming of television. It ultimately sees, as high cinema often does, the arrival of television and the usurpation of film as the end of the world, or what Baudrillard would call the "cold universe" of gutted selfhood. The center hasn't held in this Texas town; television has entered the lives of communities and routed integrity. The picture show is closed and the community scattered over a televisual wasteland.

The film can hardly bear to depict a television set. Only distracted women like Jacy and her mother Lois ever watch TV, while drinking and rehearsing their discontent. Meanwhile, the father sleeps. Ticket taker Miss Mosey (Jessie Lee Fulton) attributes the closing of the picture show to "baseball in the summer, television all the time." A final scene of the film makes an ambiguous reference to electronic media. Depressed from her breakup with Sonny, Ruth Popper doesn't have the energy to get dressed, wash the dishes, or turn off the radio or television. It plays distractingly in the background of her reunion with Sonny, adding to the pathetic banality of the scene.

The linkages between television and the end of small-town America are made more explicit, if more impassively, in a film that draws directly from *The Last Picture Show*. In Lasse Halstrom's *What's Eating Gilbert Grape?* (1993), frustrated adolescent Gilbert (Johnny Depp) resembles Sonny in that he has an older, married lover and a developmentally disabled brother, Arnie (Leonardo DiCaprio), with whom he shares a special ritual. In both films, the older boys express affection by reversing the baseball cap of "slow" boy from front to back. But despite their bonds, Sonny and Gilbert both disappoint their protégés and themselves. Gilbert's mother has eaten herself up to a weight of 600 pounds, dining in front of the television set. She is so fat that her children fear she will break through the floor and destroy the house. These characters have never had the chance to know cinema. Leaving the town, and the dead-end job that goes with it, is an inevitability rather than a heartbreak.

Ultimately, television took its revenge on *The Last Picture Show* and its melancholy by replaying it as a late-1980s commercial directed by Roger Lunn for the Guess? blue jean brand. Titled "Texas 1953," the ad recycles the black-and-white images of small-town life, including weary teenagers slumped in the movie theater and the single traffic light swaying in the wind at the end of Bogdanovich's film. Television's ravages can be seen in the film's postlapsarian homages to the great films like Hawks's *Red River*, Allan Dwan's *The Sands of Iwo Jima* (1949), and Vincente Minelli's *Father of the Bride* (1950) that we see playing in the doomed theater; in the embodiment of failed cinematic godhood Sam the Lion; and in the *Götterdämmerung* gestures of American auteur Bogdanovich. But for the town's inhabitants, the worst may be over. The sexual jealousy and suffering that Sam the Lion and Lois Farrow once felt at the end of their affair has long since faded. Cybill Shepard found enduring success on the popular TV series *Moonlighting* and *Cybill*; Cloris Leachman is best known as Phyllis on the *Mary Tyler Moore Show*; and Peter Bogdanovich's current auteurism finds expression through cable commentary on great cinema. Events have evolved past a romantic notion of noble individuality and these characters have become the stuff that television is made of.

3

Paranoia

Do you hear or fear / or do I smash the mirror?
—"Smash the Mirror" (Pete Townsend), from the film *Tommy*
(Ken Russell, 1975)

To say that cinema often presents a contemptuous view of television doesn't begin to capture the extremity of that representation. Ken Russell's 1975 *Tommy*, to take just one instance, features one of the better-known, most hysterical portraits of television paranoia. Ann-Margret, playing Tommy's careless mother, Nora Walker Hobbs, urges Tommy (Roger Daltrey) to respond to her as she cavorts in a white, mirrored room. She wants him to look in a mirror, cure himself of his hysterical blindness, and recognize himself. At the scene's climax, a television set suddenly erupts and inexplicably spews baked beans throughout the room—and all over Ann-Margret. Certainly the identity of the victim isn't random. Ann-Margret has traced a passage from one film cliché as studio system sex kitten to another as frustrated and irresponsible mother damaging her male child; or, to put it another way, from ingénue to character actress. This coda to the scene deftly invokes vomit, pornographic ejaculation shots, pollution of the virgin, hurled feces, mud, and gastrointestinal distress. This is what comes out of the television set. The media critique in *Tommy* often lacks coherence, but the protagonist's fame within the context of multiple celebrity personality cults is clearly a problem. At his mother's instigation, Tommy commercially exploits his unusual ability to play pinball. A monitor extruding effluent onto the characters is the inevitable visual metaphor that results.

The sense of pollution associated with television here echoes the polluting nature of commerce itself. It can never be forgotten or put aside that television, at least through the classic network period, is entirely fueled by an advertising model of payment. The power of television is always accompanied by paranoia that arises from our suspicion of its intents and purposes. This is the basis of the ideological critique of television, although television doesn't always fit into traditional models of power offered by established strains of ideological criticism. The content of television is like a white room filled with baked beans: It certainly makes a big mess, but what else can you say about it?

The key to television's immense power, which is its very capacity to spew ideology, comes from making sure that we don't give a damn about it. Most theoretical studies, from psychoanalysis to semiotics to post-structuralism, warn us, ideology acts by attaching itself to mechanisms that hide it. Ideology is always false consciousness, Karl Marx notes. To function, ideology must be perceived as natural, as the truth, or as a domestic and domesticating environment. As a brilliant exemplar of this strategy, television masks the falseness of ideology by making us think that what it shows and teaches doesn't matter, that this is just the fatally banal flow of the every day. Our own careless contempt for it guarantees that its meaning remains hidden.

A few observations about radio can help us grasp how television operates. Although often seen as the misbegotten progeny of cinema, classic network television is really the child of broadcast radio, the medium from which it derives its industrial model (and, to judge from Aldous Huxley, its model of critical evaluation).[1] Radio transmission, like television transmission, depends on an electromagnetic wave spectrum, the key characteristic of which is its limits. In his introduction to *Channels of Discourse, Reassembled*, Robert Allen emphasizes that this spectrum has in the United States been considered a natural resource, like coal, oil, or timber.[2] Following this logic, and overcoming dissenting voices, the U.S. Federal Radio Commission (FRC) originally licensed radio as a public utility and decreed that it be used in the public interest. The FRC, which became the Federal Communications Commission (FCC), announced this intent, but did not involve itself in programming or content. Instead, it assigned the airwaves to programmers.

Beginning with radio and certainly continuing with television, the FCC (and before it the FRC) has assumed—in the public interest, and as an obvious way that a natural resource can be allocated—that broadcast waves will be used for profit making. In keeping with the American ethos, nature is profit and the public interest is profit. As Todd Gitlin points out in "Prime Time Ideology: The Hegemonic Process in Television Entertainment," the cultural hegemony of liberal capitalist ideology assumes that the pursuit of life, liberty, and happiness is shepherded by "private commodity forms."[3] The development of commercial radio beginning in 1922 reflects these assumptions. The salesman, as always in America, has become the public trustee and guardian of our welfare. The 1927 Radio Act, passed by the FRC, led to the creation of the FCC in 1934, and the FCC became the agency authorized to assign frequencies and grant licenses to selected programmers for free. The licenses to use a bandwidth were given, not sold, to the salesmen, but—interestingly enough—the salesmen could sell the licenses. Today the appearance of high-definition television has caused another bandwidth giveaway, a broadband merger mania, and another battle over whether the FCC can impose any restrictions on the use of those bandwidths. It remains to be seen if the broadcasting of digital signals, as of this writing mandated to happen in February 2009, will actually come to pass.

If the trustee of the public good is a salesman, audiences are actually the commodities sold for profit. According to this system, your interest is served when you are sold to a sponsor, and this business transaction is believed to be for the public good. Your commodification for profit underpins the political economy of radio, television, and ultimately capitalism, through the regulation of markets outside a system of central market planning. This is not a nightmare or a horror from the perspective of advertising-based media, although it has been amply critiqued.[4] From the point of view of a capitalist economy, you are (morally) good when you are a *good* (consumer). You are being served when you are delivered as a commodity to a sponsor.

Looking at television in a way that emphasizes the commodification of the audience and a principal goal of advertising leads to an ideological approach, and advertising is often used as the key to this ideology. Critic Mimi White begins her essay "Ideological Analysis and Television" discussing a well-known commercial for cough syrup. That it has traditionally existed to advertise consumer products is the central ideological fact of classic network television, the one thing we all understand about it and claim to hate. Advertising irritates, but commercials are not something wrong with television. If we just got rid of commercials— or if we just could not figure out a way to watch them, as is increasingly happening—we wouldn't have good television, but something else entirely. As White notes, "Advertising is normal."[5] Advertising *is* American broadcast television—its very form and function. The viewer is a potential product or commodity, an entity that can be rated, gauged, valued, and sold to a sponsor. Your position as a television viewer is both as a commodity—something that gets wrapped up and sold—and as a possible consumer. It is as a "potential consumer" that you are addressed.[6]

The viewing of broadcast television is not just a torment by advertising. It is viewing in the service of buying.

This is how Eileen Meehan discusses the commodification of spectators in her 1990 essay "Why We Don't Count." Meehan argues that ratings are not a "mirror of public taste" and are entirely irrelevant as a representative sample of the public.[7] Beginning with radio, the assessment of audience size in the form of ratings was designed to reconcile the competing interests of broadcasters and advertisers. Television ratings assess and quantify that portion of the population capable of being commodified— that is, capable of consuming. This is already a rigged game. Those people who supply the ratings are already the ideal audience. You only count if you are counted. The people to whom Nielson Media Research meters are given are already people likely to consume, and therefore likely to be commodified for sponsors. Ratings, as Meehan points out, are not an attempt to find out what consumers want, but an attempt by macroeconomic systems to manufacture their own "commodity audience," which can then recirculate into sponsorship. The audience that counts is the audience that buys, and it doesn't matter at all if you don't enjoy the programming.

Ratings and statistics are not elements that reach outside the programming system; they are themselves manufactured by the system as a commercial product. You are important to television—to the extent you are—because you are important as a consumer, not because you might weigh in with a radical opinion. This may be a cynical point of view, but it's one that we should understand. To expect television to become an organ of ideal democracy, to gauge your opinions in order to change its programming or product presentation is to expect that it will no longer address you as a commodity. That would be like asking a snake not to bite you.[8] Even though television is a mass medium, with multiple producers and available to everyone with a TV set, it is, like all ideological institutions, a closed system. It is closed or nonresponsive in the sense of being insulated against outside forces—like viewers—that could disrupt its fundamental grammar or subject reproduction.

Following Antonio Gramsci, Gitlin explains that hegemony works to enforce consent rather than obedience. Even though this hegemony "leaks" and is highly complex and conflicted in its treatment, management, and absorption of oppositional forces and the variety of audience responses and social models—gay, ethnic, old-age—that it permits, television is still framed by the values and goals of a bourgeois "reality" that allows resistance to come at its own request and "in its own name."[9] Resistance is allowed to enter as a strategy of exploiting a wider consumer base, as long as it leaves unchallenged the fundamental values (family, individual success, material comfort, technical know-how, triumph over challenge, knowledge as an industry). In other words, advertising doesn't vary in its aim, although it sometimes varies in the structure of its appeal and the audience to which the appeal is made.[10] Though you might sell cough medicine to businessmen, diapers to mothers, houses to newlyweds, or household products to housewives, the consistent aim accounts for advertising's oft-criticized sameness. Even programming that may seem to be doing something different, looking to borrow cinema's auteurism in programs such as David Lynch's *Twin Peaks*, Steven Spielberg's *Amazing Stories*, or Oliver Stone's *Wild Palms*, for instance, are simply setting out to buy a different audience—perhaps educated professionals who might otherwise play movies on their TVs.

A recognition of commercial and institutional appropriation is crucial in order to understand a perceived crisis in the nature and fate of the "public intellectual" in post–World War II American life and to fully grasp the implications of the paranoia-inflected texts discussed in this chapter: the novel *What Makes Sammy Run?* (1941) and the films *A Face in the Crowd* (1957) and *Sweet Smell of Success* (1957). As Scott McLemee observes in "After the Last Intellectual," the conditions in the 1950s that fostered the "life of the intellectual freelancer … affordable rent, an abundance of magazines open to certain kinds of reviewing and essay writing, and the tendency of society to produce 'surplus intellectuals' unable to find employment in well-established institutions—were already disappearing."[11] This golden twilight of politically engaged yet independently minded critics occurs at the same moment as television's golden age and mostly within the same New York terrain. Although the social factors that contribute to the blunting of the American intellectual edge are more complex than simply television, it becomes the object of paranoid blame. When critical diversity becomes appropriated into corporate and institutional realms, the independent intellectual ceases to exist as an effective critic of society. This is the field of broadcasting: public purpose become publicity, the public intellectual become publicist.

The narrator of Budd Schulberg's 1941 novel *What Makes Sammy Run?* embodies the intellectual's anxiety in the face of a new type.[12] This new type is Sammy Glick, the huckster, a creature of radio, commerce, and new ethnicities entering the public sphere. Theater critic and ambivalent screenwriter Al Manheim narrates the story of Sammy, a Jewish character whose name will become synonymous with the midcentury huckster, an ambitious copyboy who gets his first break as a radio columnist. Manheim, who is hard-drinking, unambitious, and mostly unlucky in love, props himself up on his moral rectitude. He spends a lot of time drinking Sammy's booze and imposing a metanarrative of urban poverty to explain Sammy's embarrassing striving and eventual Hollywood success. For Schulberg, only art created outside a desire to make money or sell a brand, even the brand of the self, can be legitimate. These two incommensurable poles are represented by the New York theater and the Los Angeles film industry. When Sammy writes a play about radio so that he can get more money as a screenwriter, Al looks on in despair.

McLemee's essay jettisons the romantic nostalgia that characterizes Manheim's viewpoint as well as interventions such as Russell Jacoby's seminal 1987 book *The Last Intellectuals*.[13] For McLemee, the literary culture of "little magazines, avant-garde sects, and other marginal niches" found power in deviance, diversity, and the refusal of powerful institutions.[14] But, in the 1950s, with the ironic fact that it was television in the "front wave," the work of intellectuals became indispensable to the ideological task of mass culture. This task is to bind the centrifugal force of suburban society—its progressive privatization and professionalization—to the neutralizations and normalizations of the status quo. To forge hegemony out of a citizenry of affluent individualists, to produce these citizens as commodities and consumers, is a job requiring immense intellectual capital. The disruptions that prosperity threatened and the challenges of a race not only into outer space but a race for American scientific and cultural ascendancy in general created the conditions for a wholesale appropriation of intellectuals into the academy. Things got so bad in the urban garrets of the artist/intellectual because times got so good. The smell of smoke and scotch couldn't be fanned out of the aseptic corridors of power. It had become pervasive. The messy beans that the film *Tommy* attributes to television and its cults is mistaken; it is in fact quite ideologically tidy. Both the public good and the public intellectual are efficiently deployed into salesmanship, skepticism, and obfuscating jargon. Paranoia would seem to be a small price to pay for a system in which all alternatives are equalized in the "marketplace" of ideas.[15]

The ability of television to level fiction and truth and to monetize the culture's myths is television's modus operandi as well as its ideological power. As White notes, an actor can directly address the viewer and firmly attest, "I'm not really a doctor, but I really am an actor; and as an actor in another television text, I really play a doctor."[16] In reality he really is playing the role. Just as the barriers between the television and nontelevision worlds are permeable, there is a blurred distinction between a personality and a salesman as well as between programming and selling. There are several ways in which this takes place. At times a fictional or nonhuman character can transcend his, her, or its role in the commercial world to become a pop icon. These include Palmolive dishwashing liquid's Madge ("You're soaking in it"); Charmin toilet paper's Mr. Whipple ("Please don't squeeze the Charmin"); the Energizer battery mechanical bunny ("Keeps on going"); and Fruit of the Loom underwear's angst-ridden talking fruits. Syndicated pitchman Ernest even managed to leverage his signature shout of "Hey Vern!" into a film franchise, as did Geico Insurance's caveman into a television show.

More difficult to understand is the use of a food or beverage as pitch person—or, rather, pitch product. In this case the pitch is delivered by the actual consumable. The Pillsbury Doughboy is famous for his sub-culture of doughy erotica. A smorgasbord of plain and peanut M&Ms, wannabe Foster Farms chickens, and raisins urge viewers to eat me, choose me, or even—as one torch-singing prepubescent girl puts it with JonBenét Ramsey fervor—"Daddy, if you want to please me, then you've got to cheese me." One example of this technique appears in a movie theater advertisement. The "man" is a container of concession stand popcorn, presumably buttered. The "woman" is a cup of soda—clearly marked *Pepsi*. After escorting his companion to "her" seat, Popcorn-Box Man goes to the lobby, quickly returning with snacks including another cup of Pepsi, which he begins to suck through a straw. He's drinking a Pepsi while he's dating a Pepsi. A furor arose around a more high-profile instance: the Muppet's Miss Piggy pitching Denny's sausage and bacon combo. A comment by the advertising agency's representative, quoted in *People* magazine, suggests television's truth of fictionality when in the service of commerce: "'If we had a real live pig in there eating bacon, then there'd be issues.'"[17] Finally, new digital technologies have made it possible for dead celebrities to be salespeople. Mahatma Ghandi and Amelia Earhart "think different [*sic*]" for Apple Computers, Sammy Davis Jr. wears Gap khakis, John Wayne prefers Coors beer, and Fred Astaire dances with a Dirt Devil vacuum cleaner. As these examples demonstrate, even when television is false, it may be real and right for the televisual world: a recognized landscape of characters, settings, and situations in which the workers manning the phones for private security systems are always middle-aged white men. The appeal of television isn't that anybody really believes what it shows, but that it affirms that it's really playing at it.

Ideological criticism applied to television often originates in a Marxist critique of culture, which seeks to unmask the economic superstruc-ture that naturalizes its base. Dominant ideological positions such as patriarchy or capitalism are based primarily on economic or material interests, and they often represent the interests of a ruling class, ethnicity, or dominant gender. Marxism tells us that ideology, as expressed through culture and other social structures, is false consciousness, an illusion of truth. It's always just the truth of some fiction, always some thing that invokes the power of myth to control some other thing. It attempts in every possible way to deflect attention from itself and convince you that you act freely and naturally, that you'd have to be insane, criminal, or—in some cases—female to question it. Through culture, ideology natural-izes a position where challenge is either licensed or made deviant, a process Michel Foucault calls the "implantation of perversion."[18] Within the terms of Marxist criticism, this strategy justifies a particular power structure and presents your participation in it as a sensible choice.[19]

In this construct nothing is real. Real knowledge of the really real is seen as always inaccessible and seeking it is futile. Since reality itself is the great mask of ideology, a perception of reality is the best tool of ideology. To call one thing more real than another is either nonsense or ideological self-justification. Whatever "reality" this is, it has been invented to serve some ulterior motive. If, for Francis Bacon in the seventeenth century knowledge is power, for Foucault in our age knowledge is nothing but power. It cannot be transcended, but at best manipulated. Resistance can come through the playful request of power, yet in the words of Star Trek's Borg, "You will be assimilated."

Though classical Marxism emphasizes almost exclusively the economic base of the social superstructure, other strains—found in the work of theorists such as Louis Althusser, Mikhail Bakhtin, and Antonio Gramsci—consider different and competing ideological bases, all of which struggle for dominance. These systems are still, of course, not natural, real, or true. In fact they're still paranoid, as well as unstable and conflicted. The point is how these ideological conflicts are acknowledged within the framework of hegemonic consent.

An example of this criticism in action would be an analysis of how social and personal problems are solved. Television is characterized by variety, a range of expressions that are stabilized by institutions such as Ed Sullivan, hospitals, the family, and Oprah Winfrey. Its variety is legendary, its transitions absurd; but it always attempts to naturalize, stabilize, and domesticate. The variety of incident on dramas such as *Chicago Hope* or situation comedies such as *The Mary Tyler Moore Show* is always contained. The great multiplicity and chaos that television gen-erates is always located within a strong social order, within the confines of a state apparatus (such as a police station or a military base) or within an ideological state apparatus (such as a law firm, hospital, talk show, corporation, or family). Television creates ceaseless anxiety about crime or our health, and then reassures us that the means exist within capitalism to fix every problem. Characters who are mugged or afflicted with cancer or caught in an embarrassing scrape at work get helped out by sympathetic police, kindly doctors, or understanding bosses. In this way, television reinforces the status quo and consolidates the power base.

The products of ideology, each of which masks itself as self-evident (such as liberty, equality, fraternity), are fragile as well as multiple and competing. People inhabit culture far more fluidly than a classical Marxist critique would suggest. Ideology will constantly call out to you, interpret you, and interpellate you into standardized norms that you're meant to occupy according to your sexuality, gender, or profession. Yet, social practice is never that homogenized, single, or unified, but rather a hegemonic struggle of nationalities, ages, genders, races, and sexualities. Ideological and other cultural criticism incessantly seeks to unmask these facades of power, to unleash the competing subcultures. Yet, when your intervention is always already coded as a consumer choice, it's almost impossible to get ahead of the process.

For Mimi White, ideological analysis emphasizes the commercial message as the link between television as an information and entertainment industry and television as an industry primarily feeding consumers to the economy. The viewer is the site at which these messages meet, as television offers entertainment and information as an excuse to consume. An ideological investigation must first address television in this very obvious way—as an economy of information and entertainment designed as a pretext for a global economy of consumption. Certainly, it is hardly necessary to mention that every viewer is not going to purchase everything shown on television. Nevertheless you are still addressed as a consumer. You are not imagined as a being beyond desire, immune to its address or appeal. You are assumed to be a creature of consummate and consuming desire, although it isn't meant to be satisfied or solved. It needs only to be expressed through shopping. Your natural function is to shop and consume. It is a sign of television's great power that even as it speaks to you as a buyer it doesn't care what you buy.

Even parts of television that seem to be outside of a commercial exchange are not. The instances of televised event coverage uninterrupted by commercials—like the funeral processions of Robert Fitzgerald Kennedy or Martin Luther King Jr. in the summer of 1968 or the September 11, 2001, attacks and their aftermath—are few and far between. Assassination attempts on a pope or a president, reports of

genocide on another continent, the death of a living saint or a populist
princess all must "break away" for a "message." Perhaps only the arrival of
extraterrestrials, as in Robert Wise's *The Day the Earth Stood Still* (1951),
or an epidemic of rage, as in Danny Boyle's *28 Days Later ...* (2002)
could entirely halt the commercial flow. More likely, an invasion would
simply generate new products, audiences, and marketing strategies as in
Graham Baker's *Alien Nation* (1988).

Television is still selling, even when it's selling people—in the form
of personalities, celebrities, idols, or stars—or simply more television.
Until recently, many cable channels operated outside the paradigm of
commercially interrupted programming, yet even in these cases, cable
constantly sold more cable programming, just as "commercial-free" public television sells itself as well as its corporate sponsors. Various channels sell various audiences. They might sell children, golfers, housewives,
newsmongers, or classic film buffs. The entertainment that television
provides is a pretext for its textual address to you as a consumer.

If, in 1941, Sammy Glick enters the scene as that huckster who will
drive the intellectual Al Manheim out of the bar and into corporate re-
spectability, marriage, and a regular job, it is in the postwar years that
the huckster finds his ultimate expression and form. Two late film noirs
about television, made at a moment of advancing televisual hegemony
(1957), Elia Kazan's *A Face in the Crowd* and Alexander Mackendrick's
Sweet Smell of Success, offer examples of this type: Anthony Franciosa's
Joey DePalma and Tony Curtis's Sidney Falco, respectively.[20] Both films
argue that along with the canonical archetypes of noir characterization
and stylization—low-key chiaroscuro lighting, off-center camera angles,
shocking or grotesque close-ups, unreliable doubling of reflections,
claustrophobic atmosphere set within an impassive if not malign depth
of field—we must add television.

How can the glamour of film noir have anything to do with the
flat-out banality of television? An answer may be found lurking—just
as monitors lurk in *Sweet Smell's* cavernous television studios—in the
historical crisis of criticality and the intellectual. As we have noted above,
this is a moment when transgression is appropriated into optimism and
optimism paradoxically becomes an opportunity for repression and
corruption. As film critic Richard Schickel notes in "Rerunning Film
Noir,"[21] noir style and thematics can be newly appreciated as a return
of the intellectual repressed. In so doing he takes a revisionist stance toward Paul Schrader's essential "Notes on *Film Noir*."[22] Schrader's was an
almost exclusive concentration on postwar malaise and "a new vicious-
ness" born of disillusioned servicemen, disaffected housewives, lost jobs,

atomic anomie, McCarthyism, Korea, and "Red Scares." Schickel mirrors McLemee's revisionist reading of Jacoby in insisting that the great noir dramas of the late 1940s through the mid- to late 1950s project a far more ambivalent view toward the good times of suburban prosperity and the intact family. Characterized by melancholy for "the residual yet still-potent malevolence of the postwar city" (39), the threat of transgressive sins and buried behavior haunt the "clean, spare, safe if not very interesting" suburbs of loving wives and "healthy, normal children" (38). Schickel goes on to write, "The true tragedy of postwar American life was how ahistorical it was, how quickly those who lived it forgot the war and the Depression, how easily they settled for comfort, routine, and passivity" (42).

This analysis of ideological dynamics may help us understand why films as late in the noir cycle as *A Face in the Crowd* and *Sweet Smell of Success* failed at the box office but remain potent expressions of their times. At the center of Mackendrick's movie are its dual condemnations of its main character, J.J. Hunsecker (Burt Lancaster), an all-powerful columnist and cultural arbiter, and his slimy cohort publicist, Sidney Falco. Against their intellectual deformities and calculating opportunism is set J.J.'s much younger sister, Suzy, who has improbably maintained her innocence despite J.J.'s gifts of mink coats and paternal obsessions. Her eventual defiance in the desire to marry a jazz guitarist who is, nevertheless, completely ordinary sends J.J. into a paranoid and destructive frenzy.

In his cultural influence, J.J. resembles the real-life Hedda Hopper or Louella Parsons, or the fictional drama critic that George Sanders plays in Joseph L. Mankiewicz's *All about Eve* (1950), although he eclipses them all. From his private booth at the 21 Club, J.J. would seem to control the destiny of every artist, performer, and politician in New York, including a philandering presidential hopeful. In addition to his column, J.J. has recently gotten his own television show through which, under the guise of a self-defined Jeffersonian democracy, he proposes to cleanse America by directing "the choice and predilections of sixty million viewers in the greatest country in the world!" His fascist predilections receive stylistic analogue in the film's über-aestheticization of New York, a nighttime metropolis flashing, seething, and glistening with the sweat of ambition and a world-encompassing depth of field.

It would seem to be possible to follow the film's moral compass by reading its expressionistic noir as a metaphysical accusation. But we don't; we see it much as Schickel suggests, as "a wounded beast," obliging people "who thought they had made their escape" to return and measure their smug happiness against it (38). J.J. asks the dependent Falco to plant drugs on Suzy's fiancé and destroy their engagement; when Falco feebly demurs, J.J. seals the deal by offering access to his column and TV show. Having sold his soul, Sidney is not unaware of his own damnation, but his masochism requires him to eat J.J.'s dirt "and call it manna."

Beyond observing this milieu as a vision of social degradation requiring redemption, we identify a virulent, active protest on the part of cinema itself. J.J. and Sidney, at film's close, are and will remain irredeemable. Their efforts toward literary potency, intellectual relevance, and public mobilization are reduced, by a threatened cinema, into gossip, blackmail, and publicity mongering perpetrated by the unworthy. Eventually, television's ideological onslaught will turn the dark and doomed television studio of *Sweet Smell* into the space of prancing cigarette boxes and the domesticated movie stars that we will see in Richard Benjamin's *My Favorite Year* (set in 1954, but produced in 1982). Despite the ahistorical space that television commentary often occupies, the timing here is crucial. The commodity ecstasy of TV's *The Price Is Right* began one year before *Sweet Smell* was made, but only reached its apotheosis when Bob Barker reinvented it in 1972. By that time, the CBS television studio "in Hollywood" seemed to be always bathed in high-key lighting, and there is no shame—no fatal beatings in darkened alleys, no thugs in the guise of cops, no traumatized young women in slips threatening suicide at an open window. One just needs to guess the right price.

A Face in the Crowd shares the noir aesthetic of *Sweet Smell* as well as the character of the huckster and a cynical take on presidential politics. Sixteen years after Sammy Glick, Budd Schulberg wrote the screenplay for *A Face in the Crowd*, based on his own novel *The Arkansas Traveler*. At the beginning of the film, human-interest radio reporter Marcia Jeffries (Patricia Neal) discovers Larry Rhodes (Andy Griffith) sleeping off a bender in a Piggott, Arkansas, jailhouse and hires him as a radio personality. She's an independent woman with freedom and ideas—a loaded gun. She dubs him "Lonesome" and arranges for him to take over a local radio program. As long as Rhodes confines himself to dispensing folksy wisdom and strumming his "mama guitar," this bad good ole boy can't get into too much trouble. But he no sooner assumes control of his own television program than he gives expression to all of his baser impulses—defiling a baton twirler (Lee Remick), bullying a senator, and betraying the loyal and infatuated Marcia. His lack of restraint is symbolized by the soda fountain he has installed in his penthouse apartment.

Rhodes wants too much, but at the same time he doesn't know what he wants other than power, and that confusion threatens democracy and culture. The music of Ludwig van Beethoven accompanies a televised baton-twirling bit; elections and mass politics are reduced to money, slogans, and a fake cracker barrel with no crackers in it.[23] In a reprise of Al Manheim, the film's voice of reason—in the form of Vanderbilt-educated journalist Mel Miller (Walter Matthau)—withdraws to a bar to nurse his wounded sense of superiority along with his whiskey. Under Mel's smarmy, ultrapatriarchical tutelage Marcia is able to recognize the monster she created and accept her own responsibility to destroy him. She exposes Lonesome to the perils of a live audio feed, and he predictably disintegrates like a vampire in sunlight.

So who or what is Lonesome, really? When asked where he comes from, he replies, "Oh, from all over." He's already a virtual creature. He's from everywhere, nowhere, elsewhere. His hometown is "Riddle," described as a "compost heap." It turns out he's just a low-class, drunken jailbird intoxicated with power and possessing only contempt for his audience of good simple American folk. As it has in *Sweet Smell*, television has eroded the reliable channels of influence; popularity determines who speaks. Lonesome, abetted by an ambitious woman, shouldn't be in control of the public airwaves. Instead, Mel, the good journalist and sexual rival of Lonesome, will triumph. He doesn't bring about Lonesome's downfall, but he takes the opportunity provided by it to deliver a tongue-lashing to the beaten man and usher Marcia into a taxi. He doesn't have Lonesome's energy or charisma, but he did go to a good college.

In this film, the marginal classes, from which Lonesome is plucked, are easily led astray. Women, black folk, and the poor are particularly susceptible to his charms. Responding to an early monologue about the chore of cleaning sinks, a weary housewife rhetorically asks, "How would he know that?" Young women are unhinged by his sexual charisma—gathering in screaming crowds to greet him. In Memphis, Lonesome features a "colored" woman on his television program, asking for contributions to re-build her burnt-down house. In his understanding of his listeners and viewers, he reveals a genial contempt for institutional hierarchy. The masses are, like so much of his own motivation, personal to him; he wants always to be "a free man in the morning." Yet, after his public humiliation, Lonesome rages at the black workers assembled at his failed political fundraiser, calling them "monkeys" and crazily demanding that they love him again. Earlier, he had flaunted his power to unleash the "bush-monkeys" from traditional political control. They can be reined in only by a lack of opportunity, but opportunity is exactly what the power of television wantonly distributes.

The first hour of *A Face in the Crowd* is shattered into episodes: Lonesome in the county jail, Lonesome at the radio station, listeners reacting to broadcasts. The plot moves quickly from radio to television, reflecting the rapid deregulation and consolidation taking place in 50s broadcasting. This is also the movement from local responsibility to national impersonality and profit, from individual inspiration and creativity to the corporate boardroom. Mirroring the episodic nature of television itself, this structure isn't so much homage to television as a way to set up a second hour of high cinema's glorious narrative progression and noirish visuals. During the second half, beginning when Lonesome proposes marriage to Marcia at his penthouse, the film moves into full-fledged recuperative narrative. Now it seeks its vindication as legitimate art in contrast to the first episodic, televisual section of the film. Another specifically filmic transformation occurs: Marcia, who started out as a susceptible hick from Arkansas, suddenly loses her hick accent and assumes the star power and wardrobe of a beautiful and chic Patricia Neal. She is sexually betrayed—Lonesome marries Lee Remick's prancing Betty Lou—but she looks fabulous.

As he becomes more successful and Marcia becomes more disenchanted, although no less in love with him, Lonesome is abetted in his goals by another member of his entourage: the publicist Joey DePalma. Like Sammy Glick, DePalma starts out as a gofer, but seizes every opportunity that presents itself in order to satisfy an ambition that the film pretends not to understand. When the Memphis-based Lonesome's unconventional ways go afoul of his "Mattress King" sponsor, Joey sells the performer to New York's biggest ad agency, a guarantee of coast-to-coast influence. Joey insidiously parlays Lonesome toward a hubris about his commercial and political reach that not only betrays Lonesome's anti-hierarchical origins, but sets Joey up to take over Lonesome's entire empire—not to mention his wife. When the cuckolded Lonesome tries to fire his rival, Joey reveals he owns 51 percent of Lonesome, screaming, "You're in bed with me, Larry! In bed!" Joey's aura of perverted sexuality, stripped of carnality and driven by sheer manipulation, trumps Lonesome's, by now, quaint horniness and reveals Joey as the true new flesh.

Even as it denounces television, *A Face in the Crowd* dreams of what television really should be—not an agency of celebrity or advertisement, not a medium of exploitation. It should, we get the impression, be cinema. This film dreams of that possibility, acting out its wish through the destruction of an exemplar. In the terms of this film, good television would appear to be live, unrehearsed, unsponsored. Good television wouldn't corrupt its advertisers because it wouldn't be a medium of selling and consumption; wouldn't depend on the public's whim for success; and paradoxically wouldn't be a medium of mass manipulation. During his early rise, Lonesome seems to understand this. He self-reflexively comments on the microphone when discovered in the Piggott jailhouse and on the local radio station. After moving to a Memphis television studio, Lonesome turns the cameras around to reveal the studio audience and the monitors. This is how he "show[s] the folks" how programs are constructed, foregrounding the program's sponsorship and therefore commercial intent. His relationship to the TV apparatus becomes more problematic when he purchases his own applause machine as a domestic appliance and has a flunky operate it in response to his comments. It is hardly surprising that it is the apparatus that becomes the tool of his undoing when Marcia fiddles with the audio knobs.

Although taking pains not to be political, *A Face in the Crowd* reveals that television commodifies and corrupts its sponsors; commodifies and sells viewers; and facilitates consumption before all other purposes. And it makes the assumption that this is a catastrophe, as if entering an economy of exchange could be something to which real human beings in a real, good world could possibly be immune; something that we, as good, real people would automatically hate as a sign of corruption. In this way, *A Face in the Crowd* constructs its ideal form of being human. It assumes our horrified reaction once the nature of television is unmasked through the joint agency of cinema, a betraying woman, and the manipulation of video's own technology.

This exploitation device, wielder of opinion, medium of mass persuasion: What is it trying to persuade us to do? Does it make us want something that isn't good for us, something that will destroy our humanity? How else can we justify an attack on what has been freely chosen by people who are simultaneously viewers and citizens? *A Face in the Crowd*, like many films about television, has an unexamined nostalgia for a humanist universe filled with eternal values that are contradictory to those things that television brings with it, chief among them the perversion of watching television. Without being too shocked we have to ask, why shouldn't television do these things? Why do we assume that television is slaughtering something that we need rather than clearing away obsolete artifacts? Why shouldn't television change politics, consumption, the economy, and our souls? As Lonesome says to Senator Fuller, after recommending an entirely new television-friendly personality, "No hard feelings here; we're talking television."

A Face in the Crowd eventually exposes its own cinematic assumptions. What it hates is not so much television, as the people who watch it. The film demonstrates that television only appeals to so many because so many are so stupid, vulgar, and idiotic. A medium that would manipulate the masses is corrupted not so much by itself but by that contact. This is an old refrain. High modernism has always betrayed its revolutionary and avant-garde promises, unable to suppress its own contempt for the people it's supposed to revolutionize. It isn't so much television that we're meant to fear, but the possibility that television might incite the masses to weigh in with their own clumsy attempts to have something to do with real culture.

The film's instincts about Griffith's televisual appeal proved to be dead-on. He went on to star as the congenial patriarch of Mayberry and then as the congenial attorney Matlock. At the beginning of *A Face in the Crowd*, Griffith's character also seems congenial, but that impression is exposed as a sham as he exhibits an increasingly polarized Jekyll and Hyde personality. In this case, as in so many others, the magic transformation results from exposure to the broadcast waves themselves. Cinema takes television to the woodshed.

And yet, the beating it delivers becomes increasingly hard to cheer, and we are increasingly moved to ask: Why does the cinema of television so often subtly backfire in its attempts to demonize televisual culture and ideology? Why does the attack so often reside in characters we find it difficult to despise completely or in models of cinematic integrity we find it hard to admire totally? Doubt about the precision of the cinematic assault on television will surface in several of the films we will discuss in this book—*Being There, Network*, and *Tootsie* among others—and it is incumbent upon us to investigate this ambivalence toward television's ideology and cinema's attitudes and aesthetics. The generalized crisis of critique and of intellectual and artistic vision that is often at the source of cinema's alarm about television produces the stylistic and thematic excesses we have been noting, but the conundrum here is how these excesses, as in film noir about television, sabotage the attack even as they succeed as cinema.

We approach the texts discussed here from a far more media-saturated future than the context of their production. Furthermore, we are in the midst of a technological transformation. Increasingly, technology no longer supports the advertising model of broadcasting that has existed since 1922 and dominated during the mid-to late 50s, so much so that the quintessential protagonist of late 50s and early 60s cinema and television is the ad man.[24] It is hard to avoid the observation that many content users engage in what is technically criminal activity: duping DVDs and downloading content. Certainly this is true of anyone with sufficient bandwidth, such as the population of American college students. As an audience, Americans have become accustomed, even dependent on free content, but now can circumvent the advertisements that have traditionally paid for it all. Now, it is the corporations that have become paranoid about their own viewers, sending barrages of cease and desist letters and bringing civil actions. But these actions against viewers shouldn't be surprising. As Meehan reminds us, we were never the customers in the first place, but always the commodity. It remains to be seen what will happen should viewers refuse to give their consumer time in return for the content they expect to be cheap and plentiful, like water out of the tap.

4

New Flesh

As the previous chapter suggested, ideological criticism has proven inadequate to many of the questions that television raises. Allied with psychoanalysis, Marxist criticism assumes a particular theoretical model of a subject that misrecognizes itself; only analysis can reveal the true nature of the social formation out of which the subject arises. Television blocks this goal through decriticalization. Here we mean *critical* in the sense of engaged criticism, and also in the sense of "important" or "acute." Paradoxically, television immunizes itself from serious ideological intervention by encouraging indifference in viewers. Nothing matters, television tells us, and television, especially, doesn't matter. The dominant television series of the 1990s, after all, was *Seinfeld*, the self-proclaimed goal of which was to be "a show about nothing."

Overcoming the limits of a Marxist, Freudian, or post-structuralist critique requires the recognition that a new way to produce signs may also require a new critical model. We shouldn't be surprised, then, if television and its criticism suggest a different kind of subject or produce intimations of a different subjective evolution. This chapter borrows its title from David Cronenberg's *Videodrome* (1983), a movie about the use of television for good and evil and its agency in forging what the film terms a "new flesh."

Both Jean Baudrillard and Hans Magnus Enzensberger take positions that recognize a change in subjectivity and a changed relationship to traditional ideological criticism. Both offer possible responses to these changes. In their respective articles "Requiem for the Media" and "Constituents of a Theory of the Media" both start from a leftist view that television should somehow be better than it is. Further, these critics review the possibilities of mobilizing the medium for a revolution leading us to utopia. In chapter 8, we'll suggest ways in which the new subjectivity they describe may also originate in old fears about femininity. Both Enzensberger and Baudrillard contemplate these possibilities with differing degrees of optimism, though they both stop short of connecting the dots between women, television, and the New Flesh.

In "Constituents of a Theory of the Media," Enzensberger quickly addresses a problem that he and Baudrillard will both tackle: the impotence of the current Left and its badly aimed attacks on mass media.[1] An important Marxist philosopher and leftist critic of the media, Enzensberger observes that television represents the triumph of capitalism as a global ideology. Television and capitalism are natural allies because television, as the utmost consciousness-shaping medium, matches capitalism's status as the utmost consciousness-shaping ideology. Capitalism's great strength and great threat is its ability to evoke expressions of desire and then exploit them. It fetters and enslaves desire as privatized consumption for the many and profit for the few.[2]

This approach to the medium exposes a substantial roadblock: television can't mobilize the masses in a revolutionary way without reproducing a regressive ideology. The mass media decides what you want, offers it to you, and then guarantees that you can only get it through profit-making production and consumer activities that will serve mainly to enrich the ruling class. In the late twentieth century, the militant, Old Left encounters new media technologies with a combination of fear, surrender, and contempt—attitudes that haven't led to insight or effective action and time and again misjudge the extent to which consumers are anxious to use their cell phones to change the world. Old Left critiques point out that in their present forms media do not truly encourage user participation, and that even when they do solicit interaction, the appeal is carefully circumscribed within a status-seeking status quo of renewed obsolescence. They transmit only in order to refigure desire into fascination, and satisfaction into product consumption. The one-way transmission of media could never threaten a ruling class. Dialoging spaces such as MySpace, Wikipedia, or YouTube trespass on the privileges of power only as a pathway to effective consumption. Mimi White, in "Ideological Analysis and Television," argues that television creates a "heterogenous unity" (190). Even though a multitude of channels and programs offers a wide and often contradictory "variety of issues, voices, positions and messages" (190), this still does not mean that viewers are typically free to negotiate subversive readings. Television's mainstream ideological success and its pleasures depend on a regulated and repetitive plurality seemingly capable of speaking to everyone (190–194). The noncommunicative medium of television, as well as the communicative

medium of Internet interactivity, still only offer forced choices available
from the point of view of the ruling class. They do not allow the option
of talking back outside of rigid conversational protocols. This is true
even when the interactive communications are illegal, predatory, or
pornographic.

By reductively analyzing the media only through its function as a capitalist tool, the Left has simply stranded itself in irrelevance. Its theory of
the media is really the absence of such a theory. As Enzensberger posits,
"So far there is no Marxist theory of the media."[3] He would prefer to characterize the media as a tenable vehicle to mobilize the masses, even though
it has heretofore only been used to control and manipulate. The media
can and should be a tool for mass participation rather than exclusively a
tool for hawking and pitching. To realize these possibilities, Enzensberger
argues, we need to get over our fear of a media future. For him, visions
of a monolithic consciousness-shaping industry à la George Orwell
are frightening, but we should accept the fact that *1984* didn't happen.
We didn't become automatons to Big Brother and no all-powerful fascist bogeyman materialized. But these failed predictions continue to
create problems for the Left in the form of a theoretical hangover. It is
not enough to conjure images of happy drones "driving a Jaguar to the
Apocalypse," as one popular slogan put it. The current Left needs a more
credible threat to maintain an effective critique.

There is another problem: In its virulent criticism and hysterically outmoded vision of manipulative robots and dehumanized conspiracy, the
radicalism of the Left has slipped away. Its defensiveness has rendered it
an organ of conservatism and traditionalism so that what was previously
a voice calling for revolutionary change is now one that mostly whines.
Demonizing the power of the media, Enzensberger argues, isolates the
Left and exiles it from its traditional stance of mobilizing and radicaliz-
ing. Consumed with hatred for industrial civilization, the Left has allied
itself with bourgeois nostalgia for the "really real." This dilemma certainly
bears a resemblance to that of the characters in Elia Kazan's *A Face in the
Crowd* (1957). The revenge of the milquetoast at the film's conclusion
is seen as the triumph of reality and a return to sanity. If we could just
be writers like Mel Miller rather than a television personality like Lonesome Larry Rhodes; if we could just be a man like Mel Miller rather than
a woman like Marcia Jeffries; if we could just be liberal and upper-class
and a Vanderbilt graduate, or even just let those people stay in charge,
everything would be great.

All this *Sturm und Drang* about authenticity and real culture
has obscured the possibility that the media might *be* the revolution.

Enzensberger notes this, observing that the Left's fear of the media has been a sign of its weakness. Ideology, particularly a capitalist one, can only benefit from this paranoia, as it does whenever fear and loathing force an analytical retreat. Retreat also supports a conservative position—an old fogeyism of constant carping and harping on the "good old days" when everything was more of a struggle and yet paradoxically better. If culture could only be like it was, this position implausibly suggests, it would be good instead of what it is now: traduced and contemptible. An acceptable, nonmanipulative media, Enzensberger points out, is an impossible dream. It exists only in the imagination and is not at all threatening to television or any other organ of global ideology.

Enzensberger also rejects a bogus liberal view that tells us all to log on and be liberated through access. The idealization of universal access masks the agenda of television and the rest of the media behind notions of liberation. At present, consumers don't primarily acquire electronic devices so that they can become television producers. They're not struggling for media access in the public, bureaucratic, or political spheres. Capitalism triumphs as long as it can channel mass media into customized, private amusements, and this use of computers, the Internet, and video poses no threat to the power structure as long as everybody regards it as a hobby.[4] Though an intervention may take the form of hacking, infecting, plagiarizing, pirating, all the way to terrorizing, the production of consumers as criminals hardly overturns the consoldation of power. That power may actually request subversion as an opportunity to prosecute. The Left's despair when facing technological extensions of capitalist power is itself a hallmark of closed systems of ideology: There can be no outside that isn't anticipated and manufactured from the inside.

For Enzensberger, a new, more positive, even revolutionary theory of the media would propose that everyone is a manipulator. Everyone can be a producer of his or her own desires in addition to being a passive consumer. We can allow the media to become a mass media as long as its form and function are not simply delivered from the ruling class to the victim consumer. Enzensberger identifies radical potential in mass participation beyond mere access. The contradictions of professional and amateur, licensed broadcasters and viewers, shoppers and capitalists are liquidated through the interactive ideal: "Networklike communications models built on the principle of reversibility of circuits might give indications of how to overcome this situation: a mass newspaper, written and distributed by its readers, a video network of politically active groups."[5] In Enzensberger's model people produce the very things that they consume—a proposal with clear Marxist dimensions and a huge presumption that this is something people want to do. One might point to the rise of YouTube as a realization of this construct, but multiple uploads of karaoke-style goofs and *Saturday Night Live*'s unbleeped "Dick in a Box" skit are probably not what Enzensberger had in mind—not a nation of jackasses.

Enzensberger would expose the cult of individuality, the cult of the private, the cult of leisure; would deprogram mass consumers into public beings; would transform mass identity into public identity. The media, following the model of private car ownership, is exposed as a recognition by capitalism of collective wishes. We wanted to be more mobile; now we want to have greater access and greater opportunities for exchange. Capitalism, to its credit, recognizes our collective wishes, but it does so to trap them and rob them of any radical aspiration—in other words, to close them down and simplify: select the safest car seat, go on a beach vacation, get to work, increase productivity, then buy another car and another car seat, go to a mountain vacation, and then get a better job.

Capitalism recognizes collective wishes, but only in order to increase labor and consumption. Your time loses its public value—as opposed to its "mass"—when it is devoted to so-called personal or leisure use of the media. When this is the case, Enzensberger warns, the subversive potential of electronic media is co-opted or neutralized. Until the Left shakes off its nostalgia for authenticity and utopian thinking—until it recognizes the potential of the media as an agency of public rather than massively private expression—and drops its tedious attacks on the media as a dehumanizing agent, it will remain unable to radicalize its own critique.

Enzensberger quotes Marshall McLuhan's great dictum "the medium is the message" as provocative idiocy. To announce "the medium is the message" is to neutralize the apparatus. If the medium is the message then it really has no content; it has nothing to say. Many theorists, other than Jerry Seinfeld, have entertained the possibility that television is the great medium of nothingness: nothing matters. But if we decide on that, Enzensberger argues, we decide that its ideological content is irrelevant. Enzensberger wants to move past that point toward genuinely radical ideas. First, if we get rid of the idea of the media as monolithic, controlled, and external, we can become better—more evolved—human beings. Or we can just as easily devolve into YouTube watchers unable to distinguish the radical from the banal. Second, the media shouldn't simply be a mass organ of private consumption, but must be a mass organ of public production. That public production may have become virtually indistinguishable from mass private production is a development that Enzensberger seems not to have foreseen.

In "Requiem for the Media," Jean Baudrillard directly addresses Enzensberger's argument, beginning with the first sentence, which quotes, " 'There is no theory of the media.' "[6] But Baudrillard will go further. For him, all attempts to theorize the media are hopeless, because—he argues—the media is precisely that which demonstrates the obsolescence and irrelevance of high theory. Attempts to theorize, to come to an abstract, essential, or universal determination about the nature of the media, are what the media fights against and forbids. Its primary function may be to destroy the essentializing capacity that is at the heart of theoretical investigation. To employ Marxist theory, as Enzensberger does, to argue for a new production base in which everybody produces the very products they consume, is about as effective as Marxism has been as an economic system throughout the century—which is to say, not at all. In other words, for Baudrillard, "the radical alternative lies elsewhere" (125).

The movement known as cognitive, analytic, synthetic, or neoformalist and associated with the University of Wisconsin–Madison argues that all of film studies should lie elsewhere. In *Post-Theory: Reconstructing Film Studies*, David Bordwell and Noel Carroll reject the "vagaries," "sedimented dogma," "aggregate of doctrines," "caricatural positions," and "ethereal speculations of Grand Theory" by which they primarily mean Marxist criticism and psychoanalytic theory as they have been applied to film.[7] Putting aside the question of their own approach, the histories of film and television criticism and the histories of film and television are intertwined with these post-structuralist discourses. It seems strange to throw out the baby with the theoretical bath water, particularly when Bordwell himself employs a bit of pop psychology when he writes, "Doubtless culturalism instilled in media academics a sense of empowerment. By studying movies and TV shows one could purportedly contribute to political struggles on behalf of the disadvantaged." He does, however, correctly note the "ineradicable whiff of elitism" and the "left-wing pessimism" that pervade so much Marxist criticism.[8]

For Baudrillard, despite the promises of revolution and the imagined utopia of consumers as producers, the production base has not changed one iota. Nothing has changed, let alone been revolutionized. Baudrillard refers to what he calls the "immense retardation of classical Marxist theory" (125). Its official practice has not been able to prevent or delay capitalism's triumph over much of the world. It hasn't even managed to inspect its own presumptions, hasn't accused itself of its own failure in

purposes. One example is the rhetoric that surrounded the so-called Y2K problem or "millennium bug." Consumers were not urged to reconcile themselves with their idea of God but instead to purchase some extra, specially designed supplies. Magazines published how-to articles on hunkering down, and taste tests of survival foodstuffs. The media practices a seduction of consumption that, like all seductions, bears no relationship to authenticity. Authenticity is already constructed as a marketing drive. Buy the right brand of freeze-dried food and you will be safe and comfortable during the civil unrest. This message, be it violent or angry, can only act as diversion, flow, regulation, and an occasion to decriticalize its own address. Put a meaningful address on television and the vicious or virtuous media will instantly banalize and decriticalize it, will turn it into flow, make it an event not unlike other events. Similarity is more important than difference. Crisis is reduced to a moment of consumption.

Whether or not this is a bad thing can only be assessed in terms of what it supposedly corrupts. Perhaps we are exiled from authenticity and the sacrosanctity of our subjectivity. Nevertheless, television moves us past that realization quickly and indifferently enough to miss an occasion for holocaust or communion. By forbidding any response outside a gamelike, private manipulation, television short-circuits traditional desire. Demand is a game, our desire simply a request without any assumption of adequate or genuine fulfillment. What fool supposes television could make us content and happy? We all know that television is frustrating, irritating, and nonfulfilling, and television knows it, too.

Baudrillard advises that if we want television to be revolutionary, apocalyptic, or cataclysmic; if we want to return it to some former model of fulfilling or annihilating desire; if we want it to have a solution and a final resting place then we will have to destroy it completely. When you burn down your apartment house in order to meet your neighbors, make sure you pour extra gasoline on the television sets. You'll have to incinerate them in order to restore the community to a "public," chatting-with-the-neighbors condition.

Yet perhaps it is already too late for that remedy. Only in the destruction of the entire code of television could television become good in the way that Kazan and Enzensberger want it to. Even the most radical scorched-earth policy won't destroy TV's DNA. As viewers of Bruno Mattei's *Terminator II* (1989), Steven Speilberg's *Jurassic Park* (1993), and Jean-Pierre Jeunet's *Alien: Resurrection* (1997) have learned, it takes only the tiniest drop of blood or the tiniest e-chip to reproduce the code. Millions of years, vats of molten metal, even total mastery of space and time can't obliterate it.

Cronenberg's *Videodrome* is more ambivalent and complex than either Baudrillard's or Enzensberger's totalizing arguments, and certainly more inflected than most films about television. It represents television as an agent of "savage new times" and poses sophisticated questions about what to use it for: to control people's minds or to liberate them? It recognizes that television is an agent of evolution, of what it calls the New Flesh, although it remains murky about what that new flesh is. Is it redemption discovered in the Church of the Cathode Ray or destruction broadcast from a "Malaysian" torture chamber?

These antinomies are embodied by two women with whom the protagonist (James Wood as Max Renn) becomes emotionally involved—Nicki Brand (Deborah Harry) and Bianca O'Blivion (Sonja Smits). On one side, the sadomasochistic Videodrome produces protofascists who think that television can harden the spirit and save America from its softness, producing warriors for the coming savagery (an obscure future of seemingly Darwinian origins). Videodrome is an unclear process, with secret proponents and unknown origins. In a genetically mysterious way it fuses flesh with machine. For some reason, it can make use of the character Max. It is impossible to know what Videodrome is supposed to do, but it is conspiratorial, obsessive, repellant, and compelling—a clue, perhaps, to why only women understand it despite the fact that men deployed it.

On the side of religion, guru Brian O'Blivion (Jack Creley) and his daughter Bianca have created Videodrome to recover lost souls, but they are soon robbed of its original mission. Their noble project has been shanghaied for an evil purpose, although the difference between the two trajectories dissolved long before the action of the film commences. For them, television is the actualizer of the new flesh, the video word made flesh, the soul in the machine. They inscribe television as the messiah. Although these visions seem opposed in the film at times, they have much in common. Both organizations hope to stave off corruption, stamp out rot, replace those human parts that don't work right. Both see television as an apocalyptic agent, capable of either addressing these savage new times or bringing us into an ideal incarnation as video gods.

Both positions make the same mistake that Enzensberger makes in the idea that television is still attached to a humanist universe, still exists in a tangible world that can respond to its agency. Despite its shocking, radical qualities, *Videodrome* still subscribes to a biblical idea of the human soul. It asks whether we will preserve our souls or lose them. *Videodrome*'s sadomasochistic vision—tumors in the head, VCRs in the bowels, snuff TV as viral agent—and the O'Blivion concept of television as the new flesh messiah both imply a god machine. Like John the Baptist, *Videodrome* prepares the way for the character Neo in Andy and Larry Wachowski's *The Matrix* (1999), guiding us through the perdition of the machines toward Zion.

Regardless of what you think television is or what it is going to do, how inconsequential you think it may be, or how exclusively you focus on its profit-making aspects—the mistakes Max makes throughout *Videodrome*—television is ultimately the force and flow of evolution itself. As Max's agent Masha (Lynne Gorman) tells him, "The difference between you and Videodrome is that Videodrome has a philosophy and you don't." Our contact with television forever changes our relationship to our own subjectivity. If we believe cinema, it might grow tumors in our heads or induce us to murder, but, as Arthur Rimbaud noted more than a century ago, "after a long, involved and logical *derangement of all the senses* ... I is someone else."[12]

In *Videodrome*, Cronenberg brilliantly recognizes, as he does in other movies such as *Dead Ringers* (1988) and *Naked Lunch* (1991), that the televisual subject may be different from what the nontelevisual subject used to be. Bianca warns Max, "You will find that you are something quite different after exposure to Videodrome." Cronenberg establishes a postmodern vision of a new subject and charts the evolution to that state, but at the last moment he replaces it with apocalypse/utopia—a total vision, like those of Enzensberger and Baudrillard, of self-realization or obscene ecstasy. The new flesh in *Videodrome*—whether good or bad, evolutionary or destructive, Nicky or Bianca, fascist or religious—still represents a cinematic idea of the televisual subject. Even Cronenbergian cinema is a recuperating machine, an art form committed to resolution, narrative closure, unities, and finalities.

Videodrome, for all its televisual sophistication, continually retreats as a generic horror film into cinematic revulsion. This movement into horror is not random or arbitrary. The television is often implicated in horror films where it represents an alien or supernatural element unnaturally fused with or able to take over the body. Television operates like the pods in Donald Siegel's *Invasion of the Body Snatchers* (1956): lurking in benign domestic spaces, ready to take over the body of anyone who relaxes, turning people into automatons. In more recent horror films like Wes Craven's *Scream* (1996), old horror films play on the television in the background. Evil spirits in the form of Native American genocide victims infect the home depicted in Tobe Hooper's *Poltergeist* (1982) through the television set. The most reproduced image from that film shows the family's sweet, blond daughter ominously staring at the monitor only inches from her face. There is no image on the screen—only snow—as she solemnly intones "They're here." This is now itself an image of cinematic nostalgia for a time when television actually had dead time. The 2002 remake of a Japanese horror film visually quotes *Poltergeist*, while reversing its dynamics of possession: In Gore Verbinski's *The Ring*, the (now darkhaired) little girl is like the Native Americans in the earlier film, transformed from victim into avenging spirit. The "hook" of the film is that seven days after viewing a particular videotape, a person will die. That weeklong delay acknowledges television's most fundamental unit of programming time. Like *Poltergeist*, and akin to some images in *Videodrome*, she crawls out of the snow-covered screen. It might be the same little girl, whose family didn't take care of her properly, seeking revenge on other children watching videotapes without parental supervision. The family in *Poltergeist* can resolve its problems by moving out of the house and throwing away their TV set. Twenty years later, the situations in *The Ring*, and in the *Poltergeist* sequels, are long past the possibility of that solution. As we have said before, you can't kill TV.

A common trope of the horror film involves grafting new parts onto familiar bodies. In *Videodrome*, Brian O'Blivion observes that if television is now reality and reality is less than television, then television must assist us in mutating new organs of perception. During the film's key denouement, Max's hand becomes a gun, which he uses to shoot the evil corporate master Barry Convex (Les Carlson), who dies writhing on stage as the carapace of his body splits open and organs fly out. Convex, whose very name implies a distorting lens, has used as his "cover" the company Spectacular Optical, which produces "inexpensive spectacles for the third world and missile guidance systems for NATO." The film's ending, as the video word made flesh is announced, climaxes in the expulsion of presumably vestigial organs from a television set. The new flesh—typically brains, eyeballs, and hands—merges with the old to fulfill an exciting purpose, but it always goes wrong. The parts of the body over which one typically exerts the finest control won't obey. The hands strangle. The brain is abnormal. The remote control just won't change the channel. The New Flesh world just keeps getting creepier as new technologies advance. Digital graphics make it possible to put assorted heads and bodies together—Dustin Hoffman's Tootsie head on a body dressed in Yves St. Laurent, Oprah Winfrey's head stuck onto Ann-Margret's (!) body posing on the cover of *TV Guide*. The downside of new media technologies is always lurking, just as it lurks in other technological developments. For many years, movie mad scientists have been transplanting evil and renegade eyes, hands, faces, and brains on and into new bodies—Robert Weine's *The Hands of Orloc* (1925); James Whale's *Frankenstein* (1931); Robert Florey's *The Beast with Five Fingers* (1946); Georges Franju's *Eyes without a Face* (1959); Roger Corman's *X: The Man with X-Ray Eyes* (1963); Oliver Stone's *The Hand* (1981), and John Carpenter and Tobe Hooper's *Body Bags* (1993). New medical discoveries have now made it possible for real doctors to do the same, fastening "donor" hands and faces onto other people. As the doctors explain it, the trick isn't to sew them on, but to keep the body from rising up in rebellion to cast them off.

5

The Vidiot

Most of us who watch movies also watch television. In fact, most of us watch movies on television. One type of film character in particular, visiting our video world from another realm, demonstrates cinema's conflicted attitudes toward its rival medium. Both the "visitor" and the "video," as their common etymology suggests, appear to see and be seen, to show up and be shown: Darryl Hannah's mermaid character Madison in Ron Howard's *Splash* (1984) emerges from the sea to find a mate; and the eponymous characters in Nicolas Roeg's *The Man Who Fell to Earth* (1976; played by David Bowie) and John Carpenter's *Starman* (1984; played by Jeff Bridges) drop in from outer space, as do the sex- and pop culture–obsessed aliens in Julien Temple's *Earth Girls Are Easy* (1988). Jim Carrey's Truman spends most of Peter Weir's *The Truman Show* (1998) hatching out of an artificially controlled and constrained environment; Ed Pekurny (Matthew McConaughey) of Ron Howard's *EDtv* (1999) wanders, seemingly without direction or purpose, out of minimum-wage purgatory; and Dustin Hoffman's character Raymond Babbitt in Barry Levinson's *Rain Man* (1988) is isolated by both his institutionalization and autism. Confronting new conditions and dramatic situations, and usually operating under severe time constraints, these naïfs are educated by watching television and by television watching them.

Adapting Jerzy Kosinski's term, we call this character the *vidiot*. Kosinski's 1970 novel *Being There* and his screenplay for Hal Ashby's film of the same name (1979) depict a mediagenic, mindless protagonist. This character is perfect for television—made by TV for TV, ignorantly accepted by both the masses and the elite, functionally impotent in all senses of the word, but accepted as a seer. Through a series of improbable events over the course of only a few days, a simpleminded gardener named Chauncey (Peter Sellers) goes from being hidden in a back room to being groomed for the presidency of the United States. Until that point, his entire life had been spent tending a garden and watching television.

Kosinski first coins the term *videot* in the novel *Being There* as a disparaging reference to viewers. He ironically attributes it to "Lord Beauclerk, chairman of the board of the British Broadcasting Company," adding, "One doesn't want to work things out too finely, does one? I mean—not for the videots. It's what they want, after all: '*a god to punish, not a man of their infirmity,*' Eh?"[1]

Beauclerk is a distinctly minor character; this scornful remark, directed at what he himself has wrought, is his only utterance. In a subsequent interview, Kosinski expresses his personal concerns about the effect television has on viewers: "For me, imagining groups of solitary individuals watching their private, remote-controlled TV sets is the ultimate future terror: a nation of *videots*."[2] Kosinski looks backward—Beauclerk quotes William Shakespeare's *Coriolanus*—and forward to a televisual future, but he casts a pessimistic gaze in both directions: on the one hand is an arrogant leader presiding over a discontented people; on the other are isolated and oblivious invalids, too exhausted to get up and change the channel.

A variation on the vidiot is the naïf who finds him- or herself caught in a drama made indescribably worse by television intervention. Costa-Gavras's *Mad City* (1997) replays Billy Wilder's *Ace in the Hole* (1951) by substituting radio with television; a manipulating Chuck Tatum (Kirk Douglas) with a horde of TV reporters; and a victim of a mine accident with a victimized, but armed, Sam Baily (John Travolta). In Sidney Lumet's *Dog Day Afternoon* (1975), Al Pacino's character Sonny's laughable plan to steal money for his boyfriend's sex-change operation becomes an afternoon of performance art as the New York media quickly descend. The unrestrainable media in Joseph Rubin's *Return to Paradise* (1998), in the person of an overeager TV reporter, M. J. Major (Jada Pinkett Smith), publicly embarrasses the Malaysian government, virtually guaranteeing the execution of a hapless, hash-smoking naïf (Joaquin Phoenix).

The vidiot, or televisual naïf, functions at the opposite end of the scale from that creature of cinema, the holy fool. Holy fools, such as Billy in Peter Bogdanovich's *The Last Picture Show* (1971) and his counterpart Arnie Grape in Lasse Halstrom's *What's Eating Gilbert Grape?* (1993), are connected to nature. For them, nature is immortal and the place they assume in it is intuitive although futile and sacrificial—incessant road sweeping or incessant climbing to the top of the town water tower. They are immune to television; they don't watch it and they can't be programmed by it. Young Salvatore (Salvatore Cascio) in Giuseppe

Tornatone's *Cinema Paradiso* (1988) is a holy fool who sees the town's cinema projectionist "as his father and (this is the whole point) the movies as his mother."[3] Along these lines, Australian aborigines are very often depicted as noble savages as they are in Peter Weir's *The Last Wave* (1977); Werner Herzog's *Where the Green Ants Roam* (1984); and Wim Wenders's *Until the End of the World* (1991). Nature—as represented by the indigenous Australians—is incompatible with television. This tendency reveals something about the cultural prejudices at work when two adolescents with Down syndrome serve as narrative savants in Lars Von Trier's television-as-cinema series *The Kingdom* (1994). In Elia Kazan's *A Face in the Crowd* (1957), Lonesome Rhodes (Andy Griffith) begins as a holy fool but quickly becomes a vidiot. He is the monster who monitors, brought to life by the unnatural process of video scanning, and on his way to the new flesh.

One of the ways in which cinema and its theory view what Stanley Cavell calls "the fact of television" as different from the fact of cinema is through this archetypal character of the vidiot. The vidiot demonstrates the effects that can be made on an impressionable mind by watching or appearing on television. The process can take the form of brainwashing, as in the case of Raymond Shaw, the momma's boy (Lawrence Harvey) in John Frankenheimer's *The Manchurian Candidate* (1962), or self-diminution. Mike TeeVee (Paris Themmen) in Mel Stuart's *Willy Wonka and the Chocolate Factory* (1971) actually becomes the vidiot as new flesh when he literally "goes on television." Despite stern warnings, he insists on beaming himself through WonkaVision, a setup previously tested only on chocolate bars. When he appears on the monitor after flying through the air in "millions and millions of teensy weensy pieces," he is greatly reduced in size. His very flesh has been transformed by the encounter with television. Yet he is thrilled with the experience and wants only to repeat it. The anthropologically challenged Oompah Loompahs, in the same film, remain TV-resistant holy fools. They continually warn, in song, about many dangers, including television, demonstrating their wisdom. At the same time, they are seen as incapable of existing on their own in their native environment. They only survive under the paternalistic care of puppet master Willy Wonka (Gene Wilder).

The vidiot's psychology has not properly evolved. It may, in fact, have devolved, or disassociated itself from normal interpellation into proper subjective "place." Perhaps the vidiot has been denatured. Or perhaps he has experienced an oedipal short circuit. He resists or is forbidden all attempts at putting the family back together again. In *Being There*, the question of Chauncey's birth hangs unresolved. He could be the son rather than the employee of the old man whose death in the earliest scenes sets the plot in motion. No mention is made of a mother at all. Perhaps his isolation has been built on illegitimacy and embarrassment.

At any rate, the more alienated from the family, the more distant from the psychoanalytic *sine qua non* of reunion, the better suited one is for television performance. Guided by our reading of *Being There*, the following discussion is based on two observations about the vidiot: (1) the vidiot is not of the world, or, to put it another way, he exists in a world that has not survived him; and (2) despite his televisual construction, the vidiot is surprisingly sympathetic.

In "The Fact of Television," American philosopher Stanley Cavell asks, as does Baudrillard in "Requiem for the Media," whether or not television has any concern with the world at all. Does it realize or try to solve the world's problems? Is television something quite different in its connection to the world than art should be? These are questions that the vidiot also raises. Both Horace Newcomb and Charlotte Brunsdon argue that in order to study it seriously, television must have an aesthetic connection to the world.[4] Their position also assumes that legitimate critique must be based in this traditionalist aesthetic approach. Cavell shares this assumption; however, he discusses television textuality as quite different from the discrete, self-contained units identified with cinema or with other forms of high art. Its aesthetics are primarily serialized: repetitive and episodic. The classic structures of suspense, climax, and resolution are submitted to intermittent form and frequent interruption. The first fact of television, then—particularly classic network television—is that it doesn't create a text available for contemplation. If we approach television seeking integrity, identity, or other familiar enlightenments, we will be disappointed. Television opposes or ignores all of that, as it does the construction and placement of discrete individuality in its viewers.

A second fact concerns television's relationship to the world. Its mode is not one that is committed to realizing the world, but one that is committed to monitoring it. Television exists for all the shut-ins who feel that in-person access to the world is irrelevant or too dangerous. Television becomes really postmodern, and in a sense posthistorical, insofar as it ignores the lure of becoming cinema while refusing to see history as a force of progress and resolution. Television teaches immediate survival tactics for living in a world that didn't survive civilization with its mass exterminations; nuclear, biological, and chemical threats; and environmental chaos. The fear of television echoes the fear of what television monitors, covers, and surveys—the growing uninhabitability of the world. The key to living in a world you killed is not to kill your TV.

Cavell makes much of the distinction between the *world* and an *event*. Television is not the world, but an event standing out from the world; it is not concerned with revealing—much less redeeming—the world, as in, for instance, André Bazin's and Siegfried Kracauer's sense of cinematic realism. The truth of nature, notes Jacques Derrida, has been "affected—from without—by an overturning which modifies it in its interior, denatures it and obliges it to be separated *from itself*. Nature denaturing itself, being separated from itself, naturally gathering its outside into its interior, is *catastrophe*, a natural event that overthrows nature, or *monstrosity*, a natural deviation within nature."[5] Such is the function of writing in Derrida's critique of Ferdinand de Saussure, but it is also possible to see in this "catastrophe" the alliance of television and writing rather than their assumed antagonism. Cavell assumes, as Derrida does, the invasion of discourse into the universal problematic and locates television as a monitoring—perhaps even "writing"—of that event.

When Baudrillard says that consumers don't look for the face of production in their own faces, he makes the same separation between the world and the event as do Derrida and Cavell. For Baudrillard, consumers are not concerned with levels of involvement or commitment, but with another scene. As "obscenity begins precisely where there is no more spectacle," the consumers' "obscenity" is precisely their divorce from the main or "spectacular" scene of the world.[6] Cavell says that television doesn't have us realize or recognize anything about the world, but instead "covers it like a gun."[7] The use of the word *cover* suggests multiple ambivalences in Cavell's use of the concept, implying, as it does, protection (as in "cover me" or "cover with a blanket") as well as control and replacement (as in the recording sense of "covering" another artist's work or the cinematic production imperative of "coverage"). For Cavell, the primary function of televisual coverage, however, is not to reveal or interpret the world, nor to convey information, but to disinform, to disabuse us of the world through Baudrillard's "mortal dose of publicity." From now on, the world is just an event on television, an occasion of adaptability and management rather than readability and comprehension.[8]

Cavell's distinction between the world and an event may be broadly analyzed as a division between modernism and postmodernism. Modernism recognizes that the "catastrophe" as Derrida defines it has occurred, that something went wrong with what was supposed to be natural, real, and secure. Modernism meditates on that crisis. It offers the perception that history is moving violently against us; that the promise of infinite progress, self-realization, and freedom has been betrayed. At the end of the nineteenth century and the beginning of the twentieth, industrial and technological progress left empire after empire shattered past the ability of the king's men to put Humpty Dumpty together again. A postmodern perspective would argue, however, that there's nothing to be done except monitor the image and manage the event of that catastrophe. Postmodernist paradox—or irony—denatures the "catastrophe" of denaturation, transforming that process into the banal "monstrosity" of monitoring catastrophe. Beyond modernism's determination to resolve the world, postmodernism writes, or rewrites, without hope or as a form of empty nostalgia. As Derrida implies, the metaphor that would describe the origin of an event (built on the ground of the world) is now forbidden.

We know that modernism presents projects of resistance, rebellion, radical gesture, and radical will. Even when it assumes the form of abstract representation, it has as its goal a resolution, a solution to the problem of what to do. For postmodernism—as for television, according to Cavell—the world is not the issue anymore. Postmodernism abandons this determination to fix the world, to correct it through utopian or horrific visions. The catastrophe of the real has become a public and popular event. Rather than attempting to correct the rupture at the heart of signification or representation, or at the heart of the world or history, it likes to watch. The state of the post–O.J. Simpson legal system is a perfect expression of this strategy and may at least partly account for the happy marriage of law and television in programs such as *Law and Order* and the CourtTV network. Litigation is equivalent to managing. No one relies on a case to be fully resolved; there will be an appeal and, after that, another appeal.

Postmodernism takes modernism with absolute seriousness. It takes absolutely seriously the fact that the signifier is unhinged from the signified, that the subject is not entirely distinguishable from the object. Also absolutely serious is the fact that power is nothing but a game. We won't perform surgery on the heart of the world to excise the disease; we'll just monitor the condition.

In postmodernism, technology, ideology, and commodification are all too capable of delivering us to the status of an object. Our subjectivity is no longer a unique and authentic matter of our integrity or our identity, but something that can be mass-reproduced, commodified, and sold. Subjectivity is no longer separate in a sacred way from the object, nor is it a guarantee itself of objectivity. The arbitrary or conventional slide of signifier and signified, of modernism's differential agony, is postmodernized into sheer differentiation. It is not so much the horror of ourselves as subjects becoming objects as it is the horror of objects becoming subjects, a familiar cinematic paranoia from Donald Siegel's *Invasion of the Body Snatchers* (1957) through Stanley Kubrick's *2001: A Space Odyssey* (1968) up to David Cronenberg's *Videodrome* (1983). Television's massive repetitive formats, the endless babble of the boob tube, are an attempt to normalize our estrangement from the intuition of panic about a world that didn't survive us. The transience of television turns time and space into something that continually passes away into an experience of oblivion, into forgetting, into indifference.

Television's consumerism is, of course, part of the triumph of capitalism's global consumerist economy. In addition, consumerism—in the broader sense that we've been discussing here—also trains consumers in an attitude toward their own desire, a desire no longer imagined as coming to full satisfaction. When confronted by either a sexual overture or a television set, Chauncey Gardiner says, "I like to watch." The goal of his desire is not the end of desire or some potentially dangerous opportunity to participate. The consumerist economy in which he comes to act as an important sign—even though he has never had any money or made any purchases—ensures that the end of desire will never arrive. He appears not to have a concept of value, either in the sense of monetary exchange or in the sense of yearning for a goal. His apparent level of complacency leads other characters in the film to assign him extraordinary value.

To expect satisfaction from television is as naïve as it is irrelevant to the medium itself. As consumers, we know that what we can't have, consume, eat, or turn into a momentary event of celebrity or crisis is what we don't want. We can't "relate"—to use the current vernacular—to any part of the world that isn't a product, an event of consumption, a shopping cruise. Shopping isn't just a way to be silly; it's a survival tactic in a world where time and space don't appear to center us or lend significance. What passes for a subject now is not somebody satisfied or happy, or even capable of coherence, but someone for whom those aspirations either failed or never fully developed. What we have is Chauncey Gardiner.

Chauncey is emphatically a vidiot, someone who has never seen anything but television, and for whom politics, family, romance, culture, or any real engagement with the world are unnecessary. His idiocy becomes his brilliancy. He has the capacity to negotiate the world as if it's not there. His lack of mastery is his mastery. He is a dissolved or dispersed subject, the subject of television. While this convincing portrait of the new flesh isn't nearly as apocalyptic or monstrous as, say, that which was presented in *Videodrome*, it implies just as much the loss of identity. This is necessarily violent, but perhaps not any more violent than the traumas inherent in the construction of identity itself.

Nevertheless, *Being There* presents these ideas with the assumption that this recognition is contemptible, that we'll be appalled at the idiocy—or vidiocy—of Chauncey Gardiner. And yet, even within the terms of this film, unrelievedly hostile to television, the creature of television is seen as the representative "new man." When, early in the film, Chauncey is driven out of the old man's garden and onto the streets, Deodato's Moog synthesizer version of Richard Strauss's *Thus Spake Zarathustra* plays on the soundtrack. Chauncey is the superman of a televisual age, an empty vessel perfectly suited and entirely acquiescent to appropriation.

The film automatically allies the vidiot with femininity when Chauncey is both injured and rescued by the limo of the lonely and compassionate Eve Rand (Shirley MacLaine), the wife of ailing power broker Ben Rand (Melvyn Douglas). The alliance between Chauncey and Eve is typical of movies about television: the contemptible subject of television evolution is in many ways equivalent to what women have always been. For Eve, Chauncey is both the new Adam and the snake that comes into the garden, both close to the natural body and suspect.

Like Eve, several characters within the film talk about Chauncey as having the gift of being "natural," as if he has regained paradise. What seems to us to be the case is that he's not natural at all. This issue of the natural has interesting implications for the representation of the only person shown to be gifted with any insight—Louise, the black maid (Ruth Attaway). This character had died before the action of the novel began, but she is resurrected in the film to provide the only "common-sense" perspective. Unlike the other characters, who constantly fear social exposure, Louise is able to speak the truth. Only she recognizes that Chance "has rice pudding between his ears." As she watches him interviewed on a *Tonight Show*-like television program, she recognizes the whole affair as "gobbledygook." Louise is the most prominent of a number of marginalized black people who appear fleetingly in the film. As Chauncey initially leaves the old man's house he encounters streets peopled almost entirely with black people—including one woman from whom he requests a lunch. As he channel surfs throughout the film, many of the characters seen on the set are black, perhaps reflecting the greater racial representation—albeit stereotypical—that was seen in the late 1970s. Nevertheless, black people are absent in the film's corridors of power. Even the Rand family butler is white.

One of the oddest parts of the film's depiction of race is the inclusion, during the closing credits, of a series of outtakes showing the attempt to film a scene that was substantially cut from the completed film. In the outtakes, Chauncey repeatedly tries to tell a black actor playing an X-ray technician (Henry B. Dawkins Sellers) a story about an encounter with a group of street toughs who sent him on an errand, and Sellers repeatedly breaks up into laughter. Chauncey assumes that the technician must know the street tough "Julio" because both men are black. The fact that black men can only enter the narrative on the edge of the diegesis, and in a doubly comic way—comic through intention, and through repetition and interruption by Seller's laughter—seems to reinforce Louise's conclusions about Chauncey: "It's for sure a white man's world in America. All you got to be is white in America to get what you want." Black people may be perpetually marginalized, but they are also used to show some natural truth that continually eludes those more firmly established in culture. In the film's attempt to accuse the (white) television world, black characters are reduced to bearers of natural truth. If they were to enter the mainstream they, too, would be corrupted, not unlike the spacemen, starmen, mermaids, and mentally challenged characters seen in other movies about television.

For Chauncey it is enough to be white, to have the right look, and to be completely vacuous for complete acceptance. But, in this role, he functions not as an independent or self-motivated being, but only as a tool. In this way, Chauncey's final ascension—being put forward as a candidate for president—echoes the depiction of the previous president (Jack Warden), who is also a tool, but one shown to have a too-fragile ego, symbolized by his anxiety about impotence. Chauncey, we sense, will actually be a better president, because he has no interest in maintaining a sense of self. He permits a string of misconceptions about himself, allowing any and all interpretations.

This can be best seen through his nondefensive attitude toward language. One of the many compliments paid to Chauncey is, "You don't use words to defend yourself." Chauncey seems, at least on one level, to be aware that defense of identity is no longer the issue. He is thought to be cool and detached. But, of course, he doesn't actually possess a logocentric self to defend. The FBI and the CIA argue about which agency erased Chauncey's records, but he never *had* records. There is no conspiracy other than the television culture we inhabit that erases history. The very signifying devices of an entire culture are now dedicated to the dispersal of our identity and the invasion of our privacy; perhaps it's better not to have an identity or private life to uncover. Chauncey's relationship to written language is nonexistent. When he says, "I do not read the papers; I like TV," the comment is read by the misguided characters in the film to demonstrate a delightful lack of pretension, but is understood by viewers of the film to mean that he is unable to read. He has learned everything he knows from television—for instance, that a love scene ends before anything sexual happens, and he relates everything he experiences to television. To him, the limo ride is "just like TV only you can see farther."

The film continually hammers on the point that there is something terribly wrong with Chauncey, as if literacy in a print culture or defending oneself with words are important. When Chauncey says, "I like to watch," he is referring to watching television, but is interpreted to mean watching in a voyeuristic sense, implying something obscene or pornographic about television. But why should the vidiot wield words, or have a correspondence with nature, or be required to be literate in the old literary model? The film continually brings up standards of values to slam Chauncey, although those standards are clearly extraneous to his existence.

In a sense, Chauncey's existence is metonymic, contingent, and driven by events, but he is read by observers metaphorically. When the Russian ambassador (Richard Basehart) nods and smiles, Chauncey mimics those metonymic signs of understanding, but the ambassador reads him metaphorically, ultimately concluding that he is well-versed in Ivan Krylov's fables—in the original Russian! Nature as metaphor is an almost irresistible effect of high modernism's regret for its suspected eclipse. In this film, the garden metaphor is paradoxical. The idealistic return to nature is impossible when everything happens outside nature—the political world or the relationships between men and women. The garden is a metaphor of a natural world that never really existed except as a highly organized, artificial arena of gardening itself. It is only the garden's total irrelevance that makes it such a useful allegory.

What we see in this film, from the entourage and intrigue that surrounds the president to the huge corporation that Ben Rand administers, is that nature is hardly viable. The artificiality of Ben's world—wheelchairs, extra oxygen, elevators, transfusions, glassed-off rooms, television sets in cars—are metaphors of monitoring paradoxically implicating the film in its own insight. The panoptic eye of capitalism that caps Ben's pyramidal tomb and watches Chauncey stroll upon the water gazes with indifference on the natural world it has itself overturned.

The idea that we find Chauncey appalling has been considerably weakened since the film's release, perhaps even by a sitting president who also claims not to read the papers. Even the soothing musical background by

Erik Satie completes the aesthetic appreciation of flow and suspended judgment. Televisual subjects who see the film now, typically on DVD, can see that Chauncey occupies a metaphysics no longer dedicated to any of those values the film takes for granted. In 1979, the movie presented what it thought was a scathing attack on television subjectivity; we seem to be at a point now where it doesn't surprise us that Chauncey might be the next president of the United States, that he can walk on water, that he might be judged as a sophisticated negotiator in a world that is completely negotiated anyway. Although we're supposed to sneer at this creature rather than recognize our own spectatorial invalidism, the movie misjudges its ability to present him as an object of our contempt.

In their design for a retirement home, Robert Venturi and Denise Scott Brown choose to embrace the symbolism of television and its relationship to the more fragile members of a community by placing a large television aerial prominently on the building's facade. Robert Pinsky's poem "To Television" navigates a similar movement from "I scorned you … as I scorned so much" to "Now I like you best in a hotel room." For Pinsky—as for Venturi and Brown—there is great sympathy for viewers. Television is "escort/Of the dying and comfort of the sick," monitor of a dying world, a medium, which is

Not a "window on the world"
But as we call you,
A box a tube.[9]

6

Apocalypse

Now, everything will be different. This has been the continuing refrain of media commentary and its preoccupation with the perpetually new. Throughout television's history, and even earlier, in the growing age of mass media communications, popular rhetoric has identified a series of media apocalypses thought to have transformative power over the media that covered them, the society that gave birth to them, or humanity in general. In the Victorian era, Lizzie Borden was tried in the press (1892), and the twentieth century gave rise to numerous "trials of the century": those of Nicola Sacco and Bartolomeo Vanzetti for suspected treason (trial in 1921, execution in 1926); Nathan Leopold and Richard Loeb (1924); *The State of Tennessee v. John Thomas Scopes* (better known as the Scopes Monkey Trial), regarding the teaching of Charles Darwin's theories of evolution (1925); Richard Hauptmann, for the kidnapping of the Lindbergh baby (1935); Alger Hiss, for alleged Communist activities (1948); Ethel and Julius Rosenberg, for suspected espionage (trial in 1951, execution in 1953); Los Angeles's Rodney King police brutality trials (criminal trial in 1992, civil trial in 1993); and O. J. Simpson's trials for murder (criminal trial in 1995, civil trial in 1997). This list, limited in its scope to only American judicial actions, is still almost too tedious to recount. This tedium is already an effect of the mass media's, and later, especially television's incessant coverage. And while these events were all treated as catastrophes for the nation, they were in fact mainly only catastrophic for their participants. Society goes on as before, typically forgetting all the relevant details or even whether the defendant was found innocent or guilty. Perhaps only a final judgment of us all, in the form of the Rapture, will leave a permanent mark in anyone's memory. If we include such media events as quiz show scandals; the early 1960s Cuban Missile Crisis; the murder of Kitty Genovese in New York in 1964; the blackouts in New York City and other locations in 1965, 1977, and 2003; the Los Angeles area's Charles Manson–led Tate-LaBianca murders of 1969; New York City's Son of Sam murders in 1976–77; the wedding of Prince Charles and Princess Diana in 1981 and the death of Diana in 1996; two space shuttle explosions, in 1986 and 2003; New York's Central Park jogger attack (1989), trial, and—much later—overturning of the verdicts; the "end of history"; "Y2K"; and the September 11, 2001, terrorist attacks on the United States, it is clear that the accumulation of world-altering events is both incredibly dense and, despite the pain and upheaval they impose on the many individuals involved, ultimately inconsequential in their impact on the media and the way it conducts business.

We could make a number of observations about this list of events. For instance, we notice that the sublime is promiscuously mixed with the ridiculous. Many of these events exhibit similar narrative trajectories, featuring the search for cause and effect: either the search for outside culprits (young people, foreigners, or celebrities attempting to bring civilization down) or for weakness within ourselves (opportunity for moral self-flagellation). But mainly we are concerned here with how much we desire a world-shattering apocalyptic end and how television responds to that desire. We seek an end that will not merely mark our memories but wipe them out and destroy time as we know it. This is the mark of apocalypse from biblical times on. Even the search for causal agents is a search for the mark of the beast. Here we identify a link between the search for an apocalyptic or time-ending televisual event and Roland Barthes's notion of the *punctum*—that which we seek when looking at a photograph.

In *Camera Lucida*, Barthes defines *punctum* as that small remaining element that escapes the domestication of the real. This domestication, endless codes and interpretations that reveal the real as merely a textual fiction, is called the *studium*. The concern with the real, however, demonstrated both in popular culture and in critical and cultural studies, may really be a search for the punctum, and the search for the real is aligned with the apocalyptic search for that which exceeds history.[1] The model is both theoretical and geographical, an area in excess of textuality or outside the map. This is related to Jacques Lacan's definition of the *real*, that trauma or grief associated with endless textual negotiation, a limitless semiosis that never reaches the transcendental signified. Similarly, in *Writing Degree Zero*, Barthes isn't arguing for a writing that escapes connotation, but for an endlessly performative negotiation of signifier and signified.[2] That negotiation is all there is of the real. Barthes's poignant realization is that the more one approaches the punctum, the more it recedes. As Maurice Blanchot posits, "the end is always premature." This is the "writing of the disaster,"[3] a disaster insofar as writing's infinite approach to the beauty of closure necessarily defers its equally horrific realization. Theodor Adorno, too, is deeply suspicious of the project of totality (no poetry after Auschwitz), but is haunted by the equally totalizing logic of utopia. The nostalgic goal of reconstructing ideality must never be completed. The Frankfurt school might hate television, but television interrupts the teleology—indeed, the eschatology—of fascism. Television may be loathsome, but necessary; and perhaps more loathsome because it *is* necessary.

The punctum is the only thing that matters in the photograph, because only it can exceed or persist as a mystery beyond the encrustation of ideology and code (the studium). Therefore, it is the only real object of desire. The photograph offers that object in the form of its frozen frame, the form of time ended, an intimation of death. The punctum is a death wish. In Barthes's desperate attempt to step outside the textual systems he so masterfully understands, he resorts to his own mother's suffering and death. Discussing a photo of his now-deceased mother he writes, "My particularity could never again universalize itself (unless, utopically, by writing, whose project henceforth would become the unique goal of my life). From now on I could do no more than await my total, undialectical death. That is what I read in the Winter Garden Photograph."[4]

The search for the punctum, for the apocalypse, describes the paradoxical logic of absolute television, the entertainment of that which you know you can never have. We seek what exceeds the everyday, the regular. And in continually seeking that, everything becomes regular. By monitoring what might be a continuous apocalypse, television maintains the status quo, the chronic apocalypse of expected endings that never comes.

With this in mind, 9/11 isn't something new or something that has fundamentally changed the world, nor even the United States, nor even the way that the media covers events. As the history of apocalyptic media events demonstrates, a new equivalent—be it terrorism, an assassination, or the overthrow of a regime—has never significantly altered the media landscape. Instead, these events become an opportunity to market products (American flags, yellow ribbons, bumper stickers, or books of theory by Jürgen Habermas, Paul Virilio, or Slavoj Žižek[5]). While undeniably visually spectacular, 9/11 was not unique in terms of its nature (it has long been "the time of the assassins") or its scope. (More people become fatalities on the American highways every month or are killed in an Iranian earthquake or a heat wave in France.) Even if it were exceptional in its scope, as Jean Baudrillard notes, "An increase in violence is not enough to open up reality."[6]

Television's assumption of chronic apocalypse is the concern of both Mary Ann Doane and Patricia Mellencamp. As Walter Benjamin argues of cinema, they both posit television as a training device for spectator endurance, emphasizing not the spectacle of cinema but the discipline of time.

According to Doane,[7] time is the major category of experience in relation to which television retrains us. Television kills time and fills time, guaranteeing that something always happens. It doesn't matter what *it* is, but that it happens continually. In this way, we don't suffer television time as either unendurable or revolutionary. As poet and musician Gil-Scott Heron is famous for saying, "The revolution will not be televised."

Television doesn't produce the world that it covers—in the sense of a substance or an actual metaphysical place. It produces the event of covering through the act of covering. The question isn't *what* but *how*—how monitored, how reported, how delivered. This differs slightly from Marshall McLuhan's famous formulation, "the medium is the message." For McLuhan it was the *what*—that the content is on television—no matter *how* it was presented on television. For Doane, to cover is to create. To paraphrase McLuhan, the coverage is the message. So it doesn't matter too much what that is—a visit to the sunken Titanic, rediscovered concentration camp footage, a fashion show, or *I Love Lucy* reruns.

Doane describes three ways in which viewers actually view or "apprehend" the event on television, each based on a certain relationship to time: as (1) information, (2) crisis, or (3) catastrophe. Information includes anything imagined newsworthy on an everyday basis. Viewers continually monitor the weather, traffic, pollution, or the Dow Jones average. Information arrives in a regular continuous flow and can provide a constant sense of being "in touch." The purpose of information is not to give us facts, but to maintain connection with the flow of the everyday, to reassure us that the world still exists.[8] We are kept informed without that condition making much of a difference. No one complains when the weather report proves to be wrong or a parkway foul-up is overlooked, or if someone does complain, it isn't reported. This is, as advertising is, information as climate, and, as Doane observes, it is really disinformation.

Viewers can also view events on television as crisis. In this case, events are condensed into a limited period rather than expressed as a continuous flow. The crisis might require some response—extraordinary action by ordinary people, political or military intervention, quick decision making. Sell that stock! Get a mammogram! Bomb that ruthless dictator! Pray!

Doane's final category, catastrophe, refers to the most critical crises. Catastrophes arise instantaneously, time collapses into an instant, all bets are off. It may be the end of the world—or at least the World Trade Center towers—but most people survived it and here most of us still are. Doane argues that the televisual impulse is always toward "the perfect storm," perhaps because it assures continual viewing. As an optimistic weatherman in a *New Yorker* cartoon says, "Right now it's still being classified as a raindrop."

For Doane, television blurs the categories of information, crisis, and catastrophe. She claims there really isn't any information, and the distinction between crisis and catastrophe is really only one of some degree. It's all apocalypse, all the time. Wes Craven's film *Shocker* (1989) gives a good illustration of this point and our attitudes toward it. A serial killer, transformed by a botched electrocution, travels around town through the television signal committing heinous crimes. Although they are aware of his ability, the other characters keep switching on the set to find out what's going on, inviting death into their living rooms. We invite the Gulf Wars, as we did the Vietnam War, into our homes as a series of updates and reports.

If a catastrophe gets good ratings, maybe it can be turned into regular programming. For example, ABC's *Nightline* originally went on the air to report on the Iran hostage crisis. For twenty years it stayed on, although not always devoted to a specific global situation. Within the course of a single day, crimes are solved, celebrities divorce, space shuttles explode. By monitoring what might be a continuous apocalypse, television maintains the status quo.

In its obsession with events of destruction and extinction, television has destroyed our sense of the temporal order and the orderliness of time itself. For Doane, television is a destructive or annihilating machine that uses "liveness" as a way of staging phatic connection. But liveness is also the event of time dehistoricized. Sudden liveness is the form of catastrophe and also the norm. Doane identifies a fascination with liveness as a fascination with technology, more specifically with its dangers and failures. When technological error—or lapses such as Janet Jackson's live "wardrobe malfunction"—become televisual events, technological progress becomes the hope of both failure and the future.

Like Doane, Patricia Mellencamp emphasizes the temporal construction of television, referring to it as a "disciplinary time machine."[9] She draws on Sigmund Freud's assertion in *The Ego and the Id* that sadism is the ego turned back vindictively on its own forms of organization and mediation. Television spectators are said to position themselves in a masochistic way by placing themselves beyond pleasure through repetition and seriality. We regularize what might otherwise be unendurable: our own lack of importance. We turn ourselves into objects of consumption and into consuming machines that really can't psychologically afford to come up with self-fulfilling identities. This is the charm of television's self-referentiality. Instead of experience or memory, television evokes only its own past, evokes our laughter—hip, cynical, funny, or not—and distances us from ourselves. An example of Mellencamp's point can be found in a *Guardian Weekend* article that describes television's arrival in remote Bhutan and expresses profound dismay over television's spiritual effects on a supposedly sacred people. In this account, Bhutan is a fabled Himalayan Shangri-la, and television is a "portal ... systematically replacing one culture with another, skewing the notion of Gross National Happiness, persuading a nation of novice Buddhist consumers to become preoccupied with themselves, rather than searching [for] their self."[10]

Television instead refers to itself. Its dual logic is to create a relationship of televisual remembrance that destroys personal or historical memory, ironically preserving "me" by canceling "my" location in a past. This dual logic parallels the two poles around which Doane argues television is structured: inconceivable terror and unremitting banality. These poles continually collapse; the banality of my disavowal of an uninhabitable world finds its context in a reality that is constantly deferred or regulated and a self that feels no responsibility for it. For Doane and Mellencamp, television ensures that nothing, not even apocalypse, exceeds the studium—or ever will. With television, even Francis Ford Coppola's *Apocalypse Now* (1979) is redux.

But is television really a disinheriting technology, and is its subject really without memory, individuality, or history, as Doane and Mellencamp imply? These are both apocalyptic and cinematic assumptions. Cinema isn't necessarily apocalyptic; however, its mainstream manifestations usually insist on narrative closure. Cinema's depiction of a disenchanted future is a series of movies about apocalypse such as François Truffaut's *Fahrenheit 451* (1966), Woody Allen's *Sleeper* (1973), Norman Jewison's *Rollerball* (1975), James Cameron's *The Terminator* (1984), Wim Wenders's *Until the End of the World* (1991), Terry Gilliam's *12 Monkeys*

(1995), Andrew Niccol's *Gattaca* (1997), and Danny Boyle's *28 Days Later* ... (2002). Further, television often becomes the sign of that future, an obsession seen clearly in Annabel Jankel and Rocky Morton's *Max Headroom* (1985). It is set "twenty minutes into the future"; the cyberbeing Max (Matt Frewer) offers the cliché that "We have a great future behind us"; and Blank Reg (Morgan Sheppard) says, "Remember when we said there was no future? Well, this is it." Max's metaphysics are television. His alter ego, Edison Carter (also played by Matt Frewer), operates as a genuine, liberal humanist, primarily concerned with his own self-realization. As television destroys the future as future, Edison represents the nostalgic question: How can we become human again? This attitude toward a certain form of future and a particular kind of human are linked. A future without a progressive dynamic might as well be limitless, and infinite time cannot produce authentic narratives or heroic characters.

Robert and Marilouise Kroker call Max Headroom "[t]he first citizen of the end of the world."[11] In *Max Headroom*, worlds that are otherwise dystopian and catastrophically uninhabitable become quite banally and ordinarily uninhabitable, as long as there is nothing but the endless flow of information and coverage. The dilemma is to figure out what it means to have evolved from a subject like Edison Carter to one like Max Headroom, who is no longer concerned with issues of habitation, individuality, or autonomy—and whether it is possible to return. Revived time revives the idea of the human. The character, as much as the narrative, requires an end to time, and the most glamorous manifestation of that is the apocalypse.

One of the great cinematic genres is time travel because one of cinema's missions is to correct time. In Chris Marker's *La Jetée* (1962), an archetypal example, characters return from a ruined future to rescue themselves. Whether for good or ill, the future must be protected from the past. To save time, you must demonstrate the possibility of time's destruction, as in Robert Zemeckis's *Back to the Future* (1985), Terry Gilliam's *Time Bandits* (1981), or Stephen Herek's *Bill and Ted's Excellent Adventure* (1989). Televisual time travel is much more like sightseeing. Characters in TV series such as *The Time Tunnel* and *Quantum Leap* use their time-travel conceits to visit various pasts as they might visit exotic locations to experience sights, sounds, clothes, slang, and customs. They are more akin to the nostalgic impulses of programs like *American Dream* and *That 70s Show*.

Umberto Eco makes it clear that a desire to recover authentic humanity in a hyperreal world can only be misguided because that

recovery itself is based on a return to the "real," in the sense of high culture. High culture is hierarchically ordered, chronologically restored,
and individualistic. It doesn't treat life as if it were an amusement park,
with the disorganized activity that implies. Mass culture is flattened and
chaotic time, peopled by multitudes. As Eco notes, "If culture is an aris-
tocratic phenomenon—the assiduous, solitary and jealous cultivation of
an inner life that tempers and opposes the vulgarity of the crowd—then
even to conceive of a culture that is shared by everyone, produced to suit
everyone and tailored accordingly is a monstrous contradiction…. Mass
culture is anti-culture."[12]

Eco reveals his attitude toward this distinction through the elitist and
oblivious figure of the "apocalyptic intellectual," the critic who warns
the masses about the danger in their midst and points to television as
their greatest threat. "What emerges most strikingly," he comments, "is
a form of morbid attraction for the *mysterium televisionis*. So that, far
from helping us to free ourselves from the spell, the most the critic does
is to hold us there for even longer. Perhaps he hopes to induce his own
peers to switch off the television. But the fact that it remains switched
on for everybody else is evidently one of those things which criticism is
powerless to prevent…."[13]

Eco's perspective here resembles those expressed by Doane and
Mellencamp. What distinguishes him from them, and from the apocalyptic critic he describes, is his answer to the question, What is television's reality, and is that anything new? Apocalyptic thinking assumes
that reality has been or should be capable of being destroyed. Television
says something different: The only reality you will recognize is on television. It reveals the return of the real as what it always was: a semiotic
production, a performance, coded fiction.

It is Jacques Derrida, in "No Apocalypse, Not Now" within the
context of a discussion of the possibility of nuclear war, who really
clarifies television's textual function. Though a nuclear war would
be the "total destruction of the archive if not of the human habitat,"
the fact is, nuclear war has not taken place. The very proposal that
the archive could be destroyed is itself a textual proposition. Nuclear war, and the finitude of apocalypse, is "fabulously textual."[14]
Nothing exceeds textuality. Derrida never mentions television in this
discussion, but television is the quintessential example of what he describes, rather than "the archive" as the traditional locus of culture.
Television is the machine that continually reminds us that reality is
scripted. This idea transforms fiction away from its traditional function as (analog) mimesis toward a (digital) representation of itself. It,

too, is pure code, and when the real and fiction are both code there can be no distinction. All constantives are now performatives, and perhaps they always were.

Derrida doesn't mean that any number of texts don't adopt apocalyptic logic—the book of Revelations, after all, is the apocalypse precisely because it is a book. But, when any text—regardless of logic—enters the archive, it becomes enmeshed in a textual network. Television, in particular, makes its textuality obviously fabulous. We could also refer television to Derrida's notion of apocalypse without apocalypse, an internal movement to overcome a system's own finality. Apocalypse, in this view, can be conceived as the ever-present possibility of rupture and interruption. This is the logic of television textuality—the constant ending of its own endings. For Frank Kermode, in his book *The Sense of an Ending*, apocalypse is important in so far as it presents the fiction of an end, a textuality whereby human beings project themselves, still alive, beyond the end in order to gain or regain a perspective on history as a whole.[15] Kermode adopts the word *peripeteia* to refer to the continuous readjustment of perspective that takes place when the end doesn't occur as expected.[16] He is discussing literature here, but it is a highly relevant concept for television, one that is related to Derrida's fabulous textuality.

Nothing that appears on television does so without the specter of the televisual archive. Tributes, awards, "best of" highlights, and blooper shows all mine the greater televisual text. George Clooney's *Confessions of a Dangerous Mind* (2002) uses Chuck Barris's experiences as seminal television innovator as part of the setting for a parafictional film. Based on his "autobiography," the film presents him simultaneously as a CIA assassin and a television producer.[17] He is shown chaperoning contestants on *The Dating Game* as a cover for international CIA hits. The film is both nonchalant and unrelenting about the interpenetration of reality and fiction, banality, and excitement. We are a long way here from the modernist experiment of Gertrude Stein's *The Autobiography of Alice B. Toklas*.

Television offers a dazzling supply of such scripted spaces and tampered-with time. Its accumulation of disconnected stories, which can be perpetually cut up and rearranged, goes beyond the notion of an episodic organization. Put together, the stories don't form a larger narrative or metanarrative, but a vast index, a continual finger-pointing. This is not an index in a Piercean, existential sense, but in the sense of a literal index, to reference what is not adjacent or thematic, but arbitrary (alphabetic). Television is its own index, coextensive with itself in the same way that Jorge Luis Borges's map of the empire is coextensive with the empire: Useless for gaining an understanding of the territory, it does tell you a great deal about maps. Similarly, television as index is useless for finding anything you might want to see, resee, or recover. Unlike a classical narrative, you could never reconstruct the whole from a part and you can never reach an end, much less a conclusion, because there could always be finer separations and categorizations. In this way, television never acts to end its textuality. Against the apocalyptic critic who admonishes us to turn off our televisions, television never turns itself off. As Eco writes,

> [Neo-tv is] a complex phenomenon consisting of lots and lots of TV channels, all shot through with ads, and programmes that copy one another, taking turns to compete for the attention of the viewer who zaps compulsively on his remote control. Each pro-gramme talks about itself and addresses an audience that is part of the programmed: the message, obsessively repeated, is not "This is how the world is," but, "I am here, do you see me? This is the only reality that you will recognize from now on."[18]

In light of our discussion, Eco's "neo-tv" can only be seen as ironic because TV was never anything "old." No matter how strenuously we attempt to create a golden age of television, there was never an *ancien* TV. We might just as reasonably speak of neo-books.[19]

Because of the fabulous textuality and fabulous indexicality within television's imaginary, the apocalypse can only be rescheduled. Stay tuned. The postponement of the apocalypse doesn't mean the end of destruction and genocide, nor does it mean, to recall Cavell's fact of television, that television may not be monitoring the event, the evolution, of the world's extinction. This extinction event is not, however, a cataclysmic alien in-vasion, unleashed viruses, or asteroids hitting the earth. No one can deny television's fascination with extinction—especially "quality" or public tel-evision's documentary fascination with endangered species, dinosaurs, and Egyptian mummies. Nevertheless, an extinction event on television covers an ongoing intervention in the life of the planet by its dominant and most successful life form: us. It becomes increasingly perplexing to what degree this coverage, this intervention, is not a reduplication of alienation that defines extinction as a way of life. The toppling of the vertical ascendancy of apocalypse does not so much guarantee survival as much as it lateralizes violence and oblivion as the essential conditions of progress.

From this perspective, the terrorist attack on the United States on 9/11 and the U.S. response in a war on terror are precisely nonapocalyptic because these wars—like the war on drugs—are calculated to last forever. Any winning of the war on terror would cause a crisis in the nature of "hyperpower,"[20] which, in line with its technological imperative, requests the conditions of its own subversion in order to justify its exercise. Thomas Pynchon's *Gravity's Rainbow* revels in its exposure of the chronic nature of war and terrorism as an essential disease of a healthy empire,[21] and it's hard to resist the extrapolation that the media's coverage of disaster is not structurally part of the necessary prevention of a victory over terror. Though Jean-François Lyotard's famous anthem of postmodernism, *The Postmodern Condition*, proclaims that "the nineteenth and twentieth centuries have given us as much terror as we can take,"[22] clearly terror can never have enough of us. Similarly, for the televisual subject, for whom Max Headroom is the exemplar, the extinction of time has become a way of life.

If television is a progress report on the state of extinction, cinema is obsessed with proving that nobody has changed for the last five hundred years. Cinema would like us to all be Renaissance or Cartesian princes living in a postmodern world. The truth is that characters in post-televisual films don't know what kind of people they have become, don't always know whether they are really human or not (*Terminator*; Ridley Scott's *Blade Runner*, 1982), or even whether they are alive or dead (M. Night Shyamalan's *The Sixth Sense*, 1999; Alejandro Amjenábar's *The Others*, 2001; Richard Kelly's *Donnie Darko*, 2001). This confusion is far from the attitude expressed in earlier film movements. Celebrating Italian neorealism, André Bazin calls it "primarily a humanism and only secondarily a form of filmmaking."[23]

Although it is far from a neorealist aesthetic, *Max Headroom* expresses a frantically textual sense of the lost real, not unlike Barthes's pursuit of the punctum. As we have seen in Barthes, and with Eco's apocalyptic critic, this search for the real is inextricably involved in a humanist—and in its frustration, a cybernetic—sense of life. These possibilities both exist in the film through the characters of Edison Carter and his cyberego Max Headroom.

Edison Carter's name evokes both Thomas Edison, the celebrated individualist and genius, who subsumed mechanical technology to humanist ends—lights, phonographs, and cinema for the masses—and Jimmy Carter, a peanut farmer from the rural south who became president. Carter's well-known religious faith and support for the common people, best seen in his ongoing work with Habitat for Humanity, would no doubt strike a sympathetic chord with Bazin.

By the time of *Max Headroom*'s release, Carter's presidency had been replaced by that of Ronald Reagan, a figure who both physically and ethically resembles Max's character. Garry Trudeau made the connection explicit in a series of Doonesbury comic strips featuring the Reaganesque character Ron Headrest, a figure who, like Max, only appears on television.[24] Max's critique of the dehumanizing corporate world never goes beyond the halfhearted because it is based on a fundamental hypocrisy. Although he constantly spouts anticorporate and antinetwork slogans, it is always in a relentlessly ironic and parodic fashion. Irony is already the sign that nothing can be radicalized. With no sense of incongruity, the character was used to push New Coke in a major advertising campaign. For Max Headroom, subversion is expedience.

In "Techno-ethics and Tele-Ethics: Three Lives in the Day of *Max Headroom*," Andrew Ross writes about a dilemma among journalists, executives, and producers involved in television. Taking the liberal Hollywood high ground, they accuse the industry of degeneracy, in which ethical choices are always resolved for the sake of profit or the sponsor. This liberal mind in conflict with this degenerate industry permeates television with self-criticism, irony, and an apparently subversive self-reflexivity. For Ross, this is the code of "tele-ethics": It allows professionals to believe that their actions and decisions are not solely in the interest of exchange value, but capable of saving their souls.

Aligned with tele-ethics is what Ross deems "techno-ethics." Techno-ethics remind us that with the increasing "cyborganization" of the world we are faced with a choice; paradoxically, the only plausible exercise of free will in this situation would be to unplug the machines. Techno-ethics are an attempt to believe that our humanity remains intact against the possibility of becoming posthuman; tele-ethics argues against the inevitability of losing one's soul to profit. Ross links these two ethical stances. He refers to films such as *Blade Runner* and Ridley Scott's *Alien* (1979)—and we could certainly now include *The Matrix* trilogy—as presenting a grim, unsentimental, socially ultrarealist view of the future.

In *Max Headroom*, that future is the future of television. Messy and distopian, it is unsurvivably polluted and dangerous, twenty minutes into the future. You enter this world only at very great risk. In the first scene of the film, Edison Carter becomes disconnected from his live video feeds in the Channel 23 studios. Returning, after fighting his way back from the unregulated world to corporate headquarters, he yells, "Don't you goddamned ever do that to me!" and punches the inattentive producer.

To be left to a one-to-one relationship with the world, with no monitoring, is the worst thing that can happen. This world is far better surveilled than inhabited. Channel 23 covers the world with a camera the way a criminal is covered with a gun.

As Ross observes, in the world of *Max Headroom* nothing is going on except television. Aside from organ harvesting and transplantation, television is the only growth industry, and the only measure of all social and cultural life. In both of these realms, the human has become an expendable commodity. In a scene reminiscent of one from David Cronenberg's *Videodrome* (1983), in which Bianca O'Blivion (Sonja Smits) provides video access to those deprived of television in the Mission of the Cathode Ray, *Max Headroom* shows homeless and wandering people surrounded by television sets in an otherwise desolate plain. Television is the welfare handout or methadone fix for the masses.

The great innovation in *Max Headroom* is the "blipvert," which represents the ultimate triumph of the sponsor without the messy mediation of programming, the subliminal condensation of hundreds of commercials into a single instant. Beyond the primitive rules of broadcasting, the network's political—which is really commercial—agenda can be consumed without the possibility of channel surfing. An advantageous, though sinister, side effect of the blipvert is that it blows up overly passive or somnolent souls—who don't buy enough anyway.

This world has apparently been revolutionized, but we don't get any specific history of that revolution, and it certainly wasn't on television. What happened to the world isn't important anymore, because no one with anything to lose would venture into the world without the life-support system of a corporate carapace and continual monitoring. If the world cannot be experienced without mediation, it becomes posthistorical. Channel 23's programming parodies this in programs such as *Lifestyles of the Poor and Pitiful, Lumpy's Proletariat,* and *The Video Symptoms Show,* in which a doctor analyzes the anal pustules of home viewers. As bad as the world is, the only imaginable course is that it will get worse. Edison Carter's job is simply to report on events from a liberal humanist perspective without doing anything about it. The same corporate entity that employs Edison to broadcast critical commentaries about blipverts is the same entity that develops and uses blipverts. When the outside world is uninhabitable, no critique can come from the outside.

This is the dynamic of a number of films that deal with a corporate future. Like Edison Carter, Jonathan E. (James Caan) in *Rollerball* is hired by global oligarchs to perform a specifically televisual spectacle—in his case, a brutal combination of football, motocross, and hockey. Jonathan E., a technostud of tough individuality and male camaraderie—as opposed to the fey, new world order of the ruling party—becomes increasingly suspicious of corruption in the system. He wants to know how decisions are made, only to be told, "Corporate decisions are made by executives." Even as he becomes aware that the game is rigged, he battles to stay in the game. Similarly, in *The X-Files*—which, like *Max Headroom*, has both film and television expressions—Scully (Gillian Anderson) and Mulder (David Duchovny) cling to their jobs as agents in the FBI in the service of uncovering corruption in that agency. In all of these films, the only thing worse than a corrupt institution is being cast out of it.[25]

Max attacks both the imperial power of the network and its pretensions to imperial invulnerability. At the same time, he's only allowed that stance on television. Finally, he can only be a humanist if he's a replicant. He attacks the empire, but the empire fights back by defining all the ways in which he'll be accessible.

We sense that the values Max spouts on renegade station *Big Time TV* are obsolete, inadequate, or hypocritical. If we have to hear about what it means to be a human and how to resist the onslaught of technological power from a replicant or a corporate superstar, then the empire has already appropriated the codes of representation. Max, like the exhausted critiques of *The Daily Show*, *Late Night with David Letterman*, *The O'Reilly Factor*, or *Saturday Night Live*, proclaims that he works within the system without being serious about it. His corruption-exposing stance serves primarily to expose his own corruption. We're witnessing a spectacle of power that no longer crushes resistance, but brings that resistance into its own system. Allowing that critique, in light of its own hypocrisy, is an effective way of canceling the content of the message and maintaining the status quo.

Max Headroom presents both Edison Carter and Max Headroom as sympathetic characters. They simply negotiate their opposition to and complicity with the corporate television industry in different ways. Neither can exceed the mediated world in which they both operate. Whether we are dealing in Carter's flesh, or Max's new flesh, their rhetorical insufficiency expands paradoxically to make sexuality only texuality—their only available subjectivity.

Baudrillard identifies the seduction of the law as the call to produce and to be overcome simultaneously: what he refers to as the need to ravish or be ravished.[26] While the call to ravish seems stronger than, and at cross-purposes with, the law, it is an integral function of legality. The morality that seems to motivate, torment, and desexualize characters like Edison Carter, Jonathan E., Mulder, and Scully can only be seen as a misguided belief in their own power to change the order of things. This happens when these professionals forget they are actually mercenaries in the service of corrupt institution. Why don't they just quit (the network, the game, the FBI)?[27] The impossibility of transcending these institutions reminds us of what Žižek teaches us about the textual framework of ideology. The sublimity of ideology is enacted through the abject superego, which invites transgressions in order to formulate the law.[28] Quitting ideology is not an option. Television's own law is to seductively provoke—even as it punishes—the desire to comprehend, leave, or destroy the archive. That's what an X-File is.

7

Nostalgia

Barry Levinson's *Avalon* (1990) culminates in a highly symbolic warehouse fire on the Fourth of July. The fire itself is a highly exaggerated conflagration, apocalyptically destroying a business, a family, and the American dream, all in the form of thousands of television sets. *Avalon* depicts the struggle of immigrant patriarch Sam (Armin Mueller Stahl) to maintain his clan as both an emotional and financial unit in 1950s Baltimore by selling consumer appliances. But the promise of economic security through endless products such as washers, stoves, and TV sets in fact accelerates the passing away of the extended family. Instead of being united though production, the family is separated through consumption.

Several scenes depict television as the most dangerous appliance in the home. Early communal eating scenes are replaced by Sam's son, daughter-in-law, and grandson gathered around the set eating off TV trays. In the final scenes, Sam sits alone in an armchair, reading a paper as the television blares in the kitchen where the family now eats. He gets up and passes the empty dining room table. In the next scene, the son and wife ignore each other as they watch television in bed. A final coda to the action shows Sam in the nursing home where his grandson and great-grandson visit him. The old man indulges in a fit of nostalgia about the ironies of a life in which you spend everything you work and save for to end up in a home which is not your own. The grandson listens, but the great-grandson stares blankly at a television set.

The misfortunes that the family undergoes can be traced to the night on which everything burns—uninsured!—through a random accident. Even though the third generation has been carelessly blowing up airplanes and firecrackers in the basement of the wooden structure, the fire is actually caused by an electrical malfunction on the fourth floor. In a cinematic rather than televisual world, the characters would cause the incident that destroys them. They would matter to their world. The film attempts an apocalyptic event, but it is fatally suffused with nostalgia for a time before mass media, consumerism, and demographic changes dismantled the close-knit immigrant family as an economic unit. Certainly television is indicted in these shifts, but it is also possible to identify nostalgia for a different form of television—a golden age.

The questions posed by historicizing a nostalgic golden age for television join with those raised about the nature of televisual pleasure in Patricia Mellencamp's "TV, Time and Catastrophe" and Mary Ann Doane's "Information, Crisis, Catastrophe."[1] Film is both the apocalypse of totality and completion and the great accuser of television as an endless and boundaryless textuality, particularly in its serial form. The retrospectively designated golden age gains its legitimacy through literary and theatrical paradigms associated with the myth of "liveness" and the more discrete anthology form performed in television's ancestral home: New York City. Cinema typically prefers a literal apocalypse (the end of some world) as opposed to the loathsome and perpetual apocalypse of television. Good television can only be nostalgically accessed through reference to obsolete characteristics: New York production; theatrical form; and liveness.[2] We can approach these issues through a programming category that would seem to have little in common with theater, literature, or cinema: reality TV.

One of the most critically dismissed television programs of all time is also one of the longest running. *Candid Camera* has undergone numerous iterations since its debut in 1948,[3] both under its own name and through imitations such as *Punk'd*, *Totally Hidden Video*, *Trigger Happy TV*, and *TV's Bloopers and Practical Jokes*. In a typical *Candid Camera* stunt, unsuspecting passersby are surprised by a talking mailbox, or customers at a diner discover their spoons dissolve while stirring coffee. Into entirely regular settings such as a diner or a city street the program introduced an unexpected element and then recorded the reactions of its unwitting participants. In many ways, all reality programs are variations on this theme. "Regular" or "real" people (by which it is meant that they have no explicit ties to the entertainment industry), when placed in a recognizable place—a house, a game show studio, a taxicab, the wilderness—react to a carefully selected prompt. Their reactions are recorded, then edited to maximize some quality. Game shows—from *What's My Line?* to *You Bet Your Life* and *Queen for a Day* through *The Weakest Link*—often use many of the same strategies of nonprofessionals, artificial situations, editing for maximum effect, and confessional interludes.[4] In *Candid*

Camera, as the name implies, the camera was concealed for most of the stunt, but became a prompt itself when it was revealed with the catch-phrase, "Smile! You're on *Candid Camera!*"

To some extent, the existence of cameras themselves is a sufficient prompt. The landmark 1973 *An American Family* may have started out as a sociological experiment, but many people believed that the filming itself caused the family to fall apart, the parents to divorce, and son Lance to announce his homosexuality. *The Real World* artificially deposits groups of seven young people into overdesigned living spaces and films the results. Aside from the careful mix of residents and the extravagant decor, only the act of videotaping might be said to spur the action. Other examples of reality programming rely on increasingly baroque situations and provocative prompts—choose a wife, eat deer's eyes, date a man wearing a mask, live without modern conveniences, or redecorate your neighbor's basement.

Two contradictory observations about these programs: (1) They all crucially depend on editing; and (2) they all attempt to create an atmosphere of spontaneity or provoke a deliberate accident. *Candid Camera*'s editing style is a clear formula. Several different participants are shown encountering the same stunt while host Alan Funt provides commentary on the audio track. The most extreme or amusing reactions are saved for the end, as is the revelation of the camera (the "reveal"). In shows such as *The Bachelor*, editing heightens the personalities of participants, and story lines are developed. Goading, by off-camera interviewers who are edited out, incites emotional outbursts during the increasingly common "confessional" sections of reality programs. Whether they are reality or not, these programs, through editing, relentlessly follow formulaic patterns.

We can compare this to cinematic realism—as articulated by theorists such as André Bazin and Siegfried Kracauer—which relies to a great extent on the long take.[5] Film as a mechanical medium always allows for a chain of evidence and causality. Television, an electronic medium, side-steps Bazin's idea of an indexical bond, which he attributes to cinema and which is his basis for calling Italian Neo-Realism "primarily a kind of humanism."[6] The cinematic long take represents a world restored to immanence—meaning inherent in time and space. Television's electronic capture of a series of moments assigns no such meaning or priority to its live transmissions. Charles Barr quotes the great cinematic realist Jean Renoir, interviewed as he was approaching a 1958 television project, as saying, "'I am trying to extend my old ideas, and to establish that the camera finally has only one right—that of recording what happens....'"[7] Barr adds, "The fact that the 'magic' of live TV ... is often the focus of a

somewhat shallow and anecdotal nostalgia should not stop us from ac-
knowledging that live is different, and that Renoir knew what he was talking about."[8] Still, "what happens" in the live is not the same as cinematic
revelation of what is already meaningful, or immanent, about the world.

In post–live television configurations, the medium isn't artistically in-
ferior, but metaphysically "after." Both cinematic realism and television
reality programs rely on nonprofessional actors, location shooting, loose
or unscripted situations, and the camera as a witness rather than a character. However, cinematic realism has a tragic hope that the medium in
its role as messianic prosthesis can deliver the referent. Reality television
is less concerned with reality, in the sense of a redeemed physical world,
than the medium itself. Reality on television, whatever it may be, is never
expressed through the long take.

Despite its reliance on editing, reality programming strives for and
often achieves spontaneity, a sensation that what is happening is
unplanned, surprising, or unique—that is *live*. "Liveness" is the great
myth and ideology of television despite the fact that almost nothing is live
anymore aside from various forms of monitoring—of the weather (the
Weather Channel, Surf's Up), transportation systems (car chases, traffic
reports), the political condition (*The O'Reilly Factor, Face the Nation*)—
and miscellaneous events that can be transformed into continuing stories
(courtroom verdicts, Amber Alerts, high-profile arrests, combat footage,
and press conferences). These "breaking" items appear as almost pure
signifiers of liveness, even as they are endlessly replayed, representing a
continuing cover-up of television's fragmentation of time and space.

Jane Feuer addressed this cover-up in her 1983 article "The Concept
of Live Television." For Feuer, television isn't a seamless flow. Raymond
Williams's idea of "flow" is, for her, "pure illusion." You may watch television as a flow, but "television is constituted by a dialectic of segmentation
and flow" with segmentation "already a property of the text."[9] Though
television may define its nature in liveness and in a totality of presence
that cinema lacks, Feuer notes a key paradox: As technology advances
and takes us increasingly farther away from actual live broadcasting, the
ideology of liveness thrives:

> Indeed, as television in fact becomes less and less a "live" medium
> in the sense of an equivalence between time of event and time
> of transmission, the medium in its own practices seems to insist
> more and more upon an ideology of the live, the immediate, the
> direct, the spontaneous, the real. This is true of both program
> formats and metadiscourse (references to the "Golden Age" of live

television, "Live from New York, it's Saturday Night," the many local spots glorifying "instant" camera news coverage, "live" coverage of the Olympics, etc.). The introduction of computerized editing equipment is making video editing as flexible as film editing.... Clearly, in terms of this simplest conception of the "live," current American network television is best described as a collage of film, video and "live," all interwoven into a complex and altered time scheme. (14–15)

Feuer wonders why the ideology of liveness persists so obdurately and points to the contradictory television coinage "live on tape." She writes, "From asserting its reality to asserting its vitality, television's metadiscourse generates a circuit of meanings from the single term 'live'" (14). Feuer points to an imprecise meaning as motor to the process of television's omnipresence everywhere, elsewhere, nowhere.

What Feuer does not directly address is that all television is live not simply in the sense that it is possible to broadcast an event as it happens, but in the sense that all programming—whether it originates in an immediate transmission, videotape, or film—can be interrupted: "We interrupt this program to bring you...." Even a filmed program or a theatrical film is live by virtue of the fact that it is on television. In a discussion that moves from "live" to "real-time" to "currency," Mark Williams notes that "What began as a description of the technological relation to a referent that a medium was in the process of representing ... has become today a description of what an electronic medium is representing at this moment. What is 'live' on TV today is what TV is showing/enunciating now, regardless of the status of the referent."[10]

In *Timeshift*, Sean Cubitt connects our perception of television's ontological status—its presence—to the nature of its technology and experience of flow, with implications of passing away and grief:

The flow of images and dialogue on a TV screen is "present" in the sense that the viewer can enter into dialogue with the screen. Yet the broadcasting flow is also vanishing, a constant disappearance of what has been shown. The electron scan builds up two images of each frame shown, the lines interlacing to form a "complete" picture. Yet not only is the sensation of movement on screen an optical illusion brought about by the rapid succession of frames: each frame is itself radically incomplete, the line before always fading away, the first scan of the frame all but gone, even from the retina, before the second interlacing scan is complete. And because TV viewing is subject to constant distraction, and because it would be more accurate to say that television is constituted in a dialectic of segmentation and flow ... then viewing is also a process of missing. TV's presence to the viewer is subject to constant flux: it is only intermittently "present," as a kind of writing on a glass, to the distracted viewer, and even in moments of concentration caught in a dialectic of constant becoming and constant fading.[11]

For Cubitt, television's very technology seems to orchestrate nostalgia. Nothing ever arrives without already leaving. Television is a technology of missing, fading, and slipping away in its transmission, even as this dialectic defines television's mode of becoming. This argument, founded on metaphor, posits—according to Feuer—an "essence" that is ideologically neutral.[12] Furthermore, digital technology doesn't conform to this becoming and fading metaphor, yet it doesn't change anything fundamental about television's nostalgia. What is interesting about Cubitt's description is the melancholy sense of missing he invokes and the intrinsic, if not essential, confusion of television's ideology with what amounts to an antimetaphysics. Seen in this light, television's legendary wasteland assumes nearly Heideggerian proportions.[13]

Given the linkages among live production, vitality, currency, and presence, together with a continual "process of missing," the affinity toward liveness is hardly surprising, nor is the fact that this affinity often takes the form of nostalgia for truly live production during what is popularly thought of as a better time. In the golden age of television, New York–based hourlong dramas ruled the airways. Why has this period, roughly between 1946 and 1958, become so valorized? In its very primitiveness there is presence. In other words, something could go wrong, a line could be flubbed, and in this possibility lay an authenticity more associated with theater (New York) than cinema (Hollywood). Predictably, then, when most television production abandons New York for Hollywood, liveness ends as practice and begins as myth.

Nick Browne charts the political economy of what he calls the television "supertext"—specifically, the context of the American institutional model—as it relays its rhythms and values into the lives of spectators.[14] These spectators are no longer anchored in the live, but increasingly subject to the network manipulations of time and desire typical of Los Angeles. For Browne the very format of television—serial, endlessly repetitious, with breaks and lures that disappoint and move on—is modeled on the workaday world of the other institutions that it supports. Television achieves realism—television realism—not because of its representational reflection of what we consider the authentic or rawly real, but in the way it enforces, mirrors, and supports how we lead our everyday lives—the places we go, the products that sustain us biologically and ideologically. Television, in this way, is far more realistic than, for instance, Italian neo-realism or Hollywood's realistic modes of representation. In its essence, it naturalizes and verifies a social order. What we recognize in television is the status quo, the exterior scheduling of intimacy and domesticity, the endless renewal and destruction necessary for things merely to remain the same.

For Browne, the key aspect of the supertext is scheduling. Television scheduling means to select, place, and coordinate programs with a view to their competitive business advantage. Scheduling is how you place programming in order for it to create the most attractive lure in order to deliver audiences to sponsors, not unlike placing the appropriate fishing lure at the right depth. Television textuality is supertextual in that it must always be observed and analyzed in terms of a greater context than its internal integrity. Scheduling means to arrange a lineup calculated to deliver viewers to a set of sponsored commodities. The time of day, the day of the week, and the relationship to what precedes and follows are geared to an audience that might be piqued by the commodities for sale.

A crucial moment for Browne is when television recognizes that its aesthetic is a commercial one and stops trying to ape other arts. This is the moment when we leave the golden age—golden only because it presented live variety shows and anthology dramas as theatrically legitimate rather than serially compromised. The shift from live ensemble anthology dramas to a serial format was also a shift away from dialogue and the integrity of the speaking character. Dialogue is predicated on respect for the *you* and *I* relationship implied in it, and it continually investigates and verifies what it means to be an individual self. The shift from dialogue leads, argues Browne, to action and the image. He also identifies a shift from personal psychology (theatrical investigation) to the standardization and formulization of character types (the serial mode). The character type stands in for what used to be a self. It would be bizarre for sophisticated television watchers—and we are almost all sophisticated in viewing television—to inspect episodes of *Mister Ed* or even *Law and Order: Criminal Intent* for profound insight into the nature of the human soul. We are released from that romance.

The move from dialogue and psychology to formal character types is also a move to predictability and efficiency, and that move coincides with the transfer of production from New York to Los Angeles, from author-based, closed textuality to a producer-based medium. Further, the relatively independent control of the 1955 model—many individual stations were controlled in an independent fashion, existing more or less as theater ensembles—becomes network hegemony, with networks advancing only partial financing to program suppliers. What this means in practice is that networks had to appeal to already highly capitalized industries. What entity is in a position to make television shows? What entity has the resources to risk 80 percent of production costs on the chance that a program will become a hit or go into syndication? Exiting its own golden age, Hollywood emerges as the answer. This resolution of financing to ultimately mutual advantage leads to the televisual conquest of Hollywood, with television production representing a large proportion of "cinematic" income. Taking the familiar format of the margins striking back at the heart of the empire to an extreme, imperial Hollywood becomes servant to network mastery.

One of the chief features of the studio system was genre, which is obviously a serial format itself: musicals, gangster stories, or melodramas extravagantly repeated. Yet, Browne indicates, the seriality of television is quite different from the genre model of cinema. Television conventions evolve out of a complex negotiation of network, movie studios, advertisers, and audiences together. The network's interest is in a mass audience from the point of view of advertisement, rather than—as in genre film—the desire to repeat a formula. A traditional genre study would assess the degree to which a film realized elements of the formula. The interest of genre study is always in the completion of the formula or in its deviation. Genre films may be a low form of cinema, but they are still dedicated to the high goals of resolution or plentitude. Television seriality, however, continually violates genre demands by frustrating or ignoring them. Like the flow of broadcast television generally, which depends upon interruptions, individual programs are structured around commercial intrusions leading to a metadiscourse of genre diversion.

Viewers routinely accept astonishing variations in the established "world" of a series. The long running *Happy Days*, the failed pilot for which originally aired as an episode of *Love, American Style*, eventually featured Robin Williams as Mork, an alien from another planet, in the otherwise terrestrially bound world of 1950s Milwaukee. When Mork went on to feature in his own series, the period setting was abandoned. Violations cause breaks that metastasize into increasingly unlikely characters, situations, and story lines. This metastasizing becomes ever more frantic as a series exhausts itself, something that can happen at any point. An episode of *Happy Days*, in which Fonzie (Henry Winkler) jumps a shark on his motorcycle, inspired the website Jump the Shark where contributors vote on "a defining moment when you know that your favorite television program has reached its peak."[15]

Like Browne, Barr traces a movement from live television to a reliance on filmed programs, through five key technological developments: "(1) cuts between television cameras (mid-1940s); (2) recording of the television image on film (late 1940s); (3) shooting of television material on film (early 1950s); (4) recording of the television image on tape (late 1950s); (5) editing of the tape-recorded image (1960s)."[16] This trajectory posits television as less like theater as it becomes technically more like cinema in its raw materials and how they are manipulated and stored. However, we suggest that despite some common production elements, the nature of broadcast distribution ensures a fundamentally different response. The similarities between film and television—that they both present audiovisual material on a screen—inspires an expectation of fulfillment that cinema satisfies, but television continually violates. An absence of fulfillment leads to a particular television presence that recalls television to a golden age. Imagining ideal viewing in a simpler past—either on an individual level (childhood) or social level (the innocent 1950s)—justifies aesthetic standards through codes of realism and legitimizes the study of television through stable genres.

These observations conjure three important paradoxes. First, while anthology programs of the 1950s have becomes the most valorized, if most difficult to view of televisual products, the principle locus of liveness today can be identified in some of the most criticized programming: reality TV. Second, while some of the greatest drama—in a theatrical sense—can be found in reality programs, this drama is clearly constructed after the fact. Its drama is created through editing, rather than through some property of the original. Third, a historically recent medium has always, right from its beginning, been a locus of nostalgia.

How might television be seen as nostalgic? For some critics, television invokes nostalgia both because of its hearthlike position in the home and its historical position after World War II, when soldiers rejoined society. After all, the origin of the word *nostalgia* is *nostos*, "to return home alive."[17] Old television programs, such as those shown on Nick at Night or TVLand, are often cast as examples of nostalgia, but it's not such a simple designation. We laugh at *Bewitched* or *Leave It to Beaver*, or adopt a cynical hipster cool toward them. But if we know the program only in the form of a rerun, can we be said to be watching nostalgically?

We identify three kinds of televisual nostalgia, though it isn't always for something positive or desirable. First, there is *provideo* nostalgia, which we can compare to the profilmic. This is the unmediated world that we understand to exist before or outside the event of its reproduction—taped (provideo) or filmed (profilmic). Like the real, this world is essentially ungraspable and therefore always prone to mythologizing. Although we imagine this world to exist as historical images, worlds, events, or feelings, in practice we refer these occurrences to their televisual representation. A second order of televisual nostalgia, then, would be for this *televisual representation* in which the original has already been mediated. The only history of television is television history, and even that isn't remembered very well, and only in a presynthesized form. One example is the cheaply produced *Time after Time*, which reassembles footage from the NBC vaults. Old videotape—as well as old news anchors—are treated as recyclable commodities. The show's tagline, "We're History," expresses an internal ambivalence. It's impossible not to read "history" here in the slang sense of being over and done with. No achievement could surpass the ability to look back at history and shrug our shoulders. We can be as nostalgic as we wish for televisual representations—such as Michael Jackson's performance of "Billie Jean" at the Motown 25 celebration, the wedding of Prince Charles and Princess Diana, or—perhaps most poignant—Walter Cronkite's announcement of the assassination of John F. Kennedy.

Besides the possibility of nostalgia for an event and for its representation, we identify a third order of nostalgia for *television technology* itself. Old television footage is never hauntingly beautiful like old silent movie clips are; it is usually virtually unwatchable unless reassembled into increasingly smaller pieces so that the integrity of the original is never maintained. The demonstration of now outmoded techniques simultaneously provides an opportunity to showcase new technologies—for example, nonlinear digital editing, which is used to cut the archive into bits—and to parade the triumph of its own forms. A tension develops between quaint, charming, but unbearable technology and the call to consume even more sophisticated prototypes of the future. Some programming operates to display these technological advances—the shift from black and white to color on series such as *Bewitched*, *Gilligan's Island*, and *I Dream of Jeannie*, or the undefined image and unsophisticated sets, acting, and editing on primitive music videos. Perhaps television nostalgia is not primarily about a longing to reestablish the world and its truth, but a nostalgia that lingers over television's own substitutions and fictions, as well as its own network dominance. Television is nostalgia for itself as it watches its own unraveling. Television reviews its own textual history as precisely that secondary representation that renders old-fashioned nostalgia impossible. Resigned to loss, television re-signs and reruns that loss rather than submit to the melancholy that Cubitt essentializes.

While many theorists approach postmodernism as a largely nostalgic attitude, they maintain their own nostalgia for certain aspects of modernism as an anchor for thought and for the basis of an oppositional politics. Fredric Jameson, for instance, makes a distinction between pastiche and parody based on their relationships to nostalgia. Parody, the passing of which he laments, goes hand in hand with modernism's individual subject and personal style—a norm from which the parodist "ostentatiously deviate[s] … which then reasserts itself, in a not necessarily unfriendly way, by a systematic mimicry of their willful eccentricities."[18] In contrast, pastiche is an empty gathering of forms, "a neutral practice of [parodic] mimicry, without any … conviction that alongside the abnormal tongue you have momentarily borrowed, some healthy linguistic normality still exists" (17). With no lost value, pastiche can no longer represent loss or grief. Jameson regrets that while we used to be able to talk about "real fiction," in a postmodernist mode we can only talk about fiction as real. We live in a world in which a person can attempt to persuade by saying, "I'm not a doctor, but I play one on TV."

Jameson observes that "with the collapse of the high-modernist ideology of style … the producers of culture have nowhere to turn but to the past; the imitation of dead styles, speech through all the masks and voices stored up in the imaginary museum of a now global culture" (17–18). This leads to "random cannibalization," to "a culture of the simulacrum." He continues, "Nostalgia does not strike one as an altogether satisfactory word for such fascination (particularly when one thinks of the pain of a properly modernist nostalgia with a past beyond all but aesthetic retrieval)" (19). This nostalgia isn't history—in fact it is incompatible with genuine historicity and "lay[s] siege either to our own present and immediate past or to a more distant history that escapes individual existential memory" (19).

Another feature of this improperly articulated nostalgia is schizophrenia. Following Jacques Lacan, Jameson sees schizophrenia emerging from the infant's failure fully to enter the symbolic, to enter language, and hence the failure to enter time. Temporality issues from effective signification, the signifier and signified confidently articulated leading to the progression from a past to a future. Created in that future is a loss that can be situated, put in the past, and mourned. Schizophrenics exist in an eternal present, unable to experience the kind of loss that could lead to an authentic nostalgia.[19]

In a postmodernist mode, we're nostalgic for the very passage of time, for the experience of a spectrum of time. Authentic liveness is the link that puts golden-age television closer to theater than to cinema, and this

legitimacy trumps cinema every time. Reality TV uses editing to reestablish the progression of time, seen almost purely in terms of multiple
stories progressing or following characters, who are themselves static.
This is temporality, but without a tradition of theater or literature; it is
temporality itself as pastiche, devoid of even a parodic referent.

To see postmodernism as an improper nostalgia—as Jameson does—
is itself nostalgic in a high modernist mode. If postmodernism is nostalgic, it's in a new and fundamentally different way, not merely a debased
way. We think of nostalgia as concerning a former time or lost artifacts,
but Mellencamp's discussion of television as a "disciplinary time machine" makes it clear that nostalgia is also an attitude toward the self.[20] In
distinction to the "pleasure principle" that Mellencamp finds operating
in cinema, television pleasure frees us from finding answers and establishing fixed positions. Yet, to abandon identity implies a mythological
notion: that we once possessed an identity to abandon. Along with the
abandonment of the self, a complicated reaction toward nostalgia develops. It is nostalgic in neither the etymological sense of returning home
alive nor in the psychoanalytic sense of recovering plentitude. Mainly,
television refers to itself, and that self-referentiality is precisely the point
and pleasure of watching. We watch television watch itself. Neither the
world nor nostalgia nor apocalypse has withstood the ironic returning
and retuning of television.

Set in 1954, the favorite year of its title, before the late-1950s shift
from the glamour of New York to the crass financing of Los Angeles,
Richard Benjamin's *My Favorite Year* (1982) is steeped in nostalgia for
a time when television could be as important as theater or cinema—but
only retrospectively understood in that way. It takes place in the theatrical capital, but never mentions Broadway. It both celebrates the cinematic imaginary and reduces it and its stars to the size of a monitor.
Television's leveling of greatness is implied even in its golden age. At
the film's end, these themes are linked explicitly to the live production
model. Danger, accident, and improvisation become television magic as
the movie star accommodates himself to a lesser medium that becomes
his salvation.

In *My Favorite Year* Peter O'Toole plays Alan Swann, a John Barrymore/
Errol Flynn type, booked to guest star on the *Comedy Cavalcade* program,
a thinly disguised version of Sid Caesar's *Your Show of Shows*, which was
broadcast between 1950 and 1954 and launched the careers of such writers
as Woody Allen and Neil Simon.[21] O'Toole as Swann is certainly the star
in the film and of the film, but Mark Linn-Baker's Benjy is its protagonist.
His opening narration, set over line drawings of the Brooklyn Bridge and

the 1950s New York skyline and spoken from some unspecified later date, signals that his will be the guiding sensibility.

Benjy works as a television writer, so this will be a television sensibility, concerned with the past not as a historical place but as an alternative ontological space. The film is interested in the commodifications and derangements of television, the spectacle of girls dressed as cigarette boxes trotting around the set. What might be considered problematic here—commodification, sexism, and the promotion of tobacco products—is, through the fact of temporal distance, made innocent. In fact, history and politics of all kinds have been drained out, substituted with comic set pieces that wouldn't be out of place in the borscht belt—a bit with a fire hose, an upset dessert tray, a stolen horse, blond bimbos, the zany Jewish family sitting down to dinner: "Try the liver?" (rim shot). Nostalgia even extends to the Mafia, but this isn't surprising, both because of the way that organized crime has become a common signifier of nostalgia (home, loyalty, capitalism) in American culture and because of its obvious fakery within the context of this candy-box film. These wise guys couldn't perpetrate a hit any more than could Wile E. Coyote.

Fakery, in fact, becomes the theme and central issue in the film—that is, fakery as long as it's genuine. Swann confesses that he isn't really the hero he played in the movies: "Those are movies. Damn you, look at me. I'm flesh and blood. Life-sized, no larger. I'm not the silly goddamned hero. I never was." But to Benjy it doesn't matter: "Whoever you were in those movies, those silly goddamned heroes meant a lot to me. What does it matter if it was an illusion? It worked." He adds that Swann must possess some of the qualities of the characters he portrayed or he wouldn't have been able to play them. So much for acting. Fakery extends from playacting to personal identity in this celebration of American assimilation: Benjy and Swann both have changed their names, but they haven't repudiated anything. The fake version is better in the sense of greater utility, and these characters aren't supposed to have lost anything. Benjy is witheringly embarrassed by his Brooklyn family and changes his name, but his Jewishness is a source of comedy rather than a social impediment in a racist society: "Try the liver?"

My Favorite Year makes many of its points through a comparison of its two stars. Stanley "King" Kaiser (Joseph Bologna), although clearly a great television success and modeled on Sid Caesar, one of the great figures in television history, is never shown with fans of any kind. He is alternately abusive and pandering, the latter represented in his constant, inappropriate gift giving—steaks, whitewall tires, ties from the Bronx, used shoes. He is as crude as a hunk of meat. Swann, despite his rampant alcoholism, is unfailingly gracious to the many fans who approach him and the many who merely stare at him with admiration, gazes of which he is clearly aware. His admirers never see the seams or the strain of constant scrutiny. Like King, Swann offers gifts, but his are evanescent—little moments that fans can treasure, rather than commodities: a dance with an elderly woman, a glance, a glimpse, a kiss, a story to tell later.

Swann is an irreplaceable legend. King says, "Replace him." The television man can't imagine that anything exists without a substitute or that you couldn't pull the legendary down to the everyday. Swann's great swashbuckling movie roles devolve into "The Musketeer Skit." What makes him great—watchable, charismatic—is too self-destructive and unproductive to be encouraged, and it must be reined in, domesticated, to function in the world of television's greater utility. Swann constantly seeks to slip outside those boundaries, into alcohol, a woman's arms, or the seat of his limousine. King is only devoted to the show and only exists in the studio. His encounters with the outside world are symbolized by the ridiculous gangster subplot. Karl "Boss" Rojeck (Cameron Mitchell), outraged that King has been mocking him on the program, first threatens King, then sends in his goons—who, of course, all become part of the show. Rojeck has a bit of comic business with an oversized hat—a classic—and the goons end up on stage in an unplanned (live) melee that nevertheless plays better than anything scripted and rehearsed.

Here we see how liveness is the main source of the genuine within the fake. Benjy announces that 1954, his favorite year, was when "TV was live and comedy was king." Liveness is what the movie star doesn't understand about television. When told the show is live, Swann asks, "Live? Live! What does live mean?" What indeed? For Benjy, "It means that the exact moment you're cavorting and leaping around the stage over there, twenty million people are seeing it." Swann immediately connects this to an image of spewing: "You mean it all goes into the camera lens and then just spills out into people's houses?" and then recalls his early theatrical experience, playing a butler. Announcing "I'm not an actor. I'm a movie star!" Swann begins to guzzle booze. It is worth noting that even King has the jitters in anticipation of a live show. He stays cool and keeps the quips coming in the face of Rojeck's physical threats, but becomes a nervous wreck before showtime.

For such a charming, frothy, comic effort, this film has what seems to be a remarkably cynical ending. The audience cheers Swann saving the day and the show, but in the end, it is a television sensibility that wins out. Swann's success comes only by rejecting the habits and hubris of years, at Benjy's instigation. In a return to the retrospective mode, seemingly spoken from the distance of many years and voiced over a shot of Swann on the control room monitor, Benjy interprets the events: "I think if you had asked Alan Swann what was the single most gratifying moment in his life, he might have said this one right here." The greatest movie star in the history of cinema—modeled after figures like John Barrymore or Errol Flynn, played by the actor who embodied Lord Jim and Lawrence of Arabia—appears as an unresolved image on a tiny black-and-white screen, and this may be his most gratifying moment. The satisfaction that seems to adhere to this reduction is in keeping with another aspect of Swann's renewal. He must become a family man, be returned to the domestic, open to a sudden, sticky reconciliation with his daughter, Tess—mercifully, off camera. It's not clear what this shift means in practical terms—the mother is a complete cipher—but it does involve a Connecticut suburb rather than the city, station wagons rather than limos, and television sets rather than the great silver screen. The difference between a great movie star and a TV personality is just that distance between myth and domestic ordinariness. Television can topple legends, kill the king, reduce the idolatry of great stars to everyday personalities, daddies, or dinner guests. Television unrelentingly takes unapproachable ideality and converts it into the ordinary.

Nostalgia acts as a convenient cover for all the contradictions expressed in the film. The star of television is crude, but the true star can only be fully expressed on television. The performer can be good on television, but only while adopting an attitude of not caring. Television, which we're repeatedly told defiles family values and relentlessly attacks the family, actually supports the family.

The vision of this film is a very particular one of the 1950s, the kind of view that Stephanie Coontz would describe as "the way we never were," the same 1950s vision that renders a film like Gary Ross's *Pleasantville* (1999) self-contradictory. The 1950s would be great if only there were no racism, sexual repression, rigid social and gender roles, and hostility to minorities—and if there were more excitement. The 1950s would be great if they were different—or in color. The television *Pleasantville* appreciates is as much a cinematic dream—one in which Barney Fife (Don Knotts) plays the villain—as the world in *My Favorite Year*. The past is only as good as the protagonist's ability to go back and change it, keeping the good parts and maintaining an adopted ignorance about the world.[22]

Aside from live comedy programs, what else was happening during Benjy's favorite year? By 1954 many of the troubling issues that would dominate American politics for decades had been set in motion: racial conflict (the U.S. Supreme Court decision on *Brown v. Board of*

Education of Topeka); the threat of nuclear war (the hydrogen bomb tests in the Bikini Atoll); raging McCarthyism and anticommunism (the House Un-American Activities Committee hearings were nationally televised); the Vietnam War (Dien Bien Phu was taken by Vietnamese Communists); and a seismic shift in entertainment (twenty-nine million homes with television sets and a concomitant precipitous decline in cinema attendance). Yet, in films like *Pleasantville* and *My Favorite Year*, television refers only to its own past, and only a golden past. Willfully misunderstanding the past, these films prefer television history to all other kinds.

Karl Marx's comments on the golden age of Greece are useful in understanding the necessary distance of time, space, attitude, and understanding in constructing a nostalgic past. For Marx, Greek arts and epics can only be grasped by accepting that they "are bound up with certain forms of social development"—significantly, slavery. Going further, Marx separates past art from the present not only through a changed mythology, but explicitly in terms of technology: "Is the view of nature and of social relations which shaped Greek imagination and Greek art possible in the age of automatic machinery, and railways, and locomotives, and electrical telegraphs?"[23] We might ask, Is the view of society on which live 50s television is based possible with videotape, DVDs, time-shifting technologies, HDTV, and broadband Internet access? Arguably not, and it is in this impossibility of return that we can freely succumb to a longing for the past.

In this respect, television's past—the nostalgia *for* television rather than *of* television—is golden in the same way that Marx tells us that ancient Greece was golden. To quote Marx, the characters in *My Favorite Year* are "normal children. The charm their art has for us does not conflict with the primitive character of the social order from which it had sprung. It is rather the product of the latter, and is rather due to the fact that the unripe social conditions under which it arose and under which it could appear can never return."[24]

8

Feminization

A dangerous association with femininity is implied in most films about television and often noted in television studies. This association is so important that the present chapter will constitute the longest discussion in this book, encompassing three parts. In "Medusae and Castrati" we begin with a review of the psychoanalytic approach to feminist cinema studies associated with such theorists as Laura Mulvey and we consider whether that model is appropriate to television representation. The second section, "Drag," asks whether the best woman for a job is still a man, as we see in Sydney Pollack's *Tootsie* (1982). The alliance between television and femininity, as *Tootsie* suggests, seems to achieve its generic apotheosis in the soap opera; Tania Modelski and Robert C. Allen seek to delineate these generic conventions. Finally, in "When Men Become Women," we use an analysis of Ben Stiller's *The Cable Guy* (1996) to observe the effects on masculinity among men associated with television.

Medusae and Castrati

In "The Laugh of the Medusa," Hélène Cixous takes up the issue of "libidinal feminist" writing. This is a writing through the body meant to sweep away phallic syntax without replacing it with an essentialist feminine language. Cixous imagines a flexibility that tolerates the otherness of otherness, that carries difference within itself rather than in traumatic defense against the other. Significantly, the freedom and pleasure of this writing is associated with the woman's body. Warning against the "signifier that would take you back to the authority of a signified,"[1] she advocates a slippage, then, between the signifier and signified, between that relationship often described as two sides of a piece of paper or two sides of a coin. We might also see it as two faces of woman herself, which raises complicated issues about how liberating this construction might be.

A woman in popular culture is often two-faced, and television is two-faced as well. Television creates the threat that you will be turned to stone (or a potato), which it then works to contain or exploit. One of its faces recognizes a threat—the disintegration of the family after World War II, for instance. The other face takes advantage of that threat—exploiting its commercial possibilities.

Films such as Sidney Lumet's *Network* (1976), *Tootsie*, and *The Cable Guy* all address how television influences subjects in terms of gender. *Network* identifies the equivalence of television with femininity, *The Cable Guy* transfers that feminizing influence onto a male figure, and *Tootsie* accessorizes that economy into drag. These cinemas assume the high position in an old opposition. They consign television to its own, previous, handmaiden role. As Andreas Huyssen writes in *After the Great Divide*, "[T]he nightmare of being devoured by mass culture through co-optation, commodification, and the 'wrong' kind of success is the constant fear of the modernist artist, who tries to stake out his territory by fortifying the boundaries between genuine art and inauthentic mass culture. Again, the problem is not the desire to differentiate between forms of high art and depraved forms of mass culture and its co-optations. The problem is rather the persistent gendering of feminine of that which is devalued."[2]

There is a process, then, that we can identify involving the relationship of patriarchy, cinema, and television. First, cinema demonizes television through the figure of the woman; the culture then reciprocally demonizes woman through television. These actions depend on a relationship, both argued (women's place in the home in which television functions; the importance of genres like soap opera that appeal to women) and assumed (both women and television are debased categories). Finally, television transforms those demonizations into the status quo.

Huyssen situates woman as that source of lack and otherness against which modernism makes its recuperative depredations. Similarly, in *Haunted Media* Jeffrey Sconce traces a Victorian alliance of feminine sensibility and physiology with spiritualism and the emerging discourses of electricity and telegraphy. Though based in assumptions of the "disassociative" and "transmutable"—that is, the electromagnetic constitution of women—this alliance, Sconce argues, brought for a moment the highly gendered discourse of technology into a surprisingly paradoxical space of female empowerment. The very passivity of women allowed them an active voice in an intensely patriarchical public sphere. This utopian moment of "woman as technology" passes into more strictly modernist models of hysteria and insanity, preparing a new alliance of women and the "much more sinister" electronic "elsewheres" and "nowheres" of radio and television.[3]

As we observe throughout our study of the cinema of television, in films as seemingly diverse as *Network*, Tobe Hooper's *Poltergeist* (1982), David Cronenberg's *Videodrome* (1983), Annabel Jankel and Rocky Morton's *Max Headroom* (1985), *The Cable Guy*, and Gore Verbinski's *The Ring* (2002), this televisual space offers two very disturbing possibilities. One, which Sconce also notes, is the wholesale incorporation or absorption of real bodies into the virtualities of a new flesh. The other is the imperium of women, or at least femininity, over this new regime. Sconce himself lists a "recent glut of films concerning the electronic mediation of subjectivity and society—movies such as *Videodrome* (1983), *Robocop* (1987), *Total Recall* (1990), *Lawnmower Man* (1992), *Virtuosity* (1996), *Strange Days* (1997), and *eXistenZ* (1999)," all testifying "to the theatrical success of [a] once wholly theoretical paradigm" (170). This now postmodern paradigm, founded in Bordieu, Debord, and Baudrillard, is "the idea that we live in a world created by television (as opposed to one simply *affected* by television)."[4]

In *Network*, Diana (Faye Dunaway) *is* television. Playing a tough and ambitious television producer, she is accused by her mentor, lover, and critic (William Holden as Max Schumacher, head of the network news division) of being "universal madness and destruction." In some ways she functions in the same manner as the traditional noir femme fatale, a deadly threat to rational order and the world at large. As the noir spider-woman in this 1976 film, Diana is even more alarming than women usually are, her obvious bralessness a sign of both the femme fatale and the feminist, as she enters Max's office at night and leans provocatively against the doorjamb. Her control over the airwaves gives her the ability to broadcast her threat to the entire country.

In *Network* Dunaway doesn't simply lure a single detective into her web, as she did in another film, Roman Polanski's *Chinatown* (1974). There she destroyed Jack Nicholson's character Jake Gittes and, not incidentally, herself. When Dunaway won the 1976 Academy Award for best performance by a leading actress for *Network*, many insiders speculated that it was at least partially compensation for the Oscar she hadn't won for *Chinatown*. The earlier key, star-making Dunaway role of Bonnie in Arthur Penn's *Bonnie and Clyde* (1967) had also created a figure of threatening femininity linked to popular cultural forms. To some extent, each of these roles reflects the rise of the women's movement at the end of the 1960s and throughout the 1970s. *Bonnie and Clyde* features a critique of an emerging mass culture of celebrity, represented by the Bonnie character and the emasculated Clyde.

We don't want to assume an equivalency of feminization and emasculation. To be emasculated—as in the case of Clyde—is to be deprived of virility or strength, and this is just as likely to occur from within, as in the testicular cancer theme in David Fincher's *Fight Club* (1999) and Daniel Minahan's *Series 7: The Contenders* (2001), as it is to be imposed. To be feminized is to take on—willingly or not—the characteristics of a woman. What we will see is that feminization—in which a male character, such as, say, Dustin Hoffman in *Tootsie*, can still function like a "good" woman—often operates as a mask for emasculation. But it can be a two-faced mask: an assumption of at least some form of power—as in the case of drag—and simultaneously an accusation against women in society. Popular culture, and particularly film about popular culture, frequently depicts both of these attitudes, often oscillating between them. It is interesting to note that although a woman can be "mannish" or "handsome" there is no strictly equivalent position of defeminization. In fact, masculinity is often freely adopted by women in positions of traditional male power; Dunaway's character, Diana, explains her own femininity as "masculine temperament," by which she means that she "arouses quickly, gets off, and wants to leave." Her husband is described as having left her—for a man.

As the title character of *The Cable Guy*, Jim Carrey adopts the name Chip Douglas from one of the sitcoms that represent his only frame of reference. He is a completely televisual creature—like Chauncey Gardiner (Peter Sellers) in Hal Ashby's *Being There* (1979) or Rupert Pupkin in Martin Scorcese's *The King of Comedy* (1982)—and, like them, but in a much more explicit way, television has deranged his masculinity. The film drifts toward a subterranean accusation that he has become homosexual or that television has thwarted normal oedipal development. As in many of Carrey's roles, including the lead character in Chuck Russell's *The Mask* (1994) and as comedian Andy Kaufman in Milos Forman's *Man on the Moon* (1999), his feminization translates into insanity, with emasculation always lurking beneath.

There are two opposing and somewhat paradoxical ways to interpret the connection between femininity and television. If we accept television as the dominant signifying machine of our age, and if it employs the tactics of female subjectivity, has the day finally arrived for the reign of the woman? Does television become an historic occasion for the empowerment of femininity? Or, has the vision of the feminine remained intact, the powerful medium of television simply in league with out-of-control women—addicting the kids, inseminating violence, running off the dog, and leading to the collapse of culture?

How can this threat be exploited? This is the other face of the two-face model. There are a number of films that place the woman in a context of mass culture, advertising, and consumerism. In these films, the woman's threat is exploited ultimately to guarantee the return of men to their rightful place. We can identify this dynamic in such films as William Wellman's *Nothing Sacred* (1937; in which Carole Lombard becomes a media sensation with a bogus case of radium poisoning promoted by an ambitious reporter); George Cukor's *It Should Happen to You* (1954; in which Judy Holliday's character mounts herself on a billboard and becomes a television personality); Norman Jewison's *The Thrill of It All* (1963; in which a housewife played by Doris Day achieves media success as an advertising wizard and almost destroys her marriage); and Stan Dragoti's *Mr. Mom* (1983; in which Terri Garr's housewife character achieves media success as an advertising wizard and almost destroys her marriage). These films are all comic, which is perhaps how they're able to entertain these possibilities at all, and they don't lead to disaster—or, rather, their disasters are only temporary, retarding devices in the narrative (a swimming pool full of soap suds, etc.). Soon enough, the woman's dangerous access to media exposure is shut down in the interests of romantic harmony.

But although this is a two-faced model, it doesn't admit ambiguity. It can only see the rise of television and its equivalence with women as the decline of culture and the threat of upheaval. As in *Network*, any contact with television contaminates: all revolutionary possibilities immediately deflate. In *Network*, this view has more than a whiff of nostalgia about it. William Holden's Max—like Sam the Lion (Ben Johnson) in Peter Bogdanovich's *The Last Picture Show* (1971) or Mel (Walter Matthau) in Elia Kazan's *A Face in the Crowd* (1957)—represents imperiled male dominance, equated with reality, love, identity, and nobility—all threatened by television. But we need to ask, Why is the imperiled, noble, white male culture always represented by weak, dying, diseased, middle-aged men?

Even when television inspires people to act—as *Network*'s troubled anchorman Howard Beale (Peter Finch) does when he encourages his viewers to proclaim, "I'm mad as hell, and I'm not going to take it anymore"—it inspires them only as lemmings and sheep. The high cinema of television continually professes that we must save the masses, return them to nobility, offer them a chance at their own identity and liberation. But the fact is that these films have nothing but contempt for the

masses. These masses are capable of accepting the most insidious corporate address as inspiration for mass idolatry and consumption. Consider
the audience in *Network*: Its depiction isn't limited to prompted attendees
in the studio, but people in their homes, who are all too ready and willing
to rush to their windows and scream catchphrases.[5] The contempt for
these people is the contradiction at the heart of modernism itself. Modernism promised a revolution, but quickly withdrew into elite isolation
filled with revulsion for the very masses that it promised to liberate. This
dynamic incessantly repeats itself in the cinema of television. *Network*
shares this cynical attitude toward mobilizing the masses. Diana makes
a cheap and profitable reality TV program out of revolution featuring a
pseudo–Angela Davis character and her violent band of radicals. This organization, ostensibly devoted to racial identity and liberation, is shown
to be ridiculous. Their revolutionary planning sessions quickly devolve
into arguments over profit margins, points, and ratings. At the end of
the film, Diana orchestrates the assassination of the suicidal Howard
because of his low ratings. She pays the black radicals to do the hit, further corrupting them.

Elitist attitudes are consistently demonstrated by those writers associated with the golden age of television. *Network* was written by Paddy
Chayefsky and—like *Being There*, written by Jerzy Kosinski—it is famous
for its attack on television. Chayefsky, furthermore, is associated with
the golden age of television depicted in *My Favorite Year*, and known for
writing such famous televisual dramas as Richard Brooks's *The Catered
Affair* (1956) and Delbert Mann's *Marty* (1953), both for the Goodyear
TV Playhouse and both subsequently made into films. By the time he
came to write *Network*, television could no longer be said to be in a golden
age; it had become instead a monolithic corporate force. Like other films
about television, such as *Rollerball* (1975) or *Max Headroom*, *Network*
views the medium as a singular evil in the image of the network. Thirty
years after *Network*, we can see a television horizontally monopolized,
but far more diversified and multiple than this Goliath-like network
nightmare, itself more a failure of cinematic imagination than an accurately predicted future.

The assault of television on secure gender positions requires theoretical underpinning. Freudian psychoanalysis has profoundly influenced
film and television theory. The discourse of women in classical psychoanalytic terms can help to explain the ways in which women inhabit a
subjectivity based on lack and unstrung desire, a position closer to that
of an animal, an infant, or a psychotic than of a man. How are women
produced as subjects in this model, and how is the model of female

subjectivity made equivalent to the model of television and subject to the same kinds of attacks?

Remember, first, that psychoanalysis describes the production of subjects: how you achieve a sense of self; how you become gendered as a man or a woman; how you identify yourself with different positions of sexuality or ego. It is the job of culture to produce selves or egos—to produce subjects. It's the job of ideology to position those subjects in a structure of dominance that enfranchises particular gendered subjects and disenfranchises others. Ideology reduplicates itself through the reduplication of subjects. If the ideology of a culture is patriarchy, then the job of culture is to make natural and real the production and use of male power. Culture promotes the nuclear family as a place to raise sons and daughters in positions of relative dominance. Within this model, males enter the culture as dominant, active members, constructed on the side of desire; females enter as passive or subordinate—constructed on the side of disappointment and dependence.

In the final analysis, Sigmund Freud's importance lies in recognizing that gender and power are structured; they are not the inherent features of any human being. We aren't suggesting that Freud can't be criticized, but our purpose here is to use his model as a way of understanding our cultural relationship to television. Freud's famous question—What do women want?—can be answered by saying that it is very hard to say what women want because of their constructed nature. Culture has produced women as subordinate subjects without a particular object or logic to their desire. The question of what women want is actually unanswerable. Their desire may be produced in ways so disempowered they may simply—or quite complexly—want to want. Women desire desire.

For Freud, the production of masculinity and femininity is a project of the oedipal complex. Freud begins by saying that all children, regardless of whether they're male or female, are born with a relationship with their mothers on an imaginary integration with the mother's body and based on their needs for warmth, food, and protection. For Freud, this relationship with the mother is not only based on relatively weak instincts of survival. It is, for human beings—and perhaps uniquely for human beings—propped up by an intense sense of pleasure in the satisfaction of those instincts: food, shelter, warmth. In brief, that pleasure is the origin of infantile sexuality. Everything we may want for the rest of our lives—no matter how sophisticated, cosmopolitan, cynical, or depraved we become—expresses at least in part a desire to return to this earlier state. We seek full, immediate satisfaction, an ego-obliterating contact with presence and simultaneity, with plenitude. But obviously, this plentitude cannot persist. Babies must eventually occupy their positions as separate individuals, members of a culture as it reduplicates power structures. Civilization doesn't exist for people simply to breed, but to reinforce itself. The job of the family in civilization is to produce children structured in dominance and to empower these children in different ways. That requires the assignment of an identity and a gender.

In this Freudian construct we become individuals in a traumatic way. We are forced to recognize our separation from our mothers. We are removed from a paradise of full presence, sheer pleasure, and sameness and invited into a terrifying relationship with difference, otherness, isolation, alienation, and all those other aspects of normal adult life. Freud identifies several phases of the pre-oedipal: oral, anal, and genital. During these phases, the baby begins to investigate the limits of its own body. It stuffs things in its mouth, treasures its poop, and learns to negotiate autoerotic forms of pleasure. The three pre-oedipal stages finally introduce the individual into what Freud calls the "family romance." You enter it on one side a thumb-sucking bisexual being; you emerge on the other side sexed, gendered, and yourself.

It is here that culture actually produces masculinity and femininity and the possibility of being emasculated or feminized. Particularly in the case in which the dominant ideology is maleness, culture reproduces male dominance and female subservience. Men will be reproduced as having a relationship to power and presence. They'll assume the ability to wave a wand that will get them what they want. But women will seem lacking. The penis, in Freud's analogy, becomes the phallus, a symbol of power that men are granted and women denied. But, by naturalizing this distinction, our culture proposes that women aren't actually deniedpower; they just lack it. On behalf of the status quo, culture would rather reinforce this lack as envy rather than expose its false consciousness.

Severed first from a relationship with their mother, boys and girls will now be forced into a relationship with difference, and they must also recognize their difference from each other. According to Freud, we promote the recognition of difference by encouraging children, as they enter the oedipal cycle, to see the parent of the same sex as a rival in his or her desire for the parent of the opposite sex. Difference is constructed even as it is initiated by the structured law of the father. Girls attach themselves to their fathers and rival their mothers. Boys stand with their mothers and rival their fathers. This is another process of the reduplication of male power. The girl must drag herself away from the mother, reidentify with the father as object of desire, and rival her mother. She learns difference in this complicated negotiation. But the boy maintains the mother as his original object and rivals the father. The girl is torn away from the original object of desire; the boy maintains his original incestuous relationship with his mother. Boys maintain a continuity and integrity very different from the scatterbrained way in which girls zigzag through the family romance. Girls are taught not to know their own minds.

The father dynamizes the system as a castrating threat. He faces a dilemma associated with presenting his son to culture as a powerful man, and therefore as a potentially more powerful rival. The father threatens his son with symbolic castration. But this threat is actually an invitation, and it comes with compensations. Sublimate the mother and enter culture as anything you want. All civilization awaits you, offered up as an array of substitutions for that one thing you want most of all. Join the boy's club. Build a skyscraper; write a novel. In this way, the father displaces the forbidden desire for the mother. The boy eagerly enters culture as a fully empowered member of the William Holden Boy's Club of Real Desire, although he might have to gather an entire harem of substitutions.

The girl is not threatened by her mother with castration if she doesn't leave the father alone, and she is offered no compensatory power. The father recognizes the uselessness of sending a girl into a culture that is unwilling to enfranchise her. Girls are not threatened with castration; they realize they already are castrated. Entering gendered identity under the sign of disappointment, the girl realizes that she's not going to be invited into culture and that her dad will now primarily father her as another man's bride.

Recognizing her position—that she's already castrated, that she lacks that one thing that would give her power and civilization—she reluctantly abandons her father and reidentifies in another zigzag with her mother, who is now no longer the all-powerful phallic mother, but inadequate. The mother now represents a position of disappointment, a dead-end girl's club where camaraderie becomes rivalry for men—not for their intrinsic qualities, but for their access to culture. Few scenes are more delightful to male culture than "girls gone wild" or a catfight. This may not be a very flattering view of dominant male culture, but it does explain depressingly clearly how patriarchy works.[6] Freud's notion of femininity is one of oedipal underdevelopment and miscarriage, which leads in women to an incapacity for justice and sublimation out of an eternal masochistic envy of the potent desire represented by the penis. As Freud, in his essay "Femininity," concludes, "There are no paths open to further development; it is as though the whole process had already run its course and remains thenceforward insusceptible to influence—as though, indeed, the difficult development to femininity had exhausted the possibilities of the person concerned."[7]

Women are assigned roles of subordination that continually reinforce a vision of their desire as aimless and goalless. Laura Mulvey, in "Visual Pleasure and Narrative Cinema," has shown how women are often presented as those objects that can be fetishized, recuperated, kept barefoot and pregnant, or killed.[8] As she and many feminist critics have concluded, *woman* is a problem invented in order that she can be solved. At the point at which her threat is fully enclosed, the story is over, the curtain closes, the music comes up, and everything is fine in the world again.

Certainly, women may desire to desire in such a way that they might gain greater access to a cultural power base, yet their desire must either be attached to a man, pathologized, or dissipated into aimless consumption. Thus, women and shopping—a dyad reproduced with knee-jerk consistency every day, a model of female desire that requires encompassing structures, such as a man or a credit card. This shopoholic model of female desire represents the great danger of the femme fatale. Any contact with her is deadly because neither does she love nor does she care. Her envy is insatiable. Her goal may not be to hurt you, but she desires without aim, so she may kill you by accident.

Women on television—or rather women *as* television—often embody a desire or ambition gone awry. They represent a consumer culture not only omnivorous, but cannibalistic, a culture that might eat its children, husbands, and other victims with equanimity. In *Network*, Max asks Diana, "Do you have a favorite restaurant?" She answers, "I eat anything." She is the *vagina dentata*, castrating her way to mayhem and murder. She is television, and so is Mrs. Banks (Blythe Danner) in Costa-Gavras's *Mad City* (1997); Beverly (Kathleen Turner) in Jon Waters's *Serial Mom* (1994); the pregnant gun-toting woman Dawn Lagarto (Brooke Smith) in *Series 7*; Debbie Harry in *Videodrome*; and Suzanne (Nicole Kidman) in Gus Van Sant's *To Die For* (1995).

What power establishes these essences, and what is really at stake? What does it mean to be a "real" man or a "real" woman? What are the consequences of either assuming those roles or rejecting them? Can television—or cinema for that matter—ever answer, or even allow, these questions? If we accept the nonessentialist model of feminine (or for that matter masculine) construction, we must still, also, deliberate on how that model can be construed. Even if Diana in *Network* is not born to madness and destruction, the movie seems dedicated to essentializing that condition. Why? Cinema—at least mainstream narrative cinema—offers the opportunity for spectators to identify with completion, resolution, fulfillment, closure. We are encouraged to identify with power allied to a cohesive view of the self that is pre-egoistic. Cinema offers this identification as its pleasure, although—as Mulvey has also pointed out—at the expense of women who become the object of the male gaze at the expense of their own gaze. Women are positioned as a threat to fulfillment of the narrative, which operates in the interests of the male protagonist and the voyeuristic gaze of the male spectator. Nevertheless, narratives require this threat to function. Not so essential as she is essentially *inessential*, she has to be saved from her own abysmal desire. But Diana consistently refuses this essentialism. Capable of programming and deprogramming everything from the revolutionary agenda of black radicals to the fate of corporations and individuals, she is finally likened by a despairing Max not only to cosmic breakdown but to another great manipulator and reverser of fortune—Bugs Bunny.

Television spectators are often distracted—irresolute in a way analogous, until very recently, to the television image; glancing rather than gazing as in cinema's voyeuristic despotism. The television apparatus doesn't offer its spectators a womblike viewing environment or strong invitations to retreat into a sense of pre-oedipal integration. Instead, it offers its technology and form as an experience in disintegration, in a call to seek fulfillment outside of the text in consumption.

What we may have to conclude is that television, unlike cinema, doesn't really ask to be watched; television no longer positions a spectator who is even asked to enjoy television. But because it is different, could it be radical? Does television position spectators who are radically opposed to the cinematic model of self-fulfillment? Or, does television actually exploit that model of fulfillment in the same way it exploits women? Does it simply import into the culture a model of distraction only to consolidate the continually deferred promise of a more ultimate consolidation? That is the televisual status quo. In other words, we're being positioned by a very sophisticated ideological operation capable of requesting its own dismissal and subversion. Women are exploited as the sign of decriticalized radicality on a global scale rather than on a particular textual scale, as in cinema.

Cinema strongly suspects television of having unleashed femininity to such a degree that we may not be able to contain it again. But we return to the same paradox: Have women suddenly conquered culture? Or, as we have been shown by the cinema of television as much as by

Freud, do women enter culture in a televisual era not as empowered beings or empowered subjects but as symbolically distressed, still projected in the image of male rescue, but somehow or another escaped from the zoo or the house? Or, as in TV programs from *Knot's Landing* to *Desperate Housewives*, from a particularly nice house in the suburbs? The most damning thing about Diana is not that she is a woman or that she *is* television in *Network*, but that she's a powerful executive.[9] Power, absent the hypocritical liberal pieties of an East Coast–educated male-dominated industry, may actually be the most damming thing about television. The idea, continually reinforced, is that if you allow women access as they are, you'll destroy culture and invite universal madness. But in fact you don't get universal madness, even if it's the end of a world. You simply universalize this model of women. The power of the universal text overcomes cinematic specificity; a circuit of desire without reserve overcomes the closure of desire. Cinema may be in despair about the power of women on, in, or as television. But should it be? Naively or perversely, the single face of cinema doesn't seem able to recognize the two faces of television: that television has no intention of legitimately empowering women. It only allows this consumerist essence to escape cinema's limited—single ticket sale—textuality into a constantly deferred and connected system of consumption, a variety of goods and services purchased over a lifetime.

Diana may orchestrate the assassination of Howard, just as cinema performs a character assassination upon television at the behest of the murderous woman. But what is Diana really guilty of? All she kills is cinematic cowardice and the idea that you get what you pay for and pay for what you get. The dilemma about women on television seems to be liberating on one hand. On the other hand, nothing has really changed about the way her subjectivity is seen, the way in which it operates, what it has in mind. In the cinematic mind, television is bad and so are women. They're both bad, and the goal of high culture, good cinema and good men—like Howard Beale or Max Schumacher—should be to stay the course. Containment is the issue now, not resolution, and this diminished goal may reflect cinema's increasing marginalization in the face of new media.

Drag

The television soap opera genre has often served as a jumping-off point for an attitude that sees the whole culture—as Philip Levine puts it— "shit[ting] and squeal[ing] like a new housewife discovering television."[10] This condescending approach to the genre is rampant in a film that may seem to celebrate soap opera. Instead, *Tootsie* yearns for many of the legitimizing features of a golden age discussed previously. The film is set in the realm of television soap opera production and pays lip service to the concerns of women and gay men and to the value of camp and television, but ultimately affirms the position of the white, heterosexual man loyal to a New York theatrical tradition. It is worth noting that this perspective, together with the film's stellar ensemble cast and script, has led to great critical and financial success. In 2000, the American Film Institute named *Tootsie* number 62 on its list of the top 100 greatest movies. The film ranked number 2 on the list of 100 greatest comedies, right after Billy Wilder's *Some Like It Hot* (1959), with which it shares many similarities. *Tootsie* grossed an impressive $177.2 million during its 1982 theatrical release, Dustin Hoffman was nominated for a best actor Academy Award, and Jessica Lange won as best supporting actress.

Soap opera may be a solace and guide to women, but it takes a man (in drag, suspected to be gay) to put the world right. In this way, this film about television is wholeheartedly cinematic in its attitude toward its setting in daytime drama. A discourse of disapproval, with soap opera as its key example, continually circulates through cinematic approaches. At the same time, feminist approaches to television have often begun with analyses of programs and genres associated with women—particularly with the soap opera. The film critic Tania Modleski, for instance, has written about the intimate relationship that women form with soap operas. Modleski explains how soap opera differs from other narrative forms in terms of its constant interruptions and delays, which mimic the interrupted rhythms of women's lives in the home. With programs characterized by "repetition, interruption and distraction," reception itself "often takes place in a state of distraction."[11]

Classic cinema, as it has been traditionally theorized by Christine Gledhill, Mulvey, and others, depends on voyeurism—a pleasure in looking. Whether they are women or men, viewers are expected to assume the typically male position of the hero. That male gaze revels in female spectacle, fetishizes or destroys it, and employs the image of woman in the cause of narrative resolution. Soap opera breaks down the distance between the voyeur and the voyeurized implied in this formulation. An economy of nearness or "overidentification" circulates in soap opera between the spectator and the characters. Modleski observes a female spectator whose relationship with soap opera is both intimate and continuous. The desire to watch is fueled by complex networks of character associations leading to multiple identification. This type of identification has its own implications because no character completes an entire action. The soap opera dynamic "results in the spectator's being divested of power" (91), though simultaneously committed to the pleasure of endless deferral.

Popular ideas about soap opera viewership extend these tendencies beyond Modleski's careful and limited discussion. The stereotyped soap opera viewer doesn't respect the boundaries that separate her reality and her self from the fictional image. This dynamic is, of course, typically "female" in the sense developed for that gender category in the theoretical constructs of Western culture. Woman, who represents a difference from man, an "other" of designated lack, cannot adequately differentiate between states of being or other kinds of boundaries. Unable to say what she wants, it's not surprising that she cannot tell the difference between herself and a character in fiction. To express the problem in the terms of feminist/psychoanalytic criticism, women are trapped in an imaginary realm, exiled from the fullest symbolic expression or cultural self-recognition. The exaggerated model of how women overidentify with soap opera is to a great degree based on a traditional image of women as incapable of symbolic separations, distinctions, and obligations. For Modeleski, soap opera can at least become an outlet for feminine anger directed at the villainess, but this doesn't necessarily express a positive outcome. "Woman's anger is directed at woman's anger," she notes, "and an eternal cycle is created" (98).

Because it is so strongly associated with women, we shouldn't be surprised that soap opera is considered among the most familiar and least artistic of television narrative forms. Modleski's discussion articulates a number of recognizable features. First, a vast amount of time is devoted to telling the same story, and this story "offer[s] the promise of immortality and eternal return" (89). The narrative never stops, and no one ever expects it to. Identification is geared not so much toward stars and individuals as to a whole community of characters. The complex character networks of this community generate constant subplots. Like all broadcast television, soap operas are interrupted by commercials. They are also interrupted at the end of the day (a suspenseful moment) and the week (the most suspenseful moment); and they are interrupted within episodes as well. Scenes end after dramatic comments such as, "Do you mean ... she's alive?" "Little Billy ... he's your son!" or, "I'm not sure I want to work things out anymore ... ," and not when characters part ways or resolve their differences. Soap opera suspends its viewers in a narrative flow rather than hustling them to a conclusion. The calculated suspension of the text at the end of each episode encourages a continuous and everlasting viewing process.

Soap opera, like television in general, encourages flow rather than deliberation or an interpreted reading. Reacting to Raymond Williams's notion of televisual flow, some British cultural studies theorists consider this characteristic, seen most keenly in soap opera, to be a barrier to resistant or negotiated readings.[12] Soap opera emphasizes the relations among elements: the relations of characters rather than the linearity of the story they inhabit; the tellers and the telling rather than the progress of the plot. This repetition is less tedious than it is flattering. It flatters a networked knowledge that is dedicated to gathering and arranging useless information. It inspires the collection of facts and nuances. The crux of collection is that it supports an economy of continuous desire rather than fulfillment, a pleasure in accretion rather than completion.[13] When *this* replaces *that* we have analysis or metaphor. When we experience *this, this,* and *another this,* we have collecting or metonymy—an adjacent, partial, or apparently banal trope of displacement.

In Robert C. Allen's analysis of the genre in "Reader-Oriented Criticism and Television," however, this narrative redundancy actually results in "paradigmatic complexity."[14] Each time narrative information is retold it can be reevaluated against the teller's social position in the story community. Rather than being boring and repetitious, the viewer's knowledge of minutiae is crucial. The more you watch (know), the more reason there is to watch. Allen adapts reader-response or reception theory from literature to elucidate the power, appeal, and, perhaps, the possible threat of soap opera. Reader-response theory asks what kind of reader or viewer the text implies, induces, requires, or—one might even say—creates. This strategy is opposed to the efforts of traditional criticism to find or interpret a meaning already hidden in the text. Even though the text itself and its surrounding ideology work toward a particular end, reception theory implies that the act of reading at least partly produces the meaning of any text. The work—book, film, and so on—may start as an intentional act on the part of the author, but exists concretely only as a "set of possibilities" realized again and again in each performance of reading. The reader chooses to sustain, surrender to, or battle the author. Reading fills the "gaps" left in the text and extrapolates from partial aspects a sense of the whole—the worldview of a work. Differences of style, genre, and media enforce this worldview to different degrees.

Classical cinema works hard to resolve its elements into a unified closed text, using strategies of identification with characters, narrative, and apparatus and by employing an invisible, or seamless, technique. This can create a transcendental subject, one who operates with an illusion of omnipotence and eventual omniscience. But television creates a reader or viewer for whom the circuit of desire is not closed in the performance of the text itself, a commodified viewer, one who derives the meaning and value of a commodity from the fact that it is desired and shopped for, not because it is an end in itself. Readers of traditional texts are thought to struggle to interpret meaning from a self-sufficient text, to complete a unity out of textual signals. Watching television rarely calls for this unity or this kind of reading.

Television doesn't overcome or resolve differences, but regulates and normalizes them. It entertains and maintains difference apart from individual aberration and dictatorial enforcement. Because television's action isn't fulfilled on the screen, but diffused out into the marketplace, its effort is centrifugal. Reader-oriented criticism demystifies the sacred integrity of the self-sufficient, hermetic, or centripetal text. It locates the text in the interaction with the reader. Television is also concerned with the reader as a product not only of the text but of the entire textuality or intertextuality of the culture and its ideology. Television is rife with this intertextuality, constantly referring the reader or viewer to the culture at large rather than toward the discrete text. For Allen, viewers receive an aesthetic reward for recognizing when some element becomes inconsistent, goes wrong, or seems strange. This recognition applies both to particular soaps and to an intertextual relation with popular culture as a whole.

It's not surprising, then, that television viewers have a more fluid relationship to the text than cinematic voyeurs do to their spectacle. If a character suddenly behaves erratically, there might be a flood of protest, possibly leading to a script change. *Tootsie* plays condescendingly on this quality by showing public acclamation for Michael (the character Hoffman plays in the film) as Dorothy (the actress he plays as his drag-ego), who as Emily (the character Michael/Dorothy plays on the soap within the film) is positive, inspirational, and generally good for society—but ensures that only confused and aimless people (in a word, *women*) are expert enough to give this acclaim. The example of Elizabeth Taylor appearing as Helena Cassidine on *General Hospital* in 1981 shows intertextual cultural knowledge. Expert viewers would know Taylor as a devoted fan of the show and not be surprised that she played a relative of Luke Spencer (Anthony Geary), the show's most glamorous character. Programs might create conflict—ongoing frisson—with viewers on purpose. They kill off beloved characters and then bring them back from the dead, detained by amnesia or transformed into a long-lost evil twin. A variation is an actor leaving a program—permanently, or only for a day—with the character continuing in a new body. Soap opera writers, in their playfully perverse relationship with viewers, might split up faithful lovers, infect the innocent with a terrible disease, or make good girls turn bad.

The entire operation of a soap opera program, from production to broadcast to reception, thrives on some level of fractured—possibly discontented—but willing frustration. Producers depend on that intimacy in order to exploit all the commercial opportunities of its deferral and violation. That intimacy can be an extremely successful way to regulate and vary the relationship of viewer and program. Soaps modulate the immediate response and desire they reproduce in viewers probably better than does any other television form, and—as Allen notes in "The Guiding Light"—that relationship can be immensely profitable.[15] As he points out, the soap opera has a network profit base more secure than higher-risk prime-time programming because it can attract and hold habitual viewers, a quality audience primarily composed of women between the ages of 18 and 54. Furthermore, the costs of soap opera are low relative to prime time. They take place in a predictable, interior world of small sets that don't require much detail or expense.

Soaps engender such intimacy, such long-term devotion, that many viewers are outraged at any external disruption. Allen recalls that when news coverage of the 1981 assassination attempt on Pope John Paul II preempted daytime programming, calls from enraged viewers flooded network switchboards. For the most part, they couldn't understand why the shooting and serious wounding of the pope should interfere with their soap operas. Now, during any significant interruptions—the Olympics, or O. J. Simpson's murder trial, for instance—soaps have been rescheduled for middle-of-the-night broadcasts, intended for viewer taping or other forms of time shifting.

The cognoscenti of any soap know inherently what's right or wrong, and they respond, creating a base of viewers who help write the program. They write in to protest that "so and so" shouldn't be doing "that." This cosponsored writing could be seen as a form of Roland Barthes's ideal writerly text. The idea of such high literary value being applied to television, however, might inspire suspicion.

Both Allen and Modleski see progressive aspects about the soap opera form. Allen discusses how pejorative connotations have kept soap operas from being studied seriously, in a way not dissimilar to that of the study of television generally. Yet, the economic basis of soap opera as well as its ideology represent a community of relationships distinct from the rest of the broadcast world and worthy of some intellectual investigation. Modleski proposes "not to ignore what is 'feminine' about soap operas but to focus on it, to show how they provide a unique narrative pleasure…. Soap operas may be in the vanguard not just of T.V. art but of all popular narrative art" (87).

The entire regime of television and culture itself has assumed many dimensions once reserved for soap opera. For instance, an increasingly campy relationship, which once seemed within the preserve of soap opera, now suffuses television itself.[16] Soap opera now appeals to different viewers and is open to different types of reading—many incommensurable. We can no longer plausibly speak of a typical viewer as a woman or think of soap operas as something only women love (with a vengeance or otherwise).

Let's not make the same mistake we do with cinema and insist on redemptive readings, even if those readings come up with an appreciation of television, women, or shopping, or even an appreciation of our own self-flattering new knowledge. All of this implies a retreat to the cinematic model of the psychoanalytic subject, with everything that implies about the female spectator. Even Modleski's analysis is based on a traditional vision of the way women are—even to the extent of placing them in a domestic setting and available to watch television in the afternoon. Clearly, neither television nor women are the same as they were in 1979 when Modelski's book was written. Women viewers may form an intimate relationship with a program for reasons other than the simple fact that they are women.[17]

The ability to recognize the rightness of a particular character or plot turn according to experience and everyday values flatters viewers, but in a paradoxical way. They are flattered as being in the know, as taking the proper perspective on the most arcane details, as being hip or cool. This is hardly a progressive stance, but one that, as Nick Browne has noted about television's supertexuality in general, reinforces the status quo. The desire to know more than others can be hopelessly geeky, as all of the outside comments on Star Trek conventions, including those by William Shatner and Leonard Nimoy, make clear.

Soaps are also conventional in that they reinforce the value of the family and community as the site of all problems and all solutions. Notably, and in distinction to soaps, contemporary cinema is increasingly melodramatically impoverished. There are fewer and fewer extended families, chatty neighbors, second bananas, and secondary plotlines. The isolation of individuals and depletion of community leads to the psychopathology of such extreme examples as Adrian Lyne's *Fatal Attraction* (1987), Joseph Ruben's *Sleeping with the Enemy* (1991), Ridley Scott's *Thelma and Louise* (1991), Todd Field's *In the Bedroom* (2001),

Scott McGehee and David Siegel's *The Deep End* (2001), and Robert Zemeckis's *What Lies Beneath* (2001). Seldom do the characters in these films seem capable of getting a restraining order, consulting a grief counselor, or obtaining a prescription for antidepressants. The community is so insufficient to the problem that it cannot even be consulted. The tragic insularity of this universe is in contrast to the epic consultation that occurs in the televisual world. In television, the community is always consulted and is always adequate. Characters who reject the support of their fictional families and communities either come home again or simply disappear. Although not particularly insightful about television, Peter Weir's *The Truman Show* (1998) captures this characteristic of television drama, supplying the protagonist with a contingent of buddies, schoolmates, insurance clients, love interests, and neighbors in addition to a powerful auterist father. When Jim Carrey's Truman abandons the programmatic agenda of the TV program within the film, the world ends; it no longer has any rationale for existence.

What happens when an impoverished cinematic melodrama takes on the comic task of depicting television soap opera? Where is the family in *Tootsie*? Protagonist Michael has no family. He lives with a buddy, Jeff (Bill Murray); rejects his female friend Sandy (Teri Garr) as a romantic partner; and can't cooperate with anyone, even in terms of his profession about which he is obsessed. For her part, Sandy has left her family in San Diego for a New York theater dream. Only the divorced Julie (Jessica Lange) has a family, in the truncated form of a widowed father and a toddler. Most of the secondary characters are notably alone. The soap opera director within the film, Ron (Dabney Coleman), and lead soap actor John Van Horn (George Gaynes) are rogue males—single and predatory. Rita Marshall, the woman producer (Doris Belack) seems wedded to her job; Geena Davis's April is an available ingénue. Another film set in the world of soap opera production is Michael Hoffman's *Soapdish* (1991). Perhaps because of its more modest artistic ambitions, it provides broader comedy and a more complicated cast of characters. But like *Tootsie* its plot hinges on drag (Cathy Moriarty as a man playing a woman), and the ultimate reestablishment of the family romance.

The heterosexual coupling at the end of *Tootsie* is both inevitable and unconvincing, because the film has no positive model of any workable family. Michael's interaction with Julie's child is disastrous and clichéd, albeit hilarious. Julie's father (Charles Durning) and Michael (as Dorothy), who begin a comic dating *ronde*, might have made a great couple, but the idea is abandoned when Michael's true gender is revealed. It is interesting to compare this categorical rejection of homosexuality to *Some Like It Hot*, in which Osgood Fielding III (Joe E. Lewis) reacts to the true (male) gender revelation of the character Jerry/Daphne (Jack Lemmon) by saying, "Nobody's perfect." In 1959, when there was less threat of women's power, the joke about a man being a woman, or gay, could be funnier. Movies like *Some Like It Hot* or Howard Hawks's *I Was a Male War Bride* (1959), in which men masquerade as women, may seem more televisual from today's perspective—when men become women and women become men all the time—than does a movie like *Tootsie*, and such movies express far less "heterosexual panic."[18] However, unlike the entertaining variety of drag that television has celebrated, from Milton Berle through Flip Wilson to the Wayans Brothers, film, in general, finds the difference of gender much more threatening. When Michael does drag, he is immediately subjected to a sexual predation with incestuous implications. All of his relationships are reordered as possibly gay (or lesbian): He tells Sandy he's gay to avoid romantic involvement; he has a campy domestic relationship with his roommate Jeff; and he flirts with his agent (played by the film's director, Sidney Pollock) in the Russian Tea Room. While the character clearly doesn't want to be thought of as gay generally, if he's dressed up as a woman, he assumes that he is a beautiful and truly desirable one, and further assumes that, as a woman, he should be available for sexual conquest.

For all its women's liberation rhetoric, *Tootsie* presents a conservative vision of family, gender, and television. A man's success cannot be shown to be the result of a supportive network, whether familial or professional. Michael's success as Dorothy is based on skilled acting and on acting completely alone—against his agent, friends, co-performers, and director. It is a strategy he had attempted in his theatrical career, but that required unmanly collaboration in a gay-coded milieu. It was Michael's heterosexual individuality that sabotaged his theatrical career, yet his status within the film as the speaker of truth on the soap opera set is dependent on his being from a "higher" art.

Tootsie restores a television context back to a traditional text of romance. A complete metaphor of the theater as male and self-dominated is required to save the world not only from women and television, but on behalf of cinema. It does this by appropriating the form and the subjectivity it can identify as most at risk—the soap opera. The soap opera assumes the characteristics and the subjectivity of a damsel in distress—gullible, credulous, scatterbrained, loving, forgiving, and capable of being betrayed and getting over it, just like Julie. In *Tootsie*, Michael is actually both the rescuer (theatrical man) and the damsel in distress (television woman)—possibly because women are no longer available for that function, at least partly because of the woman's movement and per-haps partly because of television. This allows him to rescue himself and reaffirm a model of self-sufficiency. Chastened but not changed, he says he's a better man for having played a woman. And isn't that the whole point of cinema, to be a better man?

Tootsie is a canonical example of a cinematic attempt to reimpose the threat of castration, because only a real man can realize that threat leading to the revalidation of male power and of an oedipal economy. The reactionary postmodernism of this film is a return to individu-alizing (*this* replaces *that*), rather than individuating (*this*, *this*, and *another this*). However, television often exceeds psychoanalysis. When men become women on television there is no horror or unearthing of causes. Men have become women. How interesting! What would they like to buy? It becomes a function of variety, a variety of cognitive approaches rather than a Freudian nightmare. If you turn men into women or women into men—in a *Network* kind of way—then televi-sion will be devoted to making sure that any attendant hysteria doesn't alter its economy.

Though television accepts, or doesn't seem to challenge, a model of feminine castration, it exploits this castration in the general economy of consumerism as a whole. Everybody is castrated. Everybody is the same in an ever-changing status quo. Television is even better at maintaining the status quo than most forms of conservatism, which don't imagine the status quo as much as they nostalgically long for a nonexistent golden age. Television's maintenance of the status quo, where everything changes in order to stay the same, is ironically similar to cinema's ideological project, though different from cinema's reward and empowerment of the self-satisfied individual. If television shifts the ideology of individu-alism toward customized individuation, then women need not represent difference—just variety. In the long run, we may fear that we are watch-ing bad art or that we're all being turned into women, but the feminiza-tion of culture has always functioned to reproduce difference as product variety.[19]

Tootsie rescues male-dominated, theatrical/cinematic self-sufficient subjectivity, and in fact rescues soap opera from its own intolerable identity—or, rather, its own intolerable nonidentity. *Tootsie*'s feminism is paranoid, suspicious, and very specious: Sandy is still an unattractive mass of insecurities; Julie still has no idea why she's doing anything until Michael tells her; and Geena Davis is still in her underpants. The over-whelming message of *Tootsie* has a familiar ring: The best woman for the job is still a man.

When Men Become Women

We have discussed the ways in which television often positions the family as the cure for all ills, and also how feminist television criticism resists the traditional myth of the family romance. While it is true that television characters usually constellate into groups, they are not necessarily literal families. They may replicate the family structure, but television differs from film—which will go to any lengths to put the heterosexual couple back in place. Television rejects the idea that only heterosexual couples can occupy the redeeming place in culture.

An example of cinema's implausible redemption of the heterosexual couple occurs in a film that in other ways may seem postmodern or nontraditional. *Fight Club* flirts with fascist all-male structures—homosocial and homosexual bonding—and exhibits constant hostility toward women, as well as mass consumer culture, yet its implausible conclusion reconstitutes the narrator (Edward Norton) and Marla (Helena Bonham Carter) as a couple. Even as they hold hands and stare off into the apocalyptic horizon, we suspect the union may not be tranquil; the final scene also depicts total urban destruction as a re-sult of domestic terrorism and is intercut with "porn" shots of an erect penis. The incongruity of this ending only foregrounds and exaggerates the implausibility that has always lurked in the resolution of classical Hollywood cinema. Robin Wood observes that the ideal figures of clas-sical Hollywood cinema form a couple of "staggering incompatibility." The most significant feature of Hollywood cinema is that its ideology, "far from being monolithic, is *inherently* riddled with hopeless contra-dictions and unresolvable tensions,"[20] and these are often acted out on the level of the romantic couple.

Unlike film, the history of series television is the history of house-holds without a traditionally paired-up man and woman. Television is a universe of single parents and their children (*My Three Sons*, *My Two Dads*, *Valerie's Family*—which didn't even have Valerie after the first season). Fully integrated members of the family don't even need to be human. They can be machinery (*My Mother the Car*); puppets (*Greg the Bunny*); aliens (*My Favorite Martian*, *Third Rock from the Sun*); alien puppets (*ALF*); animals (*Flipper*, *Gentle Ben*, *Lassie*, *Mr. Ed*); robots (*Lost in Space*); body parts (the *Addams Family's* Thing); and even dead people (in *Dead Like Me*, *The Ghost and Mrs. Muir*, *Providence*, *Pushing Daisies*, and *Six Feet Under*). It isn't just that these fantastic characters exist, but that they fit so well into the sitcom and series drama formats. Angels and other supernatural beings are usually right at home in television's bland, domestic settings. Immortal beings with superhuman powers still worry about making dinner and keeping the house clean (*Bewitched, I Dream of Jeannie*) or getting good grades in school (*Buffy the Vampire Slayer, Sabrina, the Teenage Witch*). Like any regular television dad, Herman in *The Munsters* constantly worries about losing his job.

And despite the occasional brouhaha about same-sex kisses, television has also been a relatively welcoming environment for gender experimentation. Transvestites—starting with the beloved Milton Berle and working up through Flip Wilson's Geraldine, Tom Hanks's Kip Wilson in *Bosom Buddies*, and RuPaul—have often been popular, as have been "confirmed bachelor" characters that some interpret as gay (in such shows as *Family Affair, Frasier, Full House, Mr. Belevedere,* and *The Odd Couple*) or outright gay characters such as Ellen Degeneres's lead in *Ellen* or Will (Eric McCormick) and Jack (Sean Hayes) in *Will and Grace*. We don't argue that these are all progressive depictions of gender and sexuality, just that television can accommodate many more types of characters and many more configurations in its depiction of the family than can mainstream cinema. Certainly homosexuality or transvestitism can't be barriers to entering a televisual family when *South Park* can include a character, Mr. Hankey, who is a talking turd living in the sewer. (Not surprisingly, Mr. Hankey is a devoted family man, with a wife and kids who are also turds.)

The threat of television nourishes a very ordinary and domestic fear, one that is hinted at by these male duennas and gay subjects: feminization. The complete feminization of the subject is not just an issue for women on television, but for television's treatment of men and women alike. Men are feminized in the service of ensuring that everyday work and consumption continue in an uninterrupted way.

We know that television broadcasts a quite different idea of what it means to be a human being than cinema projects. Cinema's logic is that of suspense and delay before a final triumph. Television drama examines in endless detail the consequences of violating the everyday. The desire to rise to mighty or heroic self-fulfillment is shown in almost all television programming to be a problem, and such aspiration must often be deferred to next week's episode. The subject that follows from this worldview is a decentered, distracted, or dissolving one. Again, this is very much like a traditional view of women; only now, because of television, everybody is becoming that way. Women are women, but men are women, too. Their desire, simulated by television, threatens eccentric, if not aberrant, expression. In contrast, movie men depend on being real selves. Their mode of being can't become contaminated with disappointment and deferral without unsettling repercussions.

An important article by critic Lynne Joyrich, "Critical and Textual Hypermasculinity," argues that television shows and their positioning of men very often protect against continual disappointment.[21] Men assume what Joyrich calls *hypermasculinized* or *hyperrealized* positions through extreme violence, technology, or special effects—in programs as diverse as *Miami Vice* and *Star Trek*, and especially in cop and detective shows. Men also defend themselves by setting up a defensive space within a masculinized prime time and through masculinized products. Unlike the soap, deodorant, and dishwashing fluids offered to women during the rest of the day, these are appealing, fun, and luxurious items—gigantic cars, cutting-edge technology, fine liquor, glamorous lifestyles. Only the most extreme equipment and overmasculinized prime-time roles can save men from becoming women. The latest example of this may be the stupidly dangerous antics on MTV's all-male *Jackass,* or the stupidly dangerous counter-apocalyptic tactics on *24.*

For Joyrich, television is a medium that must modulate and manipulate the very threats it appears to broadcast. Its generalization of female subjectivity and the way it addresses its spectators keeps women as women, but also works to protect men from total feminization. Men can pretend that they are a commanding yet sensitive doctor (like Marcus Welby) or an absent-minded but efficient detective (like Columbo); they are modulated, but they are still men.

Written in the late 1980s, Joyrich's article doesn't address recent trends that show men and women competing against one another, with the women often winning, in shows such as *Fear Factor* and *Survivor.* Perhaps the "reality" context of these more recent shows argues for some standard of fairness in participation that fictional programs still don't feel compelled to share (the absurdly sexist program *The Bachelor* has been joined by *The Bachelorette*). Women can even be game show hosts—a previously unavailable role—although that may mean becoming a dominatrix à la *The Weakest Link.* But perhaps this is all simply in the interest of ratings and profit. Patriarchal privilege can't be allowed to stand in the way of making money. Women assume the place and power of men in these televisual environments with seemingly few repercussions. Unlike the textual hypermasculinity of television, about which Joyrich writes, the cinema of television has little interest in protecting men from television, but reveals in all its perverted glory what can happen to men if they get on television.

Like *Fight Club*, *The Cable Guy* is a film that struggles mightily, in the face of popular mass culture, to restore its heterosexual couple, despite the constant threat of feminization and emasculation. In both films, a nebbishy protagonist forms a close, but destructive, homosexually tinged friendship with an alter ego. As in *Fight Club*, the heterosexual couple in *The Cable Guy* ultimately triumphs, but in the most unconvincing and tenuous manner. The film itself isn't entirely convinced that it can restore order against the feminized, lisping, insatiable neediness of Jim Carrey's cable installer—who manages to survive the violent climax—or against what that figure represents: television.

Carrey's cable guy is read in several ways as womanish, or not quite a man—most notably in his association with television and the fact that he brings it into the home, first in the form of cable and then through high-end equipment. He also forms an unmanly attachment to cable client Steven (Matthew Broderick). He immediately begins to stalk Steven—a trope that, as Bobby and Peter Farrelly's *There's Something about Mary* (1998) makes painfully clear, is the dark heart of all romantic comedy. As the film goes on Chip and Steven will share a woman sexually, a common device for showing links between men. Chip even discusses the woman's "cleanliness," raising the point that in the age of AIDS, if you sleep with a person, you sleep with all of his or her sexual partners. Chip cooks eggs for Steven, creating a cozy domestic scene. Later he visits Steven in prison, reenacting the famous scene from Alan Parker's *Midnight Express* (1978) by raising his shirt and pressing his nipple to the cubicle's glass for Steven's (presumably sexual) gratification. In another scene, Chip attacks Steven's sexual rival in a men's room, forces his mouth over the hand dryer's blower, and tells him to "suck on this."

The Cable Guy opens with a montage of television clips, and this mimics the effect of flipping through the channels. Snippets of television, both real and invented, will reoccur throughout the film, most of them demonstrating intense crassness. There is, for example, a parodic replay of the infamous Menendez Brothers trial, with director Ben Stiller playing a fictional murderous brother. The last clip in the opening montage is telling. It shows a guest on the *Jerry Springer Show* announcing, "I'm really a man" immediately before the "regular" action of the film begins. This revelation suggests that there have been some doubts about gender, doubts that are often explored on television talk shows through the issues of homosexuality, transvesitism, transsexualism, and hermaphroditism.

This opening montage also hints at how and why the cable guy became what he became: he was left by himself to watch television, neglected by a promiscuous and inattentive mother. Without sufficient human

contact—without the absent father or the worthless mother—he has had
to cobble identifications together through the personalities he saw on television. The same explanation for personality formation can be seen in
the characters of Chauncey in *Being There*, Martin Tupper on the HBO
series *Dream On*, Henry in *Henry, Portrait of a Serial Killer* and Rupert
Pupkin in *King of Comedy*. In the cable guy's case, television provides his
adopted aliases, Chip Douglas and Larry Tate—both television characters and, sadly, only secondary ones. He has become a multiple personality, playing at different roles of both gender and narrative. Despite the
lure of a knee-jerk psychoanalytic explanation for this construction, the
cable guy may not be anti-oedipal, but beyond Oedipus.

In *Homos: The Straight Mind and Other Essays*, Leo Bersani speaks
of an identity that neither insists on its own externalized difference, nor
finds itself against the "other." Instead, his approach critiques subcultural
efforts to integrate identity into a "more comprehensive humanity" as
simply reduplicating the appropriational logic of the master culture. Bersani sees this eventuality as a summons to "to rethink economies of human relations on the basis of homo-ness, of sameness...."[22] The perhaps
surprising contribution of this "homo" theory to a reconsideration of
the ultimately hetereosexual romances of the cinema of television is to
request a new perspective, a "specific practice of sameness," opposing
"the defensive and traumatic nature of so-called normative development
of desire" (58–59). This sets the stage for a redefined relationship to the
law, for a "detraumatization" of difference, by internalizing it (76). The
ego is neither immobilized nor erased, but an occupant of several positions at once—"the same from the perspective of a self already identified
as different from itself" (59). In Bersani's formulation, feminization or
"homo-ization" is not seen as castrating or deviant as much as a state of
being beyond the differential calculus of straight identity.

The Cable Guy collapses a number of categories, labels them all path-
ological, and blames everything on television. But the character of the
cable guy is disturbing not because he is insane but because his identity
is so multiple. He is loathsome to some characters, and yet popular with
others—with the guests at Steven's party, for instance, who are grateful
for free cable, and with Steven's own family and girlfriend. Perhaps more
than any particular feminine trait or gesture, the cable guy can be read as
feminine because of his chronic and manic slippage among roles. His is
an ambulatory performance, and by "writing himself across the body," he
positions himself as woman. Even Steven's identity is suspect. He is not
a fine, manly protagonist. At the beginning of the film, his girlfriend has
asked for some time apart, and in response he spends much of the film

brooding, blustering, or acting ineffectually. His problems really begin when he decides to get cable. For both of these characters, although to different degrees, contamination by television has eroded something crucial to traditional notions of masculinity.

In many films, the castrating threat of loss comes not from the external agency of the father or the woman's *vagina dentata*, but from the man's inherent nature or from an internal source. The protagonist of Nicholas Roeg's *The Man Who Fell to Earth* (1976) may spend the entire film yearning for his wife and children, but he is also an alien (and so outside the usual structures of gender identification), played by a veritable symbol of androgyny (David Bowie), and forced by his alien nature to have to glue on the secondary signs of masculinity, such as body hair. *Series 7: The Contenders*, a film that parodies reality television programming such as *Survivor* by having its contestants compete to kill one another, shares with *Fight Club* the theme of testicular cancer. The "returning champion" at the beginning of the film is Dawn Lagarto (Brooke Smith) a woman who is eight months pregnant. She is ultimately supplanted by a contestant, Jeffrey Norman (Gleen Fitzgerald), who has not only had his testicles removed (depicted with graphics and voiceover explanation), but who is revealed to be gay.[23]

In *The Cable Guy*, the nature of Carrey as a performer, both manic and associated with television, is vital to the multiple constructions of identity. Carrey started his career as "the white guy" on *In Living Color*. Later, he played television-afflicted characters in *The Truman Show*, *Man on the Moon*, and Tom Shadyac's *Bruce Almighty* (2003). In all of these films we want to like the character, but it often proves impossible. Although Truman is the ostensible protagonist of a global phenomenon, he is, like contestants on some reality programs, not in on the joke. His impossible innocence, and the constant sensation that he is about to be crushed by the truth, make him an unpalatable hero. It isn't easy to identify with a dupe. Carrey's freakishly close portrayal of comedian Andy Kaufmann in *Man on the Moon* captures much of the discomfort that Kaufmann, most noted for his television work, himself elicited. Kaufmann's genius was to never make distinctions between role-playing and identity. Carrey's on-camera television reporter in *Bruce Almighty* rebels against God because he isn't given the anchor spot on the local news. Reinforcing the theme of mixing the trivial with omnipotence, God bestows on Bruce his own godly powers. Bruce uses these powers in predictably adolescent ways, such as increasing the size of Jennifer Anniston's breasts. But even the final resolution of the film is completely trivial. The experience reconciles Bruce to his role as comic relief on the news.[24]

Carrey's womanish character, infantile behavior, schizophrenic moods, and identity shifts clearly recall his comedic ancestor: Jerry Lewis. In *The Mask*, Carey plays Stanley Ipkiss—a very Lewisesque role. In his early films, Lewis played the woman in the relationship with Dean Martin. Although the two men were the same height, Lewis filed down his heels, while Martin wore lifts. Lewis frequently jumped into Martin's arms or flapped his wrists. Together they acted out a domestic relationship of care, clothing, and feeding. In Frank Tashlin's *Artists and Models* (1955), for instance, Euguene Fullstack (Lewis) wears an apron and cooks dinner. At one point Rick Todd (Martin) attempts to "break up" with him, but is lured back by the comforts of home and Jerry's plaintive looks. Not surprisingly, in this film Lewis's character ends up appearing on television.

After the real-life artistic breakup of Martin and Lewis (foreshadowed in Norman Taurog's *The Stooge*, 1952), and often discussed like a romantic breakup), Lewis adopted several quintessentially female roles: Gilbert Wooley in Frank Tashlin's *Geisha Boy* (1958) and a Cinderella clone in Tashlin's *Cinderfella* (1960). He is often gentle and graceful when not hysterical. Could Lewis's womanishness contribute to the fact that he has never been taken seriously as a filmmaker, despite having developed technical innovations such as the video assist? Lewis wins his best reviews when he "plays it straight," such as his role as the Johnny Carson-like character in *King of Comedy*. In this hyperrestrained example, his character watches classic films and lives in a cool modernist apartment as well as a gleaming white country house. And could it be that despite his successful telethons, Lewis has never been critically successful on television because he already *is* television?

In addition to Carrey, another key figure in *Cable Guy* is director Ben Stiller, himself no stranger to comic emasculations in his acting career. *There's Something About Mary* is a laugh riot of imperiled masculinity: a penis caught in a zipper, a dog biting a man's crotch, semen as a hair styling gel, male prison rape jokes. In the title role of *Zoolander* (2001), Stiller (who also directed the film) plays a male model whose imaginary is entirely colonized by television and other mass media. Stiller also played the junked out television writer in David Veloz's *Permanent Midnight* (1998), although in this case, not for laughs. Stiller hails from an old and venerable television family; mom and dad are the comedy duo Jerry Stiller and Anne Meara, who were regulars on TV's *Ed Sullivan Show*. Jerry Stiller passed further into television history as the character of George's bellicose dad on *Seinfeld*.

As both their roles and their public personas attest, Jim Carrey, Jerry Lewis, Ben Stiller and, to some extent, all television performers demonstrate the crucially proliferating nature of television celebrity. Self-promoting and self-informing, televisual desire nevertheless exceeds the self in its desire to initiate desire for the whole world. The cable guy wants to be everybody and to be everybody's friend. Rupert Pupkin wants to get on *The Jerry Langford Show*, a thinly disguised *Tonight Show*, and must establish a relationship with its host in order to establish an exchange with millions. Not content to consume products and images to gain perfection, television personalities and subjects must become the commodity, be consumed by the image. This is the logic of Guy Debord's *Society of the Spectacle*, a logic that moves from being to appearing.[25] The product doesn't nurture you; you nurture its appetite in an endless advertisement of consumption. This is a radical manner in which to deploy power, but not functionally radical because it offers a continual reverification of the normal economic order and the normal operation of power. The more things change and exchange, the more they stay the same.

Even Bersani's notion of similarity as a chain of signifiers in the homologous construction and deconstruction of identity may misjudge how easily the master culture can appropriate free play in the tactics of ideological invisibility. The cinema of television seems to mistake contempt for resistance by reinscribing its obsolete categories such as otherness, castration, and nostalgia over the "massive[ly] forgetful" regime of television. Cinema may design its spectator in a passive "readerly" way; nevertheless, television's "writerly" nihilism offers only cool comfort. You no longer aspire to be a real self—a real boy like Pinocchio or a real girl like the Little Mermaid. To become the commodity, to initiate desire—that is the only hope.

9

Noir Fatal

In 1998, at least partly in response to then-president Bill Clinton's impeachment, Toni Morrison published an article in the *New Yorker* describing Clinton as "the first black president." Clinton is, of course, a white man, but to Morrison, the story of his inquisition, the "compilation of revelations and commentary" about his adultery, can only be made sense of by recognizing that "[w]hite skin notwithstanding, this is our first black President. Blacker than any actual black person who could ever be elected in our children's lifetime.... African American men seemed to understand it right away. .... After all, Clinton displays almost every trope of blackness: single-parent household, born poor, working-class, saxophone-playing, McDonald's-and-junk-food-loving boy from Arkansas."[1] Clearly, Morrison didn't anticipate the imminent emergence of a figure such as Barak Obama.

With this article, Morrison baffled and angered many people who felt she played into stereotypes about what it means to be black in the United States, but her argument recognizes powerful narratives about powerful men, propelled by a crisis about how to exert that power. Who possesses power? How have black men become repositories of a certain kind of cultural power? Clinton's narrative, as the site of an extreme crisis of masculinity—"the President's body, his privacy, his unpoliced sexuality became the focus of the persecution ... he was metaphorically seized and bodysearched"[2]—obviously overlaps with narratives about black men in our society. We ask: How does the white man become a site of anxiety and what efforts are made to recuperate his power and equanimity?[3] This story is inextricably bound up with representations of race.

In a well-known theoretical model, older forms of cinematic recuperation deployed the woman as object either to be saved or destroyed, fetishized, or spectacularly consumed.[4] Because of social changes—and possibly because of that theoretical intervention itself—women, at least in an Anglo-American context, are less available to play that symbolic token. The well-documented crisis in masculinity reflects this shift, as does the frequent absence of women from contemporary film.[5] Even after the feminist demystification of classical spectacle and apparatus, we find ourselves enmeshed in cinematic tropes of liberation and narratives of redemption. But now the black man functions as the disturbing element that must be either desired or eliminated.[6] Just as Marlene Dietrich has become Denzel Washington, the femme fatale is now the noir fatal, and in a quintessentially postmodern twist, at once radical and appropriational, the white man becomes a black man. In the midst of Bill Clinton's tenure as the first black president, Warren Beatty, a political junkie outside his movie roles, evolves into a hip-hop political candidate in *Bulworth* (1998, Warren Beatty). He raps, smokes pot, and hangs out in South Central Los Angeles. He even dates Halle Berry in her role as Nina, the politically educated 'hood resident, who moves from suspicion to love. Berry's final line in the film says everything about the ability of a white man to be black as she tenderly addresses Bulworth; "You my nigger."

How do we go from talking about television to talking about films where a white man becomes a black man, or even films where white masculinist redemption is played out by a black woman as happens in Marc Forster's *Monster's Ball* (2001) or in Kathryn Bigelow's *Strange Days* (1995)?[7] The ideological struggles with representation that metamorphosis suggests can be valuably addressed by returning to 1970s feminist criticism of women's representation and the crucial role played in that criticism by a critique of realism.

In her influential 1978 article, "Recent Developments in Feminist Film Theory," Christine Gledhill begins by charting the "reality effect" from its deconstruction as an ideology inherent in the technological base of the cinematic apparatus itself to the challenges mounted by Louis Althusser, Roland Barthes, and Jacques Lacan. From this theoretical perspective, Gledhill points out that in mainstream cinema women are not and can not be represented as "real" women, but are instead offered as a textual problem to be solved. Particularly through psychoanalysis, feminist critics have been able to shift the debate from essentialized notions of strong or "real" women to questions of textual/sexual production.[8]

Yet Gledhill also recognizes the pitfalls in this methodology. The struggle to relocate women from the ahistorical realm of eternal value to the scene of the real can easily obscure the notion that reality itself is always coded to support and to legitimize the status quo.[9] When this occurs, nothing much has been accomplished for a so-called counter cinema.

Further, any potential feminist flight into antirealism also threatens to ignore the multiple uses of cinema as entertainment, ritual, fantasy, and escape corresponding to the multiple subject sites of women spectators and consumers. Haunted as we all are by plenitude and by the attempt to recapture it in representation, the authenticity of "lived experience" can only collapse resistance into recuperation or marginality.

How are women, then, to speak, when even those theoretical concepts used to guide them out of subordination and silence question their access to linguistic competency? Gledhill's cautious answer is speech itself, but only in a highly negotiated fashion that acknowledges differences beyond sexual and gender ones. Issues of class and race, for instance, can reassert difference in the functioning of a linguistic tradition that has "realized" itself in the repression or essentialization of sexual difference.[10] These multiple valences present a horizon, beyond the classical terrain of textuality, that promises an entertainment of difference within a single identity rather than a traumatic and monolithic identity constructed against the "other."

This is difference replayed as sameness—a possibility valorized by Foucault, Bersani, Judith Butler, and many others. This tactic may sometimes misjudge just how adept mainstream textual practice can be in managing potentially subversive substitutions and deferrals. There are two possible phases to this practice. First, tropes of brutal or noble savagery become a renewed source of primal difference in the guise of class and race consciousness, the supreme reactionary solution to a decadent, feminized, impotent masculinity. Now *men* become the problem created for its own solution. Second, this problem is too often solved by the myth of "authentic" blackness.

An early observer of this myth as it comes to be developed in the latter half of the twentieth century is Norman Mailer. His 1957 reflections on race are embedded within a larger critique of American existentialism as it finds itself confronted with "a slow death of conformity" following the "collective creation" of "*l'univers concentrationnaire*" following World War II. In the face of this mass death wish, "the only life-giving answer is to live with death as immediate danger, to divorce oneself from society, to exist without roots, to set out on that uncharted journey into the rebellious imperatives of the self."[11] With intellectual antecedents in D. H. Lawrence, Henry Miller, Wilhem Reich, and, taken to the supreme articulation, Ernest Hemingway, this postwar "frontiersman in the Wild West of American nightlife" (3) finds his urban and essentially masculine sources of rebellious chic in the Negro and in the avant-garde assimilation of the sub-world philosophy of jazz.

Access to "instantaneous existentialist states" (4) requires a profound faith in the goodness, the rightness, of one's own emotions and inner experience, especially as this individualist mysticism comes packaged in the "perversion, promiscuity, pimpery, drug-addiction, rape, razor-slash, bottle break, what-have-you" of the Negro's necessary "morality of the bottom" (10). The subcultural reality of the Negro who lives from the moment of his birth in proximity to the danger and paranoia of a world that can be neither casual nor causal, but only absurd, sets the *haute couture* of those "urban adventurers" who find the possibilities of life within death while "looking for action with a black man's code to fit their facts" (4). This hipster is the white Negro.

Of course bullfighters and superstuds share this ethic, this mysticism however atheistic of orgasmic apocalyptism.[12] But perhaps more indicative of the "arch or vulgar or irritating" assumption of black hip [-hop] authenticity is the psychopath. "At bottom, the drama of the psychopath is that he seeks love" (9), but only as a sexual outlaw and only within the psychopathology of a hatred from the outside that inspires hatred from the inside. You've got to be "Crazy, man!" and "Dig it!" for "if you do not dig you lose your superiority over the Square ... and have [not] allowed to come to consciousness a pain, a guilt, a shame or a desire which the other has not had the courage to face" (13). Mailer asks if this is the "frontrunner of a new kind of personality which could become the central expression of human nature before the 20th century is over" (7).

In *The White Negro*, Mailer recognizes, among other observations, the death symbolism associated with the white race. This is a central theme for Richard Dyer in *White*, which reminds us that whiteness is subject to its own horrific crisis of representation couched within a subjective paranoia about its own subjectlessness.[13] Dyer identifies a paradox between a historically absolute white subject and a gnawing suspicion that the logical trajectory of the concept is that there is no body. For Dyer, the question of vampiric, cannibalistic, and extraterrestrial representation becomes even more problematic when the fleshly repository of white anxiety is already black. If the hero fighting the undead is black (as he is in George A. Romero's *Night of the Living Dead*, 1968), or if the vampire/hero is black (as he is in Stephen Norrington's *Blade*, 1998), or if the otherworldly is already a black oracle (as in Andy and Larry Wachowski's *The Matrix*, 1999, or Michael Rymer's *Queen of the Dammed*, 2002) or a medium to the other side (as in Jerry Zucker's *Ghost*, 1990) or a ghost (as in *Bulworth*), then what do we need whiteness for—either its body or its metaphysics? When this crisis in horror, science fiction, or melodramatic representation occurs we see a parallel to Mailer's existentialist assumption of black authenticity in the reassignation of white redemptive power. Slayers and seers arise to take on everything, including their own racial burden. White anxiety is displaced from an uncomfortable familiarity with its own grotesque contradictions into an all-out abasement in the face of mastery—an abasement of course that donates mastery not necessarily to color, but gives color back to etiolated mastery. White is a color that cannot come too close to confronting its own reflective blankness or drift too far from its own dark superego.

Mailer and Dyer both recognize the fearsome beauty or existential hip of the symbolic association of whiteness and death, of what Dyer calls "the deathliness that white culture yearns for and spreads."[14] White death becomes bearable only through sublimity, romantic sublimation, and a metaphorization uncomfortably close to equating truth, virtue, and reality with parasitism and extinction. Metaphysics becomes melodrama, and the American story has typically been told as a melodrama, its racial dynamics particularly susceptible to melodramatic retelling. In the zeal to create a more just society, dominant culture suppresses or deconstructs symbolic meanings and metaphors, but this very suppression returns clothed in melodramatic abjection. Linda Williams writes,

> Melodrama is organized around a paradoxical quest for a full articulation of truth and virtue at precisely those junctures where truth and virtue are most vexed.... Now that we are supposed to live in an achieved era of equal rights for all, race has joined the category of the officially inexpressible. Mentioning it is considered in bad taste, a cynical ploy, "playing the race card." Increasingly, however, it is within the irrational, fantasmic, and paranoid realm of the melodramatic "text of muteness" that race takes on a heightened mode of expressivity as a dialectic of feelings—of sympathy and antipathy—that dare not speak its name. The mere appearance of the black male body on the film or television screen, for example, creates a heightened expectation for the expression of extreme good or extreme evil.[15]

Just as Gledhill does for feminism, Herman Gray clearly recognizes the problems of "realism" in critical discussions of black representation: "Alone, the argument that television representation of blackness is primarily shaped by changing industrial market conditions that enabled a small number of black producers, directors, and writers to tell stories about black life from the perspective of blacks is reductionist."[16] In "Politics of Representation in Network Television," Gray

focuses on commercial network television, especially situation comedies and variety programs, in the 1980s, but the system of categorization he establishes exceeds that period and raises more general questions about how the American racial order is constructed, reproduced,
and challenged.[17] For Gray, popular and commercial culture isn't realism—there are "multiple claims on blackness"—but it does possess
discursive power that can move people and position them in different
political and social configurations.

Gray notes that the current moment "continues to be shaped discur-
sively by presentations of race and ethnicity that began in the formative
years of television" (74). He traces a history of black representation on
television from its origins in radio, vaudeville, and cinema. These representations established a structure in which black subjectivity, though often domesticated and abused, became that otherness against which white
people defined the subjective stability necessary to be who they wanted
to be. The same dynamic that Mailer recognizes in the existential (the
jazz club) and that Dyer observes in the supernatural (cinema vampires)
is what for Gray enlivens utterly banal television variety shows. Black
people function as a guarantee.

In the early days of television, in *Amos 'n' Andy* as it moved from
radio to television; in *Beulah*; in *The Jack Benny Show*, with its depiction
of the servant Rochester; or in *Life with Father*, black actors played unrelentingly amusing domestic workers who also served as sources of essential knowledge or wisdom. That wisdom was necessary for the security
of white domestic normalcy. Without their funny and sage servants, the
white household might descend into chaos over the most trivial matters. The black characters always stood outside the existential absurdity
of white instability (75).[18]

Gray identifies in the late 1950s and 1960s a transformation that occurred
in shows such as *I Spy*, *Julia*, or *The Nat King Cole Show*, where blackness
was not funny and domestic as much as it was rendered invisible. Between
partners Bill Cosby and Robert Culp in *I Spy* there is virtually no acknowl-
edgment of black (or, for that matter, white) difference.[19] *Julia* was both a
black woman and powerful, but it was almost impossible to acknowledge
that she was powerfully black. The specious triumph of the white, liberal
values of responsibility and good taste makes of blackness perhaps an even
paler shade of white, nuanced as it was against the social deviance of black
jazz culture and its drug-addicted, sex-addicted denizens—Billy Holliday,
Charles Mingus, and Charlie Parker, let alone Miles Davis (76).

According to Gray, the 1970s, a decade of enormous social protest
in which racial and social politics were on everybody's mind, rejected

both ironic sagacity and white equivalence in favor of "authenticity." We shouldn't forget Gledhill's warnings about the appeal to authenticity and its potential for recuperability when we remember poor, urban ghetto black people struggling against hardships in such TV shows as *Good Times, Sanford and Son,* and *What's Happening,* or the "movin' on up" out of the ghetto in *The Jeffersons.* The idea that authenticity finds its wellspring in urban, working class African Americans prepares a metaphor of social flow and mobility. Stranded in tenements, or in a junkyard, eating a piece of the Manhattan pie, television's black characters never questioned the legitimacy or authenticity of economic mobility, family cohesion, and private property.[20]

In a way similar to Gledhill, Gray describes a representational landscape in which authenticity, feminine or black, exists within an ideology convinced of its own ultimate justifications. The horrors of forced emigration and forced labor (in shows such as *The Autobiography of Miss Jane Pittman, Roots,* and *Sounder*) are replayed as fruits of the white liberal establishment's self-flattering ideology. Gray's response to the theoretical cul-de-sacs of realism, authenticity, positive depictions, and the hunt for black auteurs (the same road down which the feminists traveled in the 1970s) engages Stuart Hall's model of encoding and decoding and the categories of assimilationist, pluralist, and multicultural practices.

As Gray describes it, assimilationist representations treat social and political issues of racism as personal problems and thereby erase history (of conquest, slavery, isolation, or power inequalities). They rely on the principle of racial exceptionalism on the part of blacks and individual failings on the part of both whites and blacks. People may be prejudiced because of a personal quirk or failing, but the narrative can resolve or contain the problem. These representations offer not blackness, but the invisibility of race. Pluralist or separate but equal representations place black characters in domestically centered black worlds and circumstances that parallel those of whites. They perpetuate a universal acceptance of a transparent and "normative" middle class. Pluralist representations explicitly recognize race as a basis of cultural difference and allow viewers to celebrate "others" without challenging any assumptions about American society. These representations require a "homogeneous, totalizing blackness" (88). Gray's most valorized category is multiculturalist representations, which he terms "diversity," a mode that allows the exploration of black interior lives and subjectivities. These representations don't offer a totalized blackness, but allow for complex, even contradictory perspectives. Black subjects are not forced into the role of "*the* black subject." Black life is seen as dynamic and itself diverse and is often presented in ways that are formally innovative.[21]

Gray finds a surprising place of hope in television, as impurely dedicated to entertainment for profit as it is. Unlike cinema—which persistently returns representation to melodrama—television, with its sources in radio, vaudeville, and the generally more theatrical conventions of irreality, entertains multiple and contaminated subject positions. That television as a text might be able to accommodate multilayered, intertextual, and contradictory subjectivities promises a possible release of black representation from the virus of authenticity used to inoculate cinema's diseased white male.

Cinema's melodramatic imagination always returns to "Mandingoism" in contrast to television's racial and sexual insouciance.[22] Television offers a more diverse perspective on interracial interactions, but none of them is crucial. We can see this beginning with the original *Star Trek* series' interracial kiss in 1969 between Captain Kirk and Lieutenant Uhura, the first such kiss on network television. As a gesture it was softened by the fact that it was ordered by a mind-controlling alien. Although one of the interracial relationships on the show *ER* was of concern to the actor (Eric Benet) who played the black man in the story line, it was not an issue for the characters. Music videos often adopt a self-conscious awareness of racial issues, as in Offspring's "Pretty Fly for a White Guy," and hip shows like *Ally McBeal* ignore them (as they do gender differences in the unisex bathroom). The "progressive" feature of *Will and Grace* is often thought to be the fact that it has gay characters, but Grace's casual sexual relationship with Will's black boss and Karen's polymorphous sexuality are more radical than Will's sexless gay bachelorhood.

Television's ability to show difference in a chronic rather than critical manner can be attributed to its simultaneous liveness and theatricality. During the first Gulf War, television news often presented what were called "postcards"—messages from service people in the Persian Gulf to their loved ones at home, connected by a satellite video feed. In these "live" feeds, many of the relationships depicted were visibly interracial. These postcards, along with other "reality" and news elements, demonstrate television's more fluid interaction with reality, even when it is scripted and constructed in the service of profit and propaganda.

A different fluidity is apparent in the imperatives of star casting and entertainment before all else. A 1997 television production of *Cinderella* starred Bernadette Peters as the stepmother. Not only was stepdaughter Cinderella played by a black actress, the popular Brandy, but the stepmother's two "natural" daughters were played by a black actress (Veanne

Cox) and a white one (Natalie Desselle). As the king and queen, Victor Garber and Whoopi Goldberg managed to produce a prince played by a Filipino actor. These are casting decisions closer to the conventions of theater, which doesn't need to be naturalistic. They are justified by a general artifice that is just as much at home on television as its quasi-realism and nonfictional modes.

Where is "real" difference now that television and its flattened regimes of banality and entertainment have leveled difference into nothing more than metonyms of deferral and *différance*? And who knows where the truth lies? Who can restore its metaphors? The reversal of classical cinematic logic implied in our concept of noir fatal–ity nevertheless identifies the cinematic goal of reestablishing dominant identity in opposition to television's decay of secure subject positions. Contemporary cinema installs black people as a replacement for the phallic woman, even as white masculinity succumbs to a generalized femininity. African Americans become the stopping place of sliding signification, as truth tellers and as truth itself. It is they who can see through the gobbledygook of the white man's world (in Hal Ashby's *Being There*, 1979); they who exchange witheringly ironic glances behind the back of Lonesome Larry Rhodes (in Elia Kazan's *A Face in the Crowd*, 1957); they who posses the fatal vision of an authenticating gaze (in Martin Scorsese's *The King of Comedy*, 1982, or Andy and Larry Wachowski's *The Matrix*, 1999); and they who can tell the bullshit from the Bulworth.

Unlike the genteel good taste and suave attitudes expressed in assimilationist television portrayals of blackness such as *I Spy* or *Julia*, the movie *Bulworth* is characterized by bad taste and bad behavior. It constructs a violent and excessive street culture associated with American blackness—what Mailer would celebrate as a "jazz culture" of sex, drugs, and civic contempt. By 1998, when *Bulworth* was released, popular culture, dominated by "urban" (read: African American) styles, had become another battleground, and therefore another opportunity, for the supremely endangered white man.

But acceptance into dominant popular culture isn't the only challenge facing Beatty's quintessential white man, Jay Billington Bulworth, a powerful, white, California senator. A more dangerous threat to his identity is posed by the civic and personal corruption in which he has become entangled. Corruption characterizes the interlocking system of deceptive media presence and corporate money on which his senate campaign depends. Television consolidates and replays these interests, and it is fitting that the film begins with television as a locus of false identities.

After an opening title that places the action of the film in the historical moment of the 1996 election cycle, with Robert Dole and Bill Clinton as the presidential candidates who leave the populace "unaroused," an establishing shot places the action at night in Washington, D.C. An unshaven and distraught Bulworth rewinds and replays a series of his own campaign commercials. Although Bulworth is a Democrat, the spots feature conservative bromides, such as "a hand up, not a hand out" and unsubtle appeals to "family values." An ideological disjunction is immediately presented, as the camera pans slowly across a photo of Martin Luther King Jr. with Malcolm X, a Jesse Jackson poster featuring Rosa Parks, a painted portrait of Thurgood Marshall and a drawing of Robert Kennedy. We also see photos of a young Bulworth with Julian Bond and Robert Kennedy, which create a doubled understanding: This is a young Bulworth, but it is also clearly the actual Beatty, who is well-known for his political involvement. At his desk, between the artifacts of a politically progressive past and a politically cynical present, Bulworth sits weeping. When the phone rings, Bulworth lets his answering machine pick up, and its message reinforces the theme of representation as inauthenticity. Bulworth's voice is heard saying "Hello. This is a telephone answering machine." It isn't the real Bulworth on the phone, and it isn't the real Bulworth seen in the campaign commercials. This is clearly a character who must quickly embark on a journey of personal discovery.

The theme of false representations intersects in *Bulworth*'s opening with a visual sequence frequently seen in the cinema of television: the flipping channel montage. As it appears in such films as Sidney Lumet's *Network* (1976), *Being There*, Ben Stiller's *The Cable Guy* (1996), Gary Ross's *Pleasantville* (1998), and other films, these sequences depict frequently switching channels to construct a "found" bricolage. The supposedly random nature of these sequences as symbols of television serves as antipode to the highly motivated nature of cinema. A guiding artistic sensibility, or auteur, controls the juxtaposition of sounds and images in the film. Serendipity orders, or disorders, the television text in response to a half-aware or distracted character sensibility. Yet while these random sequences serve as a rebuke to the experience of television viewing, in films like *Bulworth* they are carefully constructed, with the images selected to comment on and to collide with the action. Channel surfing is submitted to an almost Eisensteinian montage aesthetic.

The television images seen as Jay Bulworth flips mindlessly through the channels reinforce the theme of false presentations: a commercial in which a woman uses a hair removal product on her legs, lip, and underarm; a professional wrestling bout; an old-fashioned gladiator movie; a cartoon; an announcement, over the American flag, for the "American Religious Town Hall"; exercise shows; a scene from Billy Wilder's *The Seven Year Itch* (1955); women in thong bikinis; the O. J. Simpson murder trial. Bulworth's channel flipping persists as he organizes his suicide by assassination. He meets with his doctor, his insurance agent, and, finally, an organized crime figure to contract the hit.

Even though Bulworth's suicide attempt is presented as the motor of the film's plot, it is never entirely convincing. The daughter, to whom Bulworth purportedly wants to leave $10 million in insurance money, never appears, and almost immediately he seems to regret his decision, ducking and cowering every time a car backfires. The solution to the narrative problem is just as unconvincing and irrelevant: Bulworth is unable to contact assassin to call off the hit, so he must himself figure out the assassin's identity. It turns out that Nina the subcontracted (Halle Berry) has been hired for $10,000 to kill Bulworth in order to save her irresponsible brother from a black drug lord and loan shark. But other would-be assassins appear throughout the film, including the drug lord, whose car was stolen by Bulworth, and a disgruntled representative of the insurance industry, betrayed by Bulworth's Tourette's Syndrome–like truth-telling. Another potential assassin turns out to be a scandal-sheet photographer. Consistent with the film's politics, the potentially fatal final gunshot is fired by the insurance industry lackey.

The real function of the "hit" is to introduce an element of danger into Bulworth's life and to make that life meaningful. As a cosseted senator, Bulworth faces no risk; nothing is at stake for him except his own status quo, which forces him to debase himself before the moneyed interests, particularly the insurance industry, that can ensure his reelection. As a man suddenly vulnerable to gun violence everywhere he goes, Bulworth can finally experience a true sense of life. He passes from the sham of representation to become Mailer's existential white Negro.

The film pretends as if it's a cynical parody, but it is dedicated to the restoration of honesty, family values, and the institutional legitimacy of power. Bulworth is finally rescued by his contact with Nina. She joins the values of romantic love and family legitimacy with unassailable authenticity, represented by the excesses in South Central Los Angeles. Nina's family is poor, desperate, and drug-involved, but it is a more loving family than Bulworth has formed with his bored and selfish white wife. Unlike Bulworth's redemptive affair with Nina, his wife's affair with a black man is just another sign of boredom and selfishness.

Berry performs a similar function in *Monster's Ball* when her character, Leticia Musgrove, rescues Hank Grotowski (Billy Bob Thornton) from emotional paralysis through her own suffering and lust. With that Oscar-winning performance Berry became the great source of black female otherness that saves white men. Even the discovery that Hank served as executioner for Leticia's husband doesn't interrupt her redemptive project. Both femininity and blackness can be very dangerous, but in Berry's noir fatal films they are sanitized by being put in the service of solving white masculine problems.

The reversal of redemptive logic in *Bulworth* remains cinematic. The goal is always the consolidation and redemption of identity, the establishment of secure dominance over the threatening manifestations of popular culture—particularly television. Although *Bulworth* offers an often hilarious reversal of roles, nothing is more cinematic and old fashioned than Warren Beatty—close friend of Gary Hart—as politician gone astray. Women are sexually dispensible, but the homeopathic cure of dangerous black women assassins like Nina might still effect a reversal of decadence.

Ultimately, what is the status of white male power and privilege in *Bulworth*? Bulworth is never shown as "normal." His weeping disintegration has already started before the film begins. This might suggest that the white man as stable and powerful was always a lie. Or it might acknowledge that a journey from full investiture in the power structure to a willful and permanent estrangement from it is an unlikely one. Bulworth is capable of his ethical denunciation of a corrupt establishment only insofar as the movie shows him regaining his supremacy within that establishment again, and he is only able to retail his message through the agency of television. When Bulworth performs his truth-telling routine on television, his populist message resonates so strongly that he overwhelmingly wins his reelection and becomes a strong write-in candidate for president in the 1996 presidential campaign that in fact reelected Clinton, "the first black President."

As Ronald Reagan learned, getting shot on television can be good for approval ratings. Bulworth's life hangs in the balance at the end of the film, but his political viability and spiritual sanctity are unthreatened. In fact, the film's magical black seer links these characteristics when he proclaims that Bulworth is now a spirit, not a ghost. His encounters with the physical dangers and political philosophy of black Los Angeles have restored Bulworth to the nobility of the civil rights era. The cynical entertainment foisted on the public by the film's rich, liberal Hollywood Jewish establishment has been exposed, even while that industry has been exploited to distribute Bulworth's message and, more importantly, his martyrdom.

It is necessary to experience danger to feel engaged in life, but is it possible to purposefully give up power? It is politic to mock television, but is it possible to effect political change without engaging the dominant medium of our times? *Bulworth* is careful not to ask or answer those questions.

10

Seriality

The 2000 version of a long-running series of Benetton advertising campaigns features a magazine insert called "We, on Death Row." It features photographs of and interviews with convicted criminals condemned to death, many of them multiple murderers. The piece includes the United Colors of Benetton logo, a disclaimer about the legal constraints of jailhouse interviews, and a quotation from Martin Luther King Jr. It's hardly surprising that such an intersection of killers and commodities makes reference to the role of television. According to Edgar Ace Hope— convicted of two counts of first-degree murder, shown smiling in his photo—"TV is a very big influence. In here we call it Big Monster." Obviously, this advertising strategy raises a number of interesting issues. Are the prisoners wearing Benetton clothes? Is this piece a parody? Beyond parody? What does it mean when companies utilize a conscience-based opposition to capital punishment to brand a clothing company?[1]

Here, however, we're concerned with one particular intersection highlighted by "We, on Death Row"—that of seriality: the serial nature of consumerism and buying, of serial crime, and the dominant form of television programming: the serial. As a critical concept, seriality can be used to consider televisual form and the culture that surrounds it. What does television seriality as the most dominant form of television imply? A serial, at its most basic, is a story told in installments, but more than a linear progression of discrete elements. It is, as well, repetitive. Television series, although they may change from week to week or day to day, usually play out the same conflicts among the same characters. A serial depicts the repetition of the same format, conflict, or behavior.

For this reason, the end of a television series is always unnatural. The suspension of *Seinfield's* seriality on May 14, 1998, was an epic event. *Seinfield* resolved the issue by bringing back key characters and incidents in a trial and, finally, repeating a bit about shirt buttons from the first episode. The narrative problem of ending is solved by another iteration of the show's theme of "doing nothing," as the characters are sentenced to jail, a location that doesn't interrupt their usual modes of interaction in the slightest.

Despite its unusual success, *Seinfield* isn't unique. The interruption of televisual flow is often a national event as well as a formal disaster. When *M*A*S*H* ended its eleven-year run, the final episode—the most watched program ever—radically changed the show's format. It became a two-and-a-half-hour drama in which the wisecracking, nurse-chasing Hawkeye accidentally causes a baby's death and is forced to struggle with that repressed memory. It was singularly unfunny. The show assumed the proportions of catastrophic drama, or of a movie, falling into cinematic resolution in order to call off the serial nature of the format. The narrative is structured as a search for meaning, a hermeneutic: Why is Hawkeye acting so funny? Well, he accidentally killed a baby. In the normal course of television, other than artificial or inconsistent endings, there is no ending: seriality implies endlessness. Because the economic structure of television is based on advertising, in which endless desire is both the form and the message, television is particularly suited to seriality. This endless desire is offered satisfaction with a series of choices that, since they also never end but always seem the same, are themselves not really choices. When the economic model shifts to encourage subscription, as it has for pay networks such as HBO and Showtime, the imperative for seriality diminishes.

In televison's traditional endlessness and its meaningless choices lies banality. Certainly, any discussion of seriality refers to the idea of television as banal, repetitious, and undifferentiated. This is also the banality of the horrific—the serial killer is also banal, repetitious, and undifferentiated. As we will see in the discussion below, the killer Henry (Michael Rooker) in John McNaughton's *Henry, Portrait of a Serial Killer* (1990), just keeps doing the same thing repeatedly, and no narrative event is ever capable of stopping his momentum.

Two critical works raise common questions about the nature of the television text, never identified as really a text or not really a very good text. Jane Feuer, in "Melodrama, Serial Form and Television Today," borrows a model used to talk about the cinema text, specifically the ways in which film theorists have recovered film melodrama.[2] In "Playing at Being American," John Caughie builds on the shift, inaugurated by British cultural studies, from text to reader and argues for the active role that the reader can play.[3]

For Feuer and Caughie, the problem of the text-which-isn't-really-a-text is connected to questions of "subversion." But we may ask whether "subversive" is even a relevant category for talking about what is happening in television programs. Does the institution of television care what you believe as long as you watch and buy? You can watch with derision. You can buy ironically. Buy a Ken doll and use it as a gay icon; wear your underwear outside your outerwear; pick out a white Ford Bronco because you like how it performed in O. J. Simpson's slow-speed chase. Does the manufacturer care?

Feuer's article was written in the mid-1980s, so she references programs such as *Dallas* and *Dynasty*, prime-time television melodramas or soap operas.[4] Feuer discusses *Dallas* and *Dynasty* as essentially the same thing. She doesn't really differentiate these series from each other. This is a familiar way of talking about television—you watch "television" rather than a succession of individual, clearly differentiated programs. The different stations may have different logos, but you can watch the same or virtually the same trial, crisis, drama, or situation comedy on one channel or another. The version you watch may be new or a rerun or "new to you"; it might be live, live on tape, recorded earlier, or taken from the network archive, but it's still television. Undifferentiation characterizes the relationship between television programs. The viewer's choice is only between different versions—between varieties, not differences. In his observation that criticism is often displaced onto audiences, the institutions of broadcasting and markets, Caughie notes the difficulty with identifying and discussing television texts. After all, television texts are slippery entities. To claim the competency to discuss a complete television series would be to admit to a great deal of time spent over a period of years watching what could only be thought of as "too much" television.

Yet Feuer does want to talk about the text, to distinguish between different texts, and—this is also vitally important to film criticism—to discover subversive meaning. Her strategy borrows from how theorists of film have discussed melodrama, in particular the melodramatic cinema of Douglas Sirk.[5] Sirk has long been patriarchally positioned as the grandfather of melodrama and recovered as an auteur. Through formal excess, and the subversive meanings that are read through it, he can be deemed theoretically justified and his films critically valorized even though they belong to a genre that is typically demeaned. Feuer asks, Can we apply the subversive potential of melodrama criticism, as it has been applied to film, to television programs such as prime-time soap operas? Can we identify certain television texts, as we do some films texts, as good objects, as opposed to the bad object that the totality of television usually represents?

Sirk directed several films set mostly within a family unit disrupted by conflicts and confusions. Like Grand Opera, they are noted for the absurdity and unbelievability of their plots. In *All That Heaven Allows* (1955), for example, Jane Wyman plays an older widow with Rock Hudson as her sturdy gardener. She falls in love and wants to remarry, but her selfish adult children believe she should maintain her class status as the widow of a successful husband. In a memorable scene, she recognizes that she's traded a life frolicking in the woodland with a vigorous younger man for … a television set. As her children bustle around with the antenna and controls, Wyman's pursed lips communicate her regret and frustration. As well as a vivid example of Sirk's *modus operandi,* this scene shows how even the critically suspect genre of film melodrama considers itself superior to television. The year before, Sirk's *Magnificent Obsession* (1954) revealed another famously fantastical plot. Rock Hudson, as usual, gets involved with Jane Wyman. He's a wastrel playboy who accidentally blinds her, and then, later, becomes a neurosurgeon, eventually stumbling onto an opportunity to operate on her and restore her sight while excising a coincidental brain tumor.

Not only are these films similar in their lush and melodramatic plots, focused on the family, love relationships, and class, but they are also significant for their grandiose visual style, featuring wide screens, opulent sets, and a maniacally tracking camera. Film theorists, such as Geoffrey Nowell-Smith and Thomas Elsaesser, have discussed this mise-en-scène as an opportunity for "reading against the grain," a strategy that seeks ways in which the film's visual style exceeds what is happening in the narrative. In many of Sirk's films, although there is a happy ending, it is unconvincing because the viewer can't believe after all the goings-on that the characters could be happy.

The "key text" for Feuer in this context is *Written on the Wind* (1956). Lauren Bacall is married to Robert Stack, another wastrel playboy and heir to a large oil fortune. As so often happens in these stories, the true heir is unworthy, and it is an outsider, a kind of adopted son of the patriarch—in this case, Rock Hudson again—who is the true son and heir. He's also in love with the unattainable Bacall, who is suffering through Stack's drinking and abuse. Dorothy Malone plays the woman who completes the two pairs, playing the sister of Stack. She is also a wastrel, a drunken slut who likes to get sloppy at little roadside bars and throws herself sexually at an impervious Hudson. Malone is constantly moving, cavorting in negligees, trying to get some action.

Finally, after a great deal of lurid, alcohol-fueled violence—screaming, drunken shooting, a heart attack, and miscarriage—Bacall and Hudson are shown motoring off to live happily ever after. Ignore the fact that the Hudson character has resisted any form of sexuality for his entire life up until this point. Ignore the unreality of the sister's redemption accomplished instantaneously by exchanging diaphanous gowns for a sensible business suit. Ignore that her rampant sexuality might not be easily sublimated by daddy's oil business, even if that business is represented by a wonderfully phallic model of a derrick, which she caresses in the final scene.

The focus of critical discussion of these films was not so much the ridiculous and banal plots but the manner in which the visuals exceed those qualities. There are the sweeping open staircases and mirrors, the layers of glass partitions filling the frame to the edges of its wide screen. This "reading against the grain" has critics looking for disruptive elements and contradictions. They seek eruptions of excess within the text that in some manner might invalidate or make irrelevant what the plot is saying, which in most cases is, "money can't buy you happiness," "we must have a legitimate patriarchal succession," and "we must conclude with a properly paired up heterosexual couple driving off at the end." These very conservative messages are undercut by the accumulation and pressure of visual excess. Feminist and psychoanalytic critics were attracted to the study of film melodrama because of the potential for repressed meanings in the text, as in Laura Mulvey's analysis of King Vidor's *Duel in the Sun* (1946). There is the hegemonic surface, the dominant ideology that is perpetrated, but then there are the deep structural contradictions and sublimations that offer politically progressive critical readings.

Feuer describes how these readings, applied to a debased film genre, can be applied, via the same genre, to American network television. Her approach focuses on *Dallas* and *Dynasty*, in a category that could now include *Baywatch, Beverly Hills 90210, Melrose Place,* and *The OC.* She points out how visually unimaginative *Dallas* and *Dynasty* appear, noting the wide shots and opulent sets and costumes of the mise-en-scène that replace innovative camera movement and editing. When Aaron Spelling created *90210,* he specifically wanted to adopt a standard, unexciting visual style. The series is about status and consumption—about houses, schools, outfits, and hairstyles. The viewer of reruns can identify the different seasons not by what the characters do but by what they wear. These choices are partly economic—it is expensive to move the camera—and partly ideological. At a time when MTV was taking stylistic experimentation to the limit, this show for young people worked in a completely traditional visual style—one might even say boring or banal.

Feuer says that while prime-time soap operas don't necessarily display visual excess, they do demonstrate an excessive lack of closure; they don't end, just as other series typically don't. Even the politically progressive sitcoms of the 1970s such as *All in the Family* or *Maude* needed to regain their stasis by the end of each show. Feuer notes that Meathead and Archie in *All in the Family* could have a big confrontation, but by the end of the episode they still had to live together in that cramped house. Not surprisingly, when Meathead and Gloria moved out and had a baby it damaged *All in the Family* by interrupting the necessary equilibrium. The death of Edith made the show unwatchable, just as the multiple births and weddings on *Friends* produced that series' planned obsolescence.

Yet, is lack of closure sufficient to a politically progressive critique—especially, as Feuer notes, when "every marriage is just an opportunity for another divorce"? Feuer cites Laura Mulvey, who argues that while those events that interrupt narrative closure in a television series might be read as subversive, they are more often escapist safety valves allowing the show to raise potentially disturbing questions and then displace them without any decisive action being taken. Do progressive readers feel a sense of smug superiority to the hapless protagonists of television melodrama? The constructed response might be, "Well, I don't need a mansion and a convertible to be happy. Money won't buy happiness. I'm better off than those so-called elites having all those problems." This perspective applies to shows like *Dallas* and *Dynasty*, and even to a show like *90210*, significantly set in Beverly Hills, where privileged young people nevertheless suffer continual upheaval and conflict. They even have money problems when their trust funds get raided.

Despite the overblown relationships, plot lines, and visual design of prime-time soaps, these characteristics don't add up to excess in a postmodern age that calls the very concept into question. Can any excess exceed the conventional? More specifically, are there any stylistic qualities in television analogous to cinematic excess? What if television is all excess, in which case none of it is excess? What televisual standards could measure excess? Caughie asserts that there is no institutional standard of televisual form as there is for classical Hollywood cinema. Even the non-cognoscenti have a sense of classical Hollywood cinema and its parameters. Within the field of cinema studies, the classical paradigm not only measures American studio films but acts as a standard against which foreign, independent, or avant-garde films are gauged. What is the degree zero of television?

Feuer locates excess in the lack of closure, in the serial form itself rather than in content or visual form. She calls this "a resistance to teleological metaphysics" (558). She posits that the serial form itself precludes a stable political reading: "Whether [a viewer's] response is interpreted to the Right or to the Left is not a question the texts themselves can answer" (561). When people read the auteurist signature in Sirk's melodramas they are really identifying at least two texts—the hegemonic surface, available to everyone, and the potentially subversive subtext—in an attempt to make a theoretical justification for at least one of them.

Yet, who can read this second text? Does identification of the second text require a privileged reader and does the critic necessarily need to position him- or herself as an initiate of an arcane hermeneutic? The distinctions between what is available for subversive readings and what is not are already meaningless. In a postmodernist era, the question of what a text can mean becomes increasingly a function of the reader's adopted role. The enthroned cinema spectator provides a postural stability in contrast to the multipositionality available to home viewers. The televisual subject may not be in a position to offer a stable reading of anything.

Caughie also emphasizes the perspective from which this kind of viewer comes at the text. He does so as an outsider attempting to comprehend the hegemonic reach of American culture. This effort informs "Playing at Being American." Like other theorists, he is looking for some critical wiggle room; the text should not be seen as entirely determinative of its own meaning, though Caughie also does not suggest that the reader is entirely free to construct his or her own meanings.

Addressing his own feelings of marginalization as a Scotsman, Caughie notes that in the world of American television, Scotland is a fairly irrelevant entity. He distinguishes between American programs, which can be seen anywhere in the world—for instance, *Baywatch*, at one time the most watched show in the world—and American broadcast television, which, in all its particularity, can really only be found in the United States. He makes what he calls three banal reflections on the latter category. In the United States, there is greater plurality of choice, a greater variety of content than in most other countries, where there might be only two or four channels, which may broadcast for only limited periods of the day.[6] He also notes the regularity of the schedule; how there is no dead time and how in England, for instance, if a program concludes at ten minutes before the hour, it is just over. The show ends, and the broadcast ceases until the scheduled time for the next show. This characteristic can strike a sensibility accustomed to American television as extremely peculiar. In America, everything—all space and time—is filled up, is without gaps;

there is real regularity to the schedule. Finally, Caughie cites breaks and interruptions as distinguishing factors of American broadcast television. In British television a voice or title card might announce "The end of part 1 of *Baywatch*" or "resuming *Baywatch*." On American television, the screen switches immediately and unceremoniously to a commercial.

For Caughie, these characteristics comprise the American mode, to which citizens and residents of other countries are subjected. But maybe *subjected* isn't the right term. Instead Caughie seems to be asking, How *can* other nationalities watch American television? Rather than simply dismissing the product as imperial kitsch, he wonders whether there is a way in and/or a way out of the empire. Caughie compares imperial television to other examples of globalizations versus localities. These localities could be gender, race, generation, or, in his case, nation (rather than nationalism). You can play, he says, at being American without really being one. You can suspend with a certain ironic elan your own identity and occupy the American role. Caughie presents this tactic as one of empowerment, a strategy that allows you to watch dominant television rather than simply rejecting or even reading against it. American broadcast television is, after all, everywhere; it is pervasive and insistent—and enjoyable.

Continuing his strategy of implicating himself in these issues, Caughie recounts a journey he took in the company of some fellow Scots to a remote Spanish village. Their intention was to soak up some local color, to seek authenticity in the details of everyday life. Entering a local bar, they discover that the Spanish villagers have gathered to watch Sarah and Prince Andrew's royal wedding. The Scots try to leave, but the local Spanish village folk insist that they stay. They want the Scots to enjoy a wonderful spectacle, which is precisely what the Scots consider to be the height of inauthenticity. They've traveled all the way to the remote Spanish village so they can avoid just such televised events as Sarah and Andrew's royal wedding.

Nevertheless, there they are. Imagine their frustration. Caughie, like Feuer, has arrived at a difficult critical and ideological point. He can't really say to the Spanish villagers, "Don't be like this. You shouldn't really be watching this. Please be Spanish villagers for us." How can he suggest a role-playing that doesn't simply perpetuate established relationships of power? Rather than a place, Caughie proposes a procedure for viewers. As Feuer does, Caughie assigns a more active role to the spectator rather than submission to the ceaseless onslaught. He finds this to be a balancing act because of his suspicion of what he calls "a romance of radical resistance," a utopia of naturally oppositional readers. He is wary of any stance of resistance that might reproduce the totalitarian logic of the object of its subversion.

It is only in the very structure of television narratives in juxtaposition to its overall flow that Caughie finds the possibility for blurring or slippage as opposed to radical resistance. The ludic contrasts that television ceaselessly supplies create ironic (critical) distance. This is possibility based on play rather than on a place, playing at being without having to be, a suspension or refusal of knowledge rather than not knowing. It isn't simply the flow of the text in this analysis, but the flow of the psychology.

Both Feuer and Caughie seek a television that can escape the bad objectivity of television texts through the agency of multiply positioned viewers. The search for television's "good object" is the complement to accusations of television as bad object, but our project has been to avoid these issues of objectivity in a consideration of television's subjectivity. An astute portrait of television subjectivity can be seen in the film *Henry, Portrait of a Serial Killer*, which draws on melodrama, role playing, and serial form, despite the trappings of gritty cinematic realism.

The poster for *Henry, Portrait of a Serial Killer* immediately announces its attitude of realism, claiming, "It's not Jason, it's not Freddie, it's real." Upon its release, the film was discussed in these terms—as gritty, realistic, unrelenting, and broadly based on the true story of Henry Lee Lucas. But Henry is actually a very traditional and constructed American hero. For one thing, taking the main American trajectory, he is heading west in a car. He's a loner and socially isolated from family and friends. He has his own standards of conduct, typical of the American hero, reflecting a strong personal philosophy. In this case, his philosophy and conduct ensure his ability to murder people without getting caught. Henry is attractive to women and also admired by men. Like the hero of George Stevens's *Shane* (1953), at the end of the narrative he must move on. Although—unlike Henry—cinematic serial killers seldom fulfill the role of protagonists, they often bear some resemblance to those other great icons of American mythology: the cowboy and the gangster. Serial killers are a debased version of a type we know very well and actually worship within the contradictory system of American values. As protagonist, Henry doesn't really challenge traditional concepts of heroism and manhood so much as he offers a depraved, contaminated, and dispersed version. Through this identification with generic icons, Henry plays at being a cinematic hero. While it may seem strange to discuss the serial killer in these terms, the film deliberately distances us from Henry's worst crimes. In two cases, we observe stalking activity, followed by a shot of a dead body. The most disturbing crime, the torture and murder of an entire family, is only seen as a videotape after the fact. Henry is also carefully distinguished from his brutish friend Otis (Tom Towles), who is not as physically attractive, sexually attacks his own sister, and appears both more passive and ineffectual toward and enthusiastic about their criminal activities.

In addition to this generic reference, the film plays on another familiar trope of American film, one that again works against the impression of "realism": melodrama. *Henry* contemplates the viability of its characters forming a family, with Henry spending most of his time relaxing at his temporary home, watching television, washing the dishes, and drinking beer. As in *Written on the Wind*, the family disintegrates, and only the strong survive to drive down America's endless highway at the end.

After an opening montage of dead bodies, the main narrative begins when Henry arrives to stay with Otis, an old friend from prison, and Otis's sister, Becky (Tracy Arnold). Almost immediately, Becky, clearly fleeing some bad white-trash situation at home, looks to Henry as romantic partner and savior. This isn't as strange as it may seem. It is a virtue for women in popular culture to love unreservedly and unconditionally. The male character would be perfect, we conclude on her behalf, if only he wasn't a thief or a serial killer. At any rate, Becky doesn't know anything about Henry other than that he is present, polite, and not making crude sexual overtures, unlike the grotesque Otis. This threatened incest is only one of the melodramatic aspects of the plot. More significantly, Henry's "problems" are caused by his own family, specifically his mother. The serial nature of his crimes is a typically psychoanalytic return of the repressed. Maybe if his mother hadn't been a whore and made him watch her with her clients he might have turned out all right. Instead, Henry killed her, the act that led to his original incarceration.

The film certainly implies that Henry's crimes are a reenactment of his mother's murder; he speaks of her only bitterly. The victims he stalks are all attractive women, and when Henry does kill men, it is always in the context of eluding detection or a perverted "self-defense." Otis's graphic sexual attack on his sister reinforces the idea that a misfiring family romance is the basis of violence and depravity. Yet this psychoanalytic explanation is never really taken seriously. Rather, it is an almost comical prop, similar to the explanation of Norman Bates at the conclusion of Alfred Hitchcock's *Psycho* (1960). *Henry's* horror lies in its inability to offer adequate formulas to explain a compulsive repetition—in this case the compulsion to murder, which is not unlike the compulsion to continually shop and consume. The psychoanalytic paradigm, along with the formulas of melodrama, realism, traditional heroism, and genre expectations, are all offered as ways of comprehending what we are seeing and the nature of Henry, and all prove to be inadequate.

When we consider the film's realist aesthetic and its depiction of current technology, it is clear that individuals' problems are associated with contemporary social conditions rather than solely attributible to the ahistorical realm of psychoanalytic notions of the subject. The two key elements that the film puts forth as problematic are modern transportation systems, the car and the airplane, which dislocate and isolate people; and the television, with the related technology of video recording.[7]

Even in the twisted domestic scene of Henry, Otis, and Becky, television is the threat. During one crime spree, Henry and Otis kill a man with his own television set and then steal a video camera. Subsequent viewings of videotaped crimes later incite Otis and create conflict between him and his criminal mentor Henry, who, perhaps recalling his childhood with mom, takes a more cautious approach to watching. Home is what viewing destroys.

But *Henry*'s indictment of television form doesn't lie with its depiction of a television set as a lethal weapon or a video camera as an element of heinous crimes. It is, rather, through seriality as a formal property of violation and excess that exposes a horror of repetition beyond any explanation. The bodies in the opening montage—presumably those left at the scene of Henry's crimes—are quite artificial. In some cases, they appear to be mannequins. They were already turned into inert commodities. This creates a worldview that is very hard to inhabit, because on one level it's revolting and at the same time utterly ordinary.

In the opening montage, only young, pretty victims are naked. In this way, the film is coded like every other film in which young attractive women are naked, other women are not naked so much, and men are never naked. In this sense, Henry plays at being a gritty, realistic, based-on-a-true-story character in a way that is entirely in keeping with a genre film. It *is* Freddie. It *is* Jason.

11

Is There an Audience in the House?

In her seminal essay "The King of Comedy: A Crisis of Substitution," Beverle Houston claims Martin Scorsese's film ultimately produces "a crisis of identification and participation for the spectator who, when s/he leaves the theater might as well plan to stay home."[1] This crisis is brought on by a string of critical substitutions that the film precipitates and charts, but in particular by "the replacement of cinema by television within a culture where the power of spectacle and its stars is already well established" (74). Not only are classical modes of spectatorial identification and pleasure put into crisis, but classical modes of distribution, exhibition, and production—including the agency of the auteur—are threatened as well. Interpellations of the subject, of generational, gender, class, and ethnic divisions, are all endangered by television's invasion and occupation of culture, calling into question the vocabulary of subjectivity and desire inherited from film studies. The showbiz term *house* refers to the traditional space of the public theater, clearly invoking a sense of comfort and intimacy for an audience gathered as a community. But when spectators "plan to stay home" and watch television, is there still an audience in the house?

Recalling G. W. F. Hegel's notion of the absolute might provide a way of locating the space or nonspace of the television audience. In "The Preface to the Phenomenology," Hegel defines the absolute as "pure self-recognition in absolute otherness," a process of sublime self-consumption which in "pure, simple negativity ... produces its own double and opposition, a process that again negates this indifferent diversity and its opposite."[2] In Hegel's historical phenomenology this process moves progressively from realization to derealization and then onward and upward again in a dialectic that arrives at the end of history. World Historical Spirit is simultaneously immanent with history even as it transcends it. Hegel identifies Greek sculpture, Christ, and Napoleon as realizations, incarnations, and agents of Spirit—and to that list we might add television.

Television's "derealization" can be seen in its recognition of and resignation to a devalorized otherness; its dynamic of self-consumption; and its "indifferent diversity," the simultaneous production of diversity and the negation of any meaning that might attach to that difference. "Indifferent diversity" as a staple of television's critical rhetoric is, however, distinct from Hegel's progressive dialectic.[3] Television's absolute paradoxically recommends a nonprogressive, nondialectical movement toward subjectlessness, at least as subjectivity is psychoanalytically understood, and a chronic negotiation and banalization of traumatic difference and desire that never intends terminality. A subject, operating within the "laws" of television, normalizes transgression (and substitution), but disqualifies resistance and revolution, let alone apotheosis. The expendable subject of television merges into television itself and makes the concept of distance—so essential to modernist positions of imaginary signification, voyeurism, disavowal, identification, and the fictive affects of pleasure—coincidental and exhibitionist. "Pure self-recognition," "pure simple negativity," loses in television the sublime solace of pure absence, safe distance, and good form. What has been debased is the very motor of modernist creativity: a sense of loss.

The perverse absolute of television may help to explain why audience studies is perhaps the most traditional and also the most obsessively current of approaches to television studies. The same problem persists without a satisfying theoretical solution: How are television audiences able to experience pleasure and meaning, even though the process of watching lacks imaginary signification and agency? Early sociological and quantitative approaches to audience studies betray doubt about television's textual propriety for high theoretical investigation; current ethnographic and fan methodologies struggle to theorize the possibility of spectatorial agency.[4] And yet, television audiences, inexplicable as their tastes and behaviors may be, exist and must be studied.

In her essay "Audience Control," Muriel Cantor reminds us that television audiences are never just those who watch, but also critics, pressure groups, network officials, producers, writers, advertisers, and other creative gatekeepers who may be quite different from the so-called target audience and quite different from the uni-dimensional mass audience of most theoretical approaches.[5] Cantor traces the lineage of "the powerless audience" in Marxist and mass society theory; from these theoretical perspectives, the audience is victim to urbanization, industrialization, and the accompanying rise of mass communication, victim to a decline of more authentic communities and their unifying beliefs. Auguste Comte, Herbert Spenser, and Max Weber each theorize the transition from a traditional, homogeneous, familial, and ritualized society to a rationalized, industrial, and complex one. In this new society, cultural alienation and disintegration arise when an elite no longer controls the flux of cultural value. The still-influential Frankfurt school (Theodor Adorno, Herbert Marcuse, Max Horkheimer, and, far more ambivalently, Walter Benjamin) and situationist critics such as Guy Debord see the mass audience as distracted, empty, bereft of multidimensional individuality, trivialized, exploited, and "narcotized" by a technology that makes them progressively irrelevant. As audiences turn to the mass media as a substitute for real experience they deliver themselves to those very minions of spectacle that forbid authentic experience and make of subjectivity an advertisement of sheer imagery. Marxist critics see in the content and form of media textuality an enforcement of false ideological consciousness that makes viewers incapable of resistance as they hegemonically assent to their own powerlessness. The routine structures of everyday thought become the force of an ideology where wanting what you are told to want is the essence of what it means to desire at all.

The dominant paradigm of contemporary audience studies in television arises in Raymond Williams's idea of "flow."[6] Williams's original concept of flow models the way in which everyday people gain access to the cultural meaning and value traditionally denied them. Following Richard Hoggart's *The Uses of Literacy*,[7] Williams's model appeals to the possibility of a classless cultural marketplace. Nevertheless, Williams suspects that television codes of flow may neutralize an audience's appreciation of programming, enmeshing that audience in commercials, announcements, previews, and programming. Where Williams implies that the audience's agency may be confused or overwhelmed by flow, John Ellis recognizes flow as a metaphor of mindless, passive participation, one that must be challenged by audiences recast as ideological warriors.[8] Ellis echoes the possibilities put forward by Stuart Hall, who argues that the televisual material itself can be coded in any of a variety of ways, and it can be decoded by active or sensitized audiences according to dominant, negotiated, or oppositional preferences.[9] Ellis proposes the "coherent text segment" as a replacement for the concept of flow. These segments, when extracted from the flow, can be combined into larger syntagms that offer an experience more like cinema than television.

Whereas Ellis would empower the audience to transform television's flow into more cinematically discrete texts, John Fiske and John Hartley believe the term *flow* is as much an obfuscation as an explanation. It institutionalizes distraction and invites ideological submission. They prefer a flow that allows for polysemic fragmentation, or, as they call it, "bardic television."[10] For them, the ideal audience has an openness to flow, the freedom to intervene, and the ability to create meanings. Television here takes the role of the traditional bard, occupying the common center of a culture to which a highly fragmented society and highly fragmented textual delivery need to refer. If Ellis wants the television audience to construct cinema, Fiske and Hartley would have that audience compose poetry.

Charlotte Brunsdon's work on audiences represents the shift from reception theory to aesthetics. Her essay "Television: Aesthetics and Audiences" considers the status of television as aesthetic object and the difficulty for critics and scholars in identifying television as an artistically valid text.[11] As Nick Browne has argued, television textuality is so "super-" or "meta-," so huge and dispersed, that as a consequence critics often study the audience or institutional factors of television rather than the medium itself. Brunsdon observes that when people talk about good television, they generally mean television used to present, reference, or validate other arts, with all the structured hierarchies of social privilege and elitism that implies. "Good" television, as we have seen, has also historically been associated with a live relationship with real events, providing immediate information. In this way, too, television becomes "good" in service always to another purpose. A third way in which television can be considered "good" for Brunsdon is when it abandons all pretension and is simply popular or even defiantly "bad."

As it has been theorized, the concept of good television usually sidesteps the pleasure that most people get from watching it. Brunsdon understands that when people speak about good television—or what they'll let their children watch or admit to watching themselves—they typically refuse to speculate on how or why commercial television is watched at all. The question of how television addresses and positions its viewers within a continual onslaught or flow is a problem for Brunsdon because it is difficult to discuss television textuality—the realm of artistic appreciation—within that framework. Absent a legitimate text as object of pleasure, taste, and appreciation, studies of audiences lead to extreme conclusions of passivity, pathology, or revolutionary redemption.

To identify how people actually watch television presents enormous methodological, conceptual, and ethnographic problems. Brunsdon's response is to locate television aesthetics in the multiple agencies of particular audiences encountering texts—encounters that are characterized by elements of history, intimacy, and decriticalization. Her model disrupts the conceptual harmony of television flow because, she notes, television doesn't really flow—it jumps and starts. Television aesthetics are therefore created in a similarly disruptive manner: an interaction of television and the viewer, and the viewer's subjective stance toward the repetition of diverse and plural programming; the production of different forms of popular consumption; television's alternative strategies of banalization and criticalization; and the serial regularity of its disruptions. This negotiated aesthetic, both intimate and dispersed, becomes a way for audiences and critics to avoid the textual evasions of flow. While seeming to allow an openness to otherness, it also insists on the chronic substitutions and appropriations necessary to the status quo.

This paradoxical aesthetic of participatory modification neither overturns television textuality nor necessarily establishes its tyranny. In dialogue rather than passive assent, television audiences and diegetic agents may resign themselves to an experience of flow, but they also continually renavigate its course. In what we may term the *television uncertainty principle*, after physicist Werner Heisenberg's articulation of the uncertainty principle, viewing can comprise and change the nature of the event. In the television version, cinematic power, classically dependent on the spectator's misrecognition of subjective omnipotence, is replaced by horizontal dissolution into endlessly resignified otherness.

In chapter 5, "The Vidiot," we elaborated on Stanley Cavell's "fact of television," which revolved around the distinction between *world* and *event*. A *world* centers itself in metaphysical and subjective confidence, in a worldview that confirms—ideologically and psychologically—perceptual dominance and predictable outcome. An *event* arises in the monitoring of that world as it begins to shift, flow, or dissolve into a series of crises and replacements that challenge secure subject/object relations. Historical upheavals are certainly key to this shift, as are technological deconstructions of metaphysical fact. Television's postapocalyptic rise and role in monitoring late-twentieth-century upheaval is an indisputable fact of the demise of "fact," and to a certain extent accompanies Gilles Deleuze's observation in *Cinema 1* and *Cinema 2* of the shift from "movement-image" to "time-image." The "time-image" brings with it the derangement of linear and dialectical logic and movement and implies an "embodied event" that no longer follows subjective stability nor flatters its privileged point of view.

The very characteristic of an event is its mediacy and its immediacy, its state of *in medias res* embodying spectatorial participation in the midst of the event itself. This is the dynamic presented in Martin Scorsese's *The King of Comedy* (1982), a film in which the desire to display the self on television is both self-affirming and a manifestation of insanity. Rupert Pupkin (Robert de Niro), an underemployed and delusional middle-aged man in cahoots with the even more unstable heiress Masha (Sandra Bernhard), kidnaps Jerry Langford (Jerry Lewis), the host of television's most highly rated nighttime talk show. The ransom he demands is an appearance on the program. In the world of this film, late-night talk shows still engage a mass audience, and Rupert Pupkin is the disturbed avatar of that conglomeration.

From the beginning of the film, Rupert displays several markers of a problematic personality. His appearance is overly formal, creating an argument of superiority out of sync with his true status as a "loser." He wears a tailored, three-piece suit, even when he is performing his job as a delivery man. His tie and pocket handkerchief coordinate in the yellow and red "power" colors of the 1980s. At the same time, the details ring false and seem overly strained. For instance, he has a mustache, a signifier of gender appropriate for the hypermasculinity of policemen, security guards, and firemen, but not for a failed comic living at home with his mother. His hair is immaculately coiffed and slicked down with brilliantine. He wears brilliantly white shoes. In some ways, his appearance mimics that of the sleekly fashionable television personality Jerry Langford, the man into whose shoes he would like to step. But Rupert misreads the sartorial signals he tries to deploy. A similar precision of suit, accessories, hair, and manner reflects Jerry's position as a famous performer with a long and celebrated showbiz past. Jerry appropriately wears showbiz drag. For Rupert, the careful self-presentation reads as bad taste and low status. He doesn't have the social power to be casual.

In other misreadings, Rupert can't accept the gentle and politely expressed rejections he encounters in pursuit of his goal: to perform a comic monologue on *The Jerry Langford Show*. In the film's pre–opening credit sequence, Rupert "rescues" Jerry from Masha who has somehow managed to hide in the backseat of Jerry's limo as he attempts to flee a mob of fans after the taping of his show. Deflecting Masha, who we soon learn is actually Rupert's friend, as she ecstatically paws at Jerry, Rupert deftly jumps into the backseat himself. This rescue buys Rupert a few minutes in the presence of Jerry Langford, which he uses to plead his case. Jerry agrees to listen to an audition tape, but as he later explains, it's only a brush-off. Rupert's inability to "read" Jerry's social signals and to withdraw comes across as creepy, as does his unwillingness to leave the production office reception area after dropping off his tape, preferring to "wait." The opening sequence also presents an opportunity for the film's audience to misread the character dynamics. As Jerry and Rupert drive off, Masha's contorted face is freeze-framed in grainy black and white against the limo's side window as the credits begin to roll and Ray Charles sings "I'm Going to Love You." To all appearances, Masha is the stalker, and Rupert a helpful bystander. The invocation of a television screen in the frozen shot makes it clear that, in this film, television will distort all meanings and interpretations.

After his tape is rejected—it has "very good potential, but we just don't think it's ready"—Rupert takes an old high school friend, a black woman named Rita (Diahnne Abbott) with whom he seeks a romantic relationship and who functions to some degree as a noir fatal of authenticating evaluation, on a trip to Jerry's country house. It is at this point in the film that Rupert is most strange. It is difficult to know what to make of the character. Although he has several vividly rendered fantasy scenes in which he has become a successful colleague of Jerry's, he doesn't appear to be insane. In a scene of excruciating embarrassment for the spectator, heightened by the presence of the gullible Rita, Jerry kicks them out. Rupert just doesn't correctly read his own subject position, not unlike the hopeless hopefuls at an *American Idol* audition. It is almost a relief when Rupert decides to work toward his goal in a way more typical of American cinematic heroes by kidnapping Jerry and ransoming him for the shot on television. He gets a gun and a car, and he acts.

Rupert displays irritation and exasperation, but he doesn't express strong emotion. He experiences and provokes minor—or, more accurately, ambivalent—feelings that gain psychotic force by refusing emotional boundaries and fictive thresholds. He embodies a televisuality that is unable to suspend disbelief because it has never entertained disbelief. Rupert believes that Jerry is the character he plays on television. This is what makes his fanatic certainty and self-confidence so unnerving. Persistently resistant to prohibitions against imaginary reunion—becoming/replacing Jerry—Rupert crosses into blatant misrecognition, and by realizing what he should only desire he uncomfortably exposes that what we desire is designed to be ideologically impossible. Our cinematic imaginary, like Rupert's basement, is also peopled with movie star cutouts. However, in replacing established star culture, Rupert's Humphrey Bogart, Clark Gable, Marilyn Monroe, and, most prominently, Liza Minnelli (another Lewis-like figure of generic liminality), exist for him not as ego ideals but as players in an intimate fantasy with which he has promiscuously merged.[12] Rupert tips cinematic identification into overidentification.[13]

Rupert has overturned normal behavior, particularly in his relationships, by resisting normal ideological interpellation and creating for himself a new form of agency. We are reminded here of René Girard's description of "mediated" desire.[14] Rupert's need for recognition must be filtered through the figure of Jerry. This model, or mediator, simultaneously represents for him the idolized text of desire and the despised obstacle to complete achievement. As the distance between subject and mediator, disciple and model, is violated and begins to collapse, the original object of desire (self-regard in the form of fame) is contaminated by ignoble feelings of outrage, vanity, false pride, and contempt. Rupert's agency depends on his position of excessive inagency, the social entrenchment of his helplessness. His actions strain our proairetic confidence by putting the codes with which we evaluate proper behavior into crisis.

In an echo of the film's story, the most famous actor in this film is not Robert De Niro, although by 1982 De Niro had been nominated four times for an Academy Award and had won twice—for Francis Ford Coppola's *The Godfather, Part II* (1975) and Scorsese's *Raging Bull* (1981). De Niro's stature as a critically acclaimed actor and as virtual co-auteur with director Scorsese is nevertheless eclipsed by Jerry Lewis's career. Its longevity, range across various media, and international devotion constructs Lewis as a pure signifier of show business. There is certainly a conflict between the different types of renown that De Niro and Lewis represent, with the critically honored star-as-character pitted against the power of star-as-self, a reclusive and immersive acting technique against the embarrassing need for attention often noted in descriptions of Lewis even when he isn't officially performing. Lewis is that agent and agency of replacement that produces cinema's crisis of legitimacy, though it is an issue of exquisite irony and adaptability that he comes to represent high modernist legitimacy in *The King of Comedy*. Extending that irony, Lewis reportedly campaigned for a violent, more cinematically secure closure rather than the desperately parodic montage of media frenzy and subsequent celebrity (including magazine covers, a truncated prison term, a best-selling memoir, and a movie deal) that follows Rupert's coup and ends the film (Houston, 89).

We have, in chapter 8, discussed the quasi-marital relationship acted out by Dean Martin and Jerry Lewis, but there is clearly also a mimetic dimension that took place on both the level of performance and real life. Just as the "monkey," as Lewis describes his typical character, wanted to be like Martin's "sexy guy," Jerry wanted to be like Dean. As Lewis has described an early meeting with his future partner, "He gave me that smile again—warm but ever so slightly cool around the edges. It bathed you in its glow, yet didn't let you in. Men don't like to admit it, but there's something about a truly handsome guy who also happens to be truly masculine—what they call a man's man—that's as magnetic to us as it is to women. That's what I want to be like, you think. Maybe if I hang around with him, some of that'll rub off on me."[15]

In Lewis's greatest role as *The Nutty Professor* (1962, Jerry Lewis) his mimetic or mediated desire takes on a schizophrenic quality, as in his relationship with Martin, and likewise in his bizarrely unstable behavior as impresario of the annual muscular dystrophy telethon, during which he fluctuates wildly between sensible, scientifically informed medical research and blithering idiocy.

In his role as Jerry Langford, Lewis attained unprecedented critical praise, and even a British Academy of Film and Television Arts nomination. His performance is squarely in the realm of serious Jerry, and it is De Niro's Rupert who betrays an unseemly need for homosocial celebrity. In a further reversal, Rupert invents a fantasy scenario in which it is Jerry who envies him. In a scene imagined in the caricature-filled Sardi's restaurant, Jerry pleads for Rupert to take over his show. Their behavior is highly performative, played out for the restaurant patrons; Jerry's abasement is only meaningful if it is observed by others. In another fantasy sequence, Jerry surprises Rupert with a televised wedding with Rita, á la the wedding of Tiny Tim and Miss Vicky on *The Tonight Show*. Rupert imagines Jerry extravagantly praising his audition tape and extending an invitation to the country house. As Jerry gushes, "I don't know how you do it," and "I hate you, but I envy you," we not only witness Jerry put back in place as Lewis by the even more Lewis-like Rupert (played by cinema superstar De Niro), but also witness a demonstration of the endlessly interconnected chains of mediated desire that come to characterize media landscapes in general.[16]

The King of Comedy is a movie about television invoking structures of cinematic spectatorship in order to confound those sites and to conflate the resulting confusion we feel with the subjective and spectatorial dilemmas of television. The cinema of television as a whole tends to place us in the midst of a spectatorial dismay that is itself a portrayal and enactment of televisuality. *Televisuality* is a term perhaps better suited than either *subjectivity* or *spectatorship* for describing the mediated metaphysics of *The King of Comedy*. The film toggles between recognition and identification of varied and incommensurable entities: Rupert as a character, the star personas of De Niro and Lewis, the talk show format, film genre, and Scorsese as cinematic auteur. Is the film a screwball comedy, a crime caper, an expose, an art film? De Niro's cinematic signification would seem to be unchallengeable, whereas Lewis has always inhabited a cinematic/televisual no man's land.

Houston uses the utter recognizability of the talk show host, "himself not a figure of ecstatic desire," to explore these liminal challenges. She locates the host's identity "somewhere between that of a star and a family member ... allowed to mediate between [the stars'] imagined location in pure desire and the living room where television delivers them.... Rupert's obsession involves a contradiction or transition marked by the talk show itself—the nostalgic power of cinema negotiated through the medium of television" (78–79).

The King of Comedy is altogether marked by "a contradiction or transition," a "negotiation" of uncertainties, reversals, and replacements that is televisuality itself. Movie spectatorship is forced to rely on televisual skills in order to find the film funny or enjoyable at all. This calling "into question the nature or possibility of spectator pleasure in the new medium" (88) is, for Houston, Scorsese's auteurist mark on the film, and—we might note—television's placement of auteurism under erasure.

Though we struggle throughout the film "to find funny this confusion of registers as a reflection of auteurist wit under the pressure of television" (86), too often we find ourselves abandoned to an uneasy tittering closer to embarrassment than spectatorial mastery. When Rupert triumphs in his scheming and delivers his final monologue of parental perversion, alcoholism, and vomiting to a nationwide audience, we can't find ourselves in that imagined audience, in the alarming laugh-track hilarity of an unseen studio audience, nor finally in recourse to the elite assurances of a Scorsese audience. Even auteurism's reactionary cult of individuality takes a body blow from television. Houston quotes Scorsese's own perplexity toward television comedy, television desire, and the medium as a whole: "'(People) want something. It's like the Maltese falcon, nobody knows what the hell it is'" (88).

Scorsese's bewildered suspicion of television audiences doesn't extend to the creative personnel—producers and performers—with whom he identifies to the extent that he casts himself as the director of *The Jerry Langford Show*. The twin objects of that suspicion exist entirely within the realm of the audience, through the characters of Rupert and his friend Masha. Masha functions to make Rupert, who is, after all, the protagonist, more acceptable through her inconsistencies and fanaticism. She is the stereotypical audience member of televisual contempt: an idle woman. She is rich, as her townhouse, shopping, and preppy clothes reinforce, and she doesn't have a husband or children to tend to. Without the constraints of domestic duty, she is therefore too susceptible to over-identification with what she sees on television. We recognize in Masha a highly exaggerated version of what critical thinking and writing about television continually tell us about the nature of television audiences, and fans in particular.

Rupert, particularly when he begins to behave like a more typically goal-oriented cinematic figure, operates within a normalized rhetoric of subjective delusion, allowing some small basis to identify with him. There is a familiar oedipal revenge in his actions and his appallingly unfunny final monologue. Masha, on the other hand, whose life fluctuates between the high status of comfort and privilege and stalker-like fandom, is far more narratively incoherent. Abandoned by her parents to an ivory-towered townhouse, her distress imagines rescue by a gallant Jerry domesticated by hand-knit sweaters, candlelit intimacy, and dining with expensive crystal. Hers is an imaginary that money might buy, a sad hallucination of standardized romance that makes her fragility deranged but stripped bare nevertheless. Masha bears the burden of redeeming Rupert as protagonist and redeeming Scorsese as auteur, despite the embarrassing subject matter of his film. Although she disappears, somewhat inexplicably, from the narrative before Rupert's final triumph, it is hard not to imagine Masha's derision at the final monologue and hard not to think she would find it unfunny. The creepy feeling left at the end of *The King of Comedy* arises from several quarters, not least an agreement with Masha's skepticism. To be aligned with such a creature can only engender unease.

The very assumption of cinema as enlightened address to the vulnerable and addicted body of television spectatorship is the central issue of *The King of Comedy* and of the cinema of television, one that assumes a complicated and ironic negotiation that cannot be resolved by quality programming or even the elimination of television. Houston writes of this cinematic aftermath that "television, unlike cinema, does not offer its own viewing as the fulfillment of the circuit of desire it opens up" (82). Indeed, it is precisely the disposability, the mediation, the transformation of desire into an agency beside itself that strips it of its single-minded subjective imperative. Contaminated, "the will to representation [becomes] 'pure,' offered without psychological explanation or motivation, a fact of culture rather than personality or individuality" so that it becomes possible for the televisual subject—the televisual spectator and fan—"no longer to struggle unsuccessfully to become the desire of the Other, but, finally, to become the Other who initiates desire for the world, as it was initiated for him in television" (82). Exceeding the rules of the cinematic endgame, television nonchalantly induces disgust at the heart of classically driven subjectivity. The bad objectivity of televisual practice argues against the proper practice of pleasure, entertaining desire's eschatology into endless consumption. A desiring machine infinitely capable of replicating our own desire, television replaces erotic integrity with pluralized, irritating consensus.

Houston concludes her article "Viewing Television" by positing the possibility that "the spectator of television is not so barred from producing a knowledge of his or her position even while taking television's pleasures. Indeed the link between the level of the economic base and television's role in furthering it seems deceptively clear in comparison with that of cinema. Yet since it is based on a mechanism of desire in which both the dream and its interruption seem to power the viewer toward consumption, it is difficult for a knowledge to be effective."[17]

The dream of desire and its interruption, this possibly ineffective and bad example of epistemological agency: what Houston's conclusion stops short of is the possibility that this knowledge *is* consumption. Blocked from catharsis and completion, this pitiless knowledge presumes a capitalist co-optation of modernism's empty presentation of loss. A powerful postspectatorial obsolescence then triumphs, as Rupert does, in pursuing an exceedingly pleasurable solution it knows is never going to last: "Better to be king for a night, than schmuck for a lifetime."

Rupert Pupkin emerges as representative of television at the pinnacle of the network domination of cinema's established culture of "spectacle and star." Rupert's motto—"I can wait"—reflects this power as a Bartlebyan capacity for passive aggression and the serial drive to repeat and persist. After 1982—the year of the film's release—and following television's internal logic of replacement and substitution would come a series of network diminutions as a result of cable and satellite distribution and the programming and audience niching they make possible. The mass marketing of time-shifting digital technologies and an era of federal deregulation would further accomplish this lateralization.

In "TV and the Family Circle" Lynn Spigel sees in television's origin its eventual teleology of crisis and substitution, an aesthetic of its own overcoming. In the post–World War II family, in which husbands were returning to an economy that had empowered their wives and scattered their children throughout the suburbs, television arrived to foster a paradoxical unity out of disunity, to exploit a crisis in order to offer its own management of that crisis. Even as a piece of furniture, the television offered a hearthlike center around which dispersed families might gather. At the same time, it broadcast variety, multiplicity, and a fractured experience of flow as its defining textuality, as the textual accommodation of postwar differences. Television masterfully recommends itself as a unifier by structuring diversity, and the *enjoyment* of television arises in large part from learning to handle that diversity. Across television's history, instability becomes an opportunity to negotiate stability, stability itself the status quo of chronically normalized disruption.

In the twenty-five years following *The King of Comedy*, the craving for invasive access and American idolatry in the eyes of tens of millions of fans will have become all too decriticalized, and the problematic power and pleasure Rupert takes in achieving his goals and abandoning respectable subjectivity and spectatorship will have devolved into cinemas of renewed impotence in the face of television. In films from Tobe Hooper's *Poltergeist* (1982) to M. Night Shyamalan's *Signs* (2002) to Michael Haneke's *Caché* (2005) and Steven Spielberg's *War of the Worlds* (2005) we see not only a common crisis of viewer/victim/auteur in the face of television and video culture but a similarity of causes and responses to the crisis that constitutes a phenomenon very like a return to cinematic faith. *Poltergeist*, released in the same year as *The King of Comedy*, is nominally directed by Hooper, though it is certainly producer/writer Steven Spielberg's film. A hapless father (Craig T. Nelson) promotes real estate built over a sacred Indian burial ground, and so unwittingly and witlessly invites hell into the family circle. The portal of hell is the static screen of a television set after programming has ceased for the day, and its chief victim is the youngest daughter, whose innocent susceptibility and prescience makes her a prime sacrifice to the TV demons. "They're here!" announces the electromagnetic threat, and only the quasi-religious intervention of psychic experts, midget exorcists, and that other feminine intimate of television's chaos—the mother—can save the day. The patriarch, who can't even get his keys into the car's ignition as caskets and corpses erupt in his backyard, is reduced to throwing the television set out on the balcony of the Holiday Inn where the family takes refuge.

In Shyamalan's *Signs* Mel Gibson plays a family patriarch and ex-priest haunted into atheism by the memory of his wife's seemingly senseless death. Mysterious crop circles keep appearing all over the world until finally television records evidence of an alien invasion. Television becomes the only way of comprehending and banalizing what is happening by paradoxically inciting a mass hysterical response to the rather quaint and surprisingly vulnerable aliens. Media coverage guarantees that their arrival will be sensationalized back into normalized place. And that is apparently what Graham (Gibson) cannot abide about television, that it is hyperrealizing a normalized, secularized catastrophe rather than allowing a true apocalypse. He initially bans his family from watching television in order to guarantee the sanctity of the event. The rejection of television's ceaseless interpretation leads to the restoration of family, planet, and the mysticism of recovered faith. Graham finds the priesthood again, and television finds its true place when its semiotics of narrating otherness into sameness are exiled by the semiotics of God. Aliens and dead wives must remain senseless in order that they may command faith.[18]

Under the thrall of television, audiences are potentially capable of overcoming a threat they create in order to resolve it. This is the perverse flow of technology in general, and of the everyday. In *Poltergeist* and *Signs*, when the programming signal goes blank it is a terrifying event that suspends television's eventfulness, its origins in paranoid surveillance and its continuing form and function in monitoring and domesticating a world otherwise too dangerous to inhabit. There are interesting parallels among *Poltergeist*, *Signs*, and Spielberg's *War of the Worlds* in this regard. In all three films, the loss of the terrestrial broadcast signal signals the magnitude of the extraterrestrial peril and the "opportunity" to abandon merely human agency. A Reformation-like agenda takes hold where even though the patriarchs (Tom Cruise in *War of the Worlds*) remain central to the films' narrative, they are irrelevant to solving the catastrophic problem. In all cases, demons and alien invaders are brought down by factors unconnected to their actions, except insofar as they are willing to examine their souls for signs and emblems of predetermined grace—the homogenized and ritualized values of family and faith.

Spielberg and Shyamalan seem almost desperate to believe anything that would mitigate the continuously flowing tragedy of life and death that television entertains as the mass cultural relationship between pleasure and the real. Authorship becomes that authority in cinema that insists on a reconstructed reminder that audiences are the ideological prey of mass culture. Peter Weir's *The Truman Show* (1998) springs immediately to mind, and Scorsese's auteurism in *The King of Comedy* is no exception. Andy and Larry Wachowski's *Matrix* trilogy (*The Matrix*, 1999; *The Matrix Reloaded*, 2003; *The Matrix Revolutions*, 2003) gives Neo (Keanu Reeves) ultimate authority in destroying the godless metaphysics of the machines (though not the film's own digital inferno of *haute couture* and special effects). "The One," Neo, slays the signifier whose names are legion; as the holy signified, the Word reborn, he redeems the world of sheer eventuality, and with the authenticating assistance of his black disciples and oracles he rises beyond the terrestrial pleasures of illusory enjoyment (obscenely delicious steak and wine!) into the passion of the Christ.

Finally, the authorless gaze at an unexamined life in Haneke's non-Hollywood film *Caché* sees video surveillance swivel into a fascinating recovery of authorial accusation. Another father (Georges Laurent, played by Daniel Auteuil) can do nothing to stop the videotapes that mysteriously arrive at his house and seem simply to stare at the *dasein*, the brute "being there" of his life. Soon enough, however, the terror of this passive investigation grows to destabilize his relationship with his wife, son, and profession. His is the privileged life of a literary intellectual within high bourgeois French culture, though his fame comes—as we should by now be wary of—from disseminating his views on a television talk show. As he searches for some accusatory logic in the events that threaten his smug metropolitan life, the repressed returns in the oedipal details of Algerian negritude, and we are left searching for clues as to how the sins of the father and the mother will continue to fall on the helpless heads of the sons. In this biblical context of historical betrayal where we can positively blame no one, we fall back on the relentlessly emptied gaze of European auteurism Haneke inherits from Michelangelo Antonioni and Ingmar Bergman.

Haneke's film is a brilliant vision of a story that doesn't, and can never, add up. One cannot reconcile what the video footage shows with any rational account of production, motivation, or camera placement. Who is showing us these images and why? Why do we watch even though, by watching, we might discover some guilt about our own actions? These questions are pertinent outside the context of *Caché*. The conflicts and complications of watching television, finally, are what we are left with.

We identify a myth of channel infinity—the myth that channels will continuously proliferate until there is programming for everyone at every moment, even though we know that there are fewer and fewer independent producers of content. We also see that television's ideology of liveness is increasingly dependent on programmed and scripted impressions of simultaneity, a televisuality defined by immediacy, proximity, interactivity, and omnipresence. Yet, immediacy is performed through encrustation in the very technology that produces it; spontaneity is increasingly channeled through technological control (DVR, TiVo, pay-per-view technology, video on demand, and the cinematic nostalgia of high-definition and home theater apparatus).

Despite these contradictions, what remains is the curious promise of viewer agency. As Slavoj Žižek argues (often in regard to popular cinema) in such works as *Enjoy Your Symptom!* and *The Sublime Object of Ideology*, mass culture does not necessarily steal our power and pleasure, but enacts it. Nor does mass culture automatically dupe us into submission. "*Les non-dupes errant*" are actually those enlightened authors, protagonists, critics, and auteurs who believe they can see through the capitalist deceptions of the mass cultural ornament. For Žižek, the endless threat of subjective dissolution constitutes the vital dynamic of mortality; out of that menace comes the fearsome work of enjoyment. If you resolve all the dilemmas, whether they are ideological or narrative, you ruin your opportunity for pleasure. Viewers seeking the transcendent and ecstatic pleasures of cinema may find the quotidian rhythms, familiar situations, likable personalities, and petty competitions of television too humdrum, poorly constructed, or inconsequential. But the joys and skills of television may be as useful as they are guilty, and the viewer agency of technological control may be more than just that of an automaton.

We have discussed many ways in which cinema takes television to task and the ways in which television criticism often reproduces these attitudes. In fact, these attitudes also reflect mainstream opinion, highly infected with that distinct style of American anti-intellectualism. It is apparently somewhat unseemly to watch television, to like television, or to write about television in a way that suggests it has anything interesting to say about American life. But these mainstream opinions are really out of phase with what people actually do. When we ask students, friends, and colleagues what television programs they really like and watch, they offer up a strong, if slightly defensive, affection for *America's Next Top Model*, *The O.C.*, and *Robot Chicken*. Although masterpieces may sometimes occur on television (*Seinfeld*, *The Sopranos*, and *Star Trek* among them), perhaps it is time to stop making the search for masterpieces—and the failure to find them everywhere— the inevitable goal of television criticism. Cinema has only been able to make a stark distinction between its pleasures and that of other media forms because cinematic specificity in style and narrative construction often depends on the challenges of a rival like television. Movies, then, offer a key to transvaluing television—beyond the categories of masterpiece and kitsch, if not entirely beyond good and evil. In both cinematic and televisual paradigms of viewer address, the difficult work of remaining human, of being called into being, is assumed. Though television's diversions can produce hostile reactions, pleasure remains—complicated, precarious, and guilty.

Notes

Chapter 1

1. As Paul Young, *The Cinema Dreams Its Rivals: Media Fantasy Films from Radio to the Internet* (Minneapolis: University of Minnesota Press, 2006), 249, notes, "Intermedia studies have become an important subfield within cinema and media criticism. The revisionist histories of the beginnings of particular media and technologies ... during the past two decades have helped push media studies past its understandable tendency to think of the question of media identity primarily as one of technological specificity and ontology."

2. Ibid., xxii.

3. See also Richard W. Hubbell, *Four Thousand Years of Television: The Story of Seeing at a Distance* (New York: G. P. Putnam's Sons, 1942).

4. Jane Stokes, *On Screen Rivals: Cinema and Television in the United States and Britain* (New York: St. Martin's Press, 2000).

5. Mitchell Stephens, in *Rise of the Image, Fall of the Word* (Oxford: Oxford University Press, 1998), historicizes the crisis raised by electronic media by locating similar crises, from Plato to Johannes Gutenberg to the pencil eraser. Yet, while Plato argues that we must exile the poets from the republic, Stephens suggests that we become visually literate as we incorporate new imaging technologies into our culture. Friedrich Kittler, developing notions discussed by Marshall McLuhan, argues that machines (technology) have replaced the traditional function of the central nervous system. We experience all objects and events as an experience of "mediality."

6. A similar juxtaposition can be seen in an even earlier film: Marcel L'Herbier's 1924 *L'Inhumaine*. The impetuous Einar (Jaque Catelain) introduces his inamorata Claire (Georgette Leblanc) to his invention—television—by showing her scenes from around the world, including China. It is never clear how the cameras got to the exotic locations, nor how the foreign people are able to hear Claire as she warbles an accompaniment to their activities. The travelogue/ song format is employed, and, as in Clifford Sanforth's *Murder by Television* (1935), television is quickly reduced to a mere device in a familiar tale.

7. Anna McCarthy, *Ambient Television: Visual Culture and Public Space* (Durham, NC: Duke University Press, 2001).

8. The precise meaning and dating of "network era" or "network age" varies. Michele Hilmes refers to the "Network Age" as lasting from 1926 to 1940. Jeremy Butler defines "network-era television" as beginning with a system dominated by three networks, which multiply and then "explode[e] into dozens of channels in the 1980s" with "the widespread acceptance of cable and satellite delivery" (4).

9. Mark Williams, "real-time fairy tales: Cinema Prefiguring Digital Anxiety," in *New Media: Theories and Practices of Digitextuality*, ed. Anna Everett and John T. Caldwell (New York: Routledge, 2003), 159–78, argues for the continued relevance of apparatus theory traditionally located in film studies in the analysis of electronic media.

10. James Lardner, *Fast Forward: Hollywood, the Japanese, and the Onslaught of the VCR.* New York: W. W. Norton, 1987.

11. The impact of technology on the nature of television can be seen in such work as that by Patricia Clough in *Autoaffection: Unconscious Thought in the Age of Teletechnology* (Minneapolis: University of Minnesota Press, 2000), and Richard Dienst in *Still Life in Real Time: Theory after Television (Post-Contemporary Interventions)* (Durham, NC: Duke University Press, 1994). Their emphasis is not so much on televisual texts, but on placing television within the context of a technological metaphysics.

12. Jean-Louis Comolli, "Technique and Ideology: Camera, Perspective, Depth of Field," trans. Diana Matias, in *Movies and Methods*, vol. 2, ed. Bill Nichols (Berkeley and Los Angeles: University of California Press, 1985), 40–57.

13. Brian Winston, *Media Technology and Society: A History: From the Telegraph to the Internet* (London: Routledge, 1998), 6–7.

14. The U.S. Department of Commerce Bureau of Economic Analysis National Income and Product Accounts Table 2.5.5. Personal Consumption Expenditures by type of Expenditures *(http://www .bea.gov/national/nipaweb/TableView.asp?SelectedTable=73& FirstYear=2002&LastYear=2004&Freq=Qtr.* Accessed Jan 9, 2009) reports that in 2006 Americans spent $9.3 billion on admissions to motion picture theaters. Compare this to the $90.1 billion spent on video and audio goods or the $17.2 billion on spectator sports. Consumers spent more than half as much ($5.4 billion) for the repair of their radios and television as they paid for movie tickets.

15. Susan Sontag adopts the term *cinephilia* to refer to an attitude that is no longer possible; see Sontag, "A Century of Cinema," in *Where the Stress Falls* (New York: Picador, 2002), 117.

16. See Gene F. Jankowski and David C. Fuchs, *Television Today and Tomorrow: It Won't Be What You Think* (New York: Oxford University Press, 1995).

17. Robert C. Allen, ed., *Channels of Discourse, Reassembled*, 2nd ed. (Chapel Hill: University of North Carolina Press, 1987); Patricia Mellencamp, ed., *Logics of Television* (Bloomington: Indiana University Press, 1990); Horace Newcomb, ed., *Television: The Critical View*, 7th ed. (New York: Oxford University Press, 2006).

18. Toby Miller, "Turn Off TV Studies!" *Cinema Journal* 45, no. 1 (2005): 98–101.

19. Lynn Spigel, "TV's Next Season," *Cinema Journal* 45, no. 1 (2005): 83–90, refers to "umbrella terms like new media studies and visual culture studies."

20. Paul A. Cantor, *Gilligan Unbound: Pop Culture in the Age of Globalization* (Lanham, MD: Rowman and Littlefield, 2001).

21. Ibid., 27.

22. Along with Clough and Dienst, Bernard Stiegler's dialogue with Jacques Derrida, *Echographies of Television: Filmed Interviews* (Malden, MA: Blackwell Publishers Ltd., 2002), also offers a profoundly philosophical approach to television. Although not imbued with high philosophical rhetoric, Stephen Johnson's *Everything Bad Is Good for You* (New York: Riverhead Books, 2005) argues for a positive and intellectually complex view of television narrative.

23. Jerzy Kosinski, *Being There* (New York: Bantam Books, 1972).

24. Charlotte Brundson, "Television: Aesthetics and Audiences," in *Logics of Television*, edited by Patricia Mellencamp (Bloomington: Indiana University Press, 1990), 59–72.

25. Philosopher and anthropologist Thomas de Zengotita, in *Mediated: How the Media Shapes Your World and the Way You Live in It* (New York: Bloomsbury, 2005), mounts a critique of the mass narcissism resulting from a media-saturated world that reflects a field of representation packaged as sheer entertainment and customized to flatter whatever we want to be. Not unlike Jean Baudrillard's accusation of "obscenity" in his "The Ecstasy of Communication," De Zengotita goes beyond publicity and celebrity as modes of performance and considers, without naive condemnation, the advent of reality TV, blogs, and iPods as evidence of a shift in human consciousness toward an increasingly impenetrable and inescapable solipsism.

Chapter 2

1. George W. S. Trow, *Within the Context of No Context* (New York: Atlantic Monthly Press, 1997), 82.

2. Ibid., 119.

3. Marie Winn foregrounds the metaphor of addiction in the title of her book, *The Plug-In Drug: Television, Computers, and Family Life* (New York: Penguin, 2002). Winn's book, like others, focuses its critique on what television does to children.

4. William F. Baker and George Dessart, *Down the Tube: An Inside Account of the Failure of American Television* (New York: Basic Books, 1999), xiii.

5. Trow, *Within the Context of No Context*, 45.

6. Jerry Mander, *Four Arguments for the Elimination of Television* (New York: Quill, 1978); Neil Postman, *Amusing Ourselves to Death: Public Discourse in the Age of Show Business* (New York: Penguin, 1986); David Marc, *Bonfire of the Humanities: Television, Subliteracy and Long-Term Memory Loss* (Syracuse, NY: Syracuse University Press, 1995), Todd Gitlin, *Media Unlimited: How the Torrent of Images and Sounds Overwhelms Our Lives* (New York: Henry Holt, 2001); Pierre Bourdieu, *On Television*, trans. Priscilla Parkhurst Ferguson (New York: New Press, 1998); George Ritzer, *The Globalization*

of *Nothing* (Thousand Oaks, CA: Sage, 2003); George Ritzer, *The McDonaldization of Society* (Thousand Oaks, CA.: Sage, 2003).

7. Kurt Vonnegut, *Timequake* (New York: G. P. Putnam's Sons, 1997), 17–18.
8. John Hartley, *Uses of Television* (London: Routledge, 1999), 206.
9. Vonnegut, *Timequake*, quoted in John Hartley, *Uses of Television*.
10. Gore Vidal, *Live from Golgotha: The Gospel According to Gore Vidal* (New York: Penguin, 1992), 15.
11. Kathleen Fitzpatrick, *The Anxiety of Obsolescence: The American Novel in the Age of Television* (Nashville, TN: Vanderbilt University Press, 2006), 5, 2.
12. Joyce Maynard, *At Home in the World: A Memoir* (USA: Picador, 1998), 95.
13. The AAP recommends "10 things parents can do" to develop positive viewing habits, including setting limits, watching with your child, and providing other options such as "playing, reading, activities with family, friends or neighbors and learning a hobby, sport, instrument, or an art"; see American Association of Pediatrics website (*http://www.aap.org/healthtopics/mediause.cfm*, accessed January 9, 2008). Depictions of television used as a substitute for correct parenting are often shown as both disastrous and comic, as in the colonized minds of Martin Tupper (Brian Benben) in the TV series *Dream On* (1990, HBO; 1995, Fox) and Jim Carrey's lead character in Stiller's *The Cable Guy* (1996).
14. Stan Brakhage refused to allow his work to be released on videotape or DVD during his lifetime because of the mind-altering technology of the cathode ray. (Personal interview with Jon Wagner, 1990, Boulder, Colorado). He did, however, authorize a DVD collection to be distributed after his death, which occurred in 2003.
15. Meaghan Morris, "Banality in Cultural Studies," in *Logics of Television*, ed. Patricia Mellencamp (Bloomington: Indiana University Press, 1990), 14.
16. Ibid., 19.
17. Ibid., 14.
18. For example, in Antononi's film about television, *Professione: Reporter*, television reporter Jack Nicholson assumes another identity on a whim. By the end of the film, he has been killed for it, but the film itself is sublimely indifferent to his fate; the camera tracks past the murder scene, into the town square, and then travels on

with its mission, suggesting that subjectivity itself may be obsolete. Antonioni's *Zabriski Point*, yet another film with exploding television sets, ends with the apocalyptic image of a house thoroughly blown up in the desert. It's apocalyptic but without resolution. The scene has now been set for the posthuman.

19. Susan Sontag, "A Century of Cinema," in *Where the Stress Falls* (New York: Picador, 2002), 117.

20. Ibid.

21. Robert Thompson, "Too Many Cooks Don't Always Spoil the Broth: An Authorship Study of *St. Elsewhere*," in *Critical Approaches to Television*, ed. Leah R. Vande Berg, Lawrence A. Wenner, and Bruce E. Gronbeck (Boston: Houghton Mifflin, 1998), 78; hereafter, page numbers cited parenthetially in the text.

22. Jane Feuer, Paul Kerr, and Tise Vahimagi, eds., *MTM "Quality Television"* (London: BFI, 1984) also discusses Grant Tinker's production company MTM in auteurist terms. Jim Collins, "Television and Postmodernism," in *Media Studies: A Reader*, 2nd ed., ed. Paul Marris and Sue Thornham (New York: New York University Press, 2000), 375–84, analyzes the appeal of David Lynch's *Twin Peaks* to a microculture of elite liberal cinephiles yearning for auteurist signatures in their television. As John Thornton Caldwell, "Boutique; Designer Television/Auteurist Spin Doctoring," in *Televisuality: Style, Crisis, and Authority in American Television* (New Brunswick, NJ: Rutgers University Press, 1995), 105, observes, "the whole point, however, is not to argue over which creative craft dominates television," since the auteurism of directors like Lynch and producers like Tinker is an "excessively intentional" and "conceptual mytholog[y]" servicing corporate-sponsored "counter-programmed sensitivity."

23. A significant early variation on this approach is David Morley's 1970 study of audience reactions to selected episodes of the British current affairs series *Nationwide*. Inflected by a concern for subcultural resistance, Morley is working in the British cultural studies tradition, identifying oppositional, negotiated, and dominant readings.

Chapter 3

1. As Aldous Huxley, *The Perennial Philosophy* (New York: Harper and Brothers, 1945), posits, "That most popular and influential of all recent inventions, the radio, is nothing but a conduit through which

pre-fabricated din can flow into our home. And this din goes far deeper, of course, than the eardrums. It penetrates the mind, filling it with a babble of distractions, blasts of corybantic or sentimental music, continually repeated doses of drama that bring no catharsis, but usually create a craving for daily or even hourly emotional enemas."

2. Robert C. Allen, "Introduction to Second Edition, More Talk About TV," in *Channels of Discourse, Reassembled*, 2nd ed., ed. Robert C. Allen (Chapel Hill: University of North Carolina Press, 1987), 1–30.
3. Todd Gitlin, "Prime Time Ideology: The Hegemonic Process in Television Entertainment," in *Television: The Critical View*, 5th ed., ed. Horace Newcomb (New York: Oxford University Press, 1994), 533.
4. See, for example, *Adbusters* (*http://www.adbusters.org*).
5. Mimi White, "Ideological Analysis and Television," in *Channels of Discourse, Reassembled*, 2nd ed., ed. Robert C. Allen (Chapel Hill: University of North Carolina Press, 1987), 161.
6. Ibid.
7. Eileen R. Meehan, "Why We Don't Count: The Commodity Audience," in *Logics of Television*, ed. Patricia Mellencamp (Bloomington: Indiana University Press, 1990), 127.
8. Dallas Smythe, "On the Audience Commodity and Its Work," in *Media and Cultural Studies: Keyworks*, ed. Meenakshi Gigi Durham and Douglas M. Kellner (Oxford: Blackwell, 2001), 253–79, argues that the time consumers spend working to buy products, the time spent to select products, and the time spent working to purchase newspapers and televisions, which exposes them to advertising, is all work and time that benefits advertisers and not consumers. It "makes a mockery of free time and leisure" (272). He recommends that "the most important way by which consumers can cope with commodities and advertising is to limit the time spent per purchase in thinking about what to buy" (268).
9. Gitlin, "Prime Time Ideology," 533.
10. White, "Ideological Analysis," 171.
11. Scott McLemee, "After the Last Intellectual," *Bookforum* 14, no. 3 (2007): 15.
12. Budd Schulberg, *What Makes Sammy Run?* (New York: Random House, 1941).

13. Russell Jacoby, *The Last Intellectuals: American Culture in the Age of Academe* (New York: Basic Books, 1987).

14. McLemee, "After the Last Intellectual," 15.

15. As Terry Eagleton, *The Function of Criticism* (London: Verso, 2005), 102, posits, "One is reminded of the anthropological tale of the tiger which regularly disrupted a tribal ceremony by leaping into its midst; after a while the tiger was incorporated into the ritual."

16. White, "Ideological Analysis," 162.

17. Unauthored piece. *People* (July 19, 2002): 17. Peter Taylor is quoted.

18. Michel Foucault, *The History of Sexuality*, vol. 1, trans. Robert Hurley (New York: Vintage Books, 1980), 36.

19. Althusser calls these mechanisms "ideological state apparatuses" in his essay "Ideology and Ideological State Apparatuses (Notes towards an Investigation)," in *Lenin and Philosophy and Other Essays*, trans. Ben Brewster (New York: Monthly Review Press, 1971), 127–86. He employs Lacan's notion of *méconnaissance*, or imaginary misrecognition of an ideal ego in the mirror stage, to construct an ideological imaginary exploited—indeed, created—by the symbolic.

20. Note how Glick's Jewish identity has here been displaced by a vaguely Italian ethnicity.

21. Richard Schickel, "Rerunning *Film Noir*," *Wilson Quarterly* 31, no. 3 (2007): 36–43; hereafter, page numbers cited parentheticaly in the text.

22. Paul Schrader, "Notes on *Film Noir*," *Film Comment* 8, no. 1 (1972): 8.

23. Inappropriate uses of classical music are often a marker of televisual degeneracy. In Stanley Donan's *It's Always Fair Weather* (1955), Franz Liszt's *Hungarian Rhapsody* is used to sell detergent. Television's paradoxical relationship to politics can also be seen in John Ford's *Last Hurrah* (1958), in which Spencer Tracy plays an Irish mayor whose backroom—though authentically working-class—political machine comes undone partly because of his ignorance of and contempt for television's power.

24. The films of Rock Hudson, Doris Day, and Tony Randall come to mind, as does Billy Wilder's *The Apartment* (1960). On television, the Darrin Stephens character (played by both Dick York and Dick Sargent) on *Bewitched* is relevant; currently the series *Mad Men* addresses the early 1960s through the figure of the ad man.

Chapter 4

1. Hans Magnus Enzensberger, "From *The Consciousness Industry*," trans. Stuart Hood, in *Video Culture: A Critical Examination*, ed. John G. Hanhardt (Layton, UT: Peregrine Smith Books/Visual Studies Workshop Press, 1986), 96–123.

2. Raymond Williams's work has provided an influential model of this ambivalent form of cultural studies for Enzenberger and other theorists. Of the advertising on which television relies, Williams, in "Advertising: The Magic System," in *The Cultural Studies Reader*, ed. Simon During (London: Routledge, 1993), 336, writes, "It's perfectly true to say that modern capitalism could not function without it."

3. Enzensberger, "Constituents," 97.

4. Jean-François Lyotard, in "Answering the Question: What Is Postmodernism?" in *The Postmodern Condition: A Report on Knowledge*, trans. Geoff Bennington and Brian Massumi (Manchester: Manchester University Press, 1984), 108, notes that "capitalism inherently possess the capacity to derealize familiar objects, social roles, and institutions to such a degree that the so-called realistic representations can no longer evoke reality except as nostalgia or mockery, as an occasion for suffering rather than for satisfaction."

5. Enzensberger, "Constituents," 108.

6. Jean Baudrillard, "Requiem for the Media," trans. Charles Levin, in Hanhardt, ed., *Video Culture: A Critical Examination*, 124; hereafter, page numbers cited parenthetically in the text.

7. David Bordwell and Noel Carroll, eds., *Post-Theory: Reconstructing Film Studies* (Madison: University of Wisconsin Press, 1996). A concentrated example of their contempt is the use of the acronyms SLAB (for Saussure, Lacan, Althusser, and Barthes) and SLAG (for Saussure, Lacan, Althusser, and Gramsci).

8. David Bordwell, "Contemporary Film Studies and the Vicissitudes of Grand Theory," in Bordwell and Carroll, eds., *Post-Theory*, 11, 3–36.

9. Jean Baudrillard, "The Ecstasy of Communication," trans. John Johnson, in *The Anti-Aesthetic: Essays on Postmodern Culture*, ed. Hal Foster (Port Townsend, WA: Bay Press, 1983), 130.

10. We'll save ourselves by selling ourselves. Like "pornography," the depiction of prostitutes, we will turn ourselves into graphic signs and be known. As Baudrillard, in "The Ecstasy of Communication," 130, notes, "Obscenity begins precisely when there is no more spectacle,

no more scene, when all becomes transparence and immediate visibility, when everything is exposed to the harsh and inexorable light of information and communication."

11. Guy Debord, *Society of the Spectacle*, trans. Donald Nicholson-Smith (New York: Zone Books, 1995), 146.

12. Arthur Rimbaud, "Letter to Paul Demeny," in *Rimbaud Complete* (New York: The Modern Library, 2002), 366–67.

Chapter 5

1. Jerzy Kosinski, *Being There* (New York: Bantam Books, 1972), 79.

2. Jerzy Kosinski, "A Nation of Videots" (interview by David Sohn), in *Television: The Critical View*, 2nd ed., ed. Horace Newcomb (New York: Oxford University Press, 1979), 345.

3. Roger Ebert, review of *Cinema Paradiso*, *Chicago Sun-Times*, March 16, 1996.

4. Stanley Cavell, "The Fact of Television," in *Video Culture: A Critical Examination*, ed. John G. Hanhardt (Layton, UT: Peregrine Smith Books / Visual Studies Workshop Press, 1986), 192–218; Jean Baudrillard, "Requiem for the Media," trans. Charles Levin, in Hanhardt, ed., *Video Culture: A Critical Examination*, Horace Newcomb, ed., *Television: The Critical View*, 3rd ed. (New York: Oxford University Press, 1982), 124–43. Charlotte Brunsdon, "Television: Aesthetics and Audiences," in *Logics of Television*, ed. Patricia Mellencamp (Bloomington: Indiana University Press, 1990), 59–72.

5. Jacques Derrida, "Linguistics & Grammatology," in *Of Grammatology* (Baltimore: Johns Hopkins University Press, 1979), 41.

6. Jean Baudrillard, "The Ecstasy of Communication," trans. John Johnson, in *The Anti-Aesthetic: Essays on Postmodern Culture*, ed. Hal Foster (Port Townsend, Wa: Bay Press, 1983), 130.

7. Cavell, "The Fact of Television," 205.

8. Of this state of siege, of the invalid (in the sense of "not valid") world held at bay by the chronic surveillance of its invalid citizens, Paul Virilio, "The Last Vehicle," trans. David Antal, in *Looking Back on the End of the World*, ed. Dietmar Kamper and Christoph Wulf (New York: Semiotext(e), 1989), 199, posits, "[R]elief [is] no longer the reality. From now on the latter is concealed in the flatness of pictures, the transferred representations. It conditions the return to the house's state of siege, to the cadaver-like inertia of the interactive

dwelling, this residential cell that has left the extension of the habitat behind it and whose most important piece of furniture is the seat [*siege*], the ergonomic armchair of the handicapped's motor, and—who knows?—the bed, a canopy bed for the infirm voyeur, a divan for being dreamt of without dreaming, a bench for being circulated without circulating."

9. Robert Pinsky, "To Television," *New Yorker*, August 10, 1998, p. 34.

Chapter 6

1. Roland Barthes, *Camera Lucida: Reflections on Photography*, trans. Richard Howard (New York: Hill and Wang, 1981).
2. Roland Barthes, *Writing Degree Zero*, trans. Annette Lavers and Colin Smith (New York: Hill and Wang, 1977).
3. Maurice Blanchot, *The Writing of the Disaster*, trans. Ann Smock (New York: New Press, 1998).
4. Barthes, *Camera Lucida*, 72.
5. Theoretical approaches to 9/11 include three in a Verso series published on the first anniversary of the attacks: Jean Baudrillard, *The Spirit of Terrorism: And Requiem for the Twin Towers*, trans. Chris Turner (London: Verso, 2002); Paul Virilio, *Ground Zero:* trans. Chris Turner (London: Verso, 2002); and Slavoj Žižek, *Welcome to the Desert of the Real: Five Essays on September 11 and Related Dates* (London: Verso, 2002). See also Giovanna Borradori, *Philosophy in a Time of Terror: Dialogues with Jürgen Habermas and Jacques Derrida* (Chicago: University of Chicago Press, 2004).
6. Jean Baudrillard, "L'Esprit Du Terrorisme" [The Spirit of Terrorism], trans. Donovan Hohn, *Harpers* 304, no. 1821 (February 2002): 13–18.
7. Mary Ann Doane, "Information, Crisis, Catastrophe," in *Logics of Television*, ed. Patricia Mellencamp (Bloomington: Indiana University Press, 1990), 222–39.
8. This is related to Nick Browne's "supertext" and Raymond Williams's concept of "flow."
9. Mellencamp, "TV, Time and Catastrophe, or Beyond the Pleasure Principle of Television," in *Logics of Television*, ed. Patricia Mellencamp (Bloomington: Indiana University Press, 1990), 240.
10. Cathy Scott-Clark and Adrian Levy, "Fast Forward into Trouble," *Guardian Weekend* (June 14, 2003): 20. Another movie that charts

the changes modern civilization can bring to an idyllic way of life is Nikita Mikhalkov's *Close to Eden* (1999). When a peasant farmer leaves the inner Mongolian steppe for the big city to obtain birth control (Chinese law forbids him and his wife from having another child), he brings home a TV, which proves even more effective than birth control.

11. Arthur Kroker and Marilouise Kroker, "Panic Sex in America," in *Body Invaders: Panic Sex in America* (New York: St. Martin's Press, 1987), 19.

12. Umberto Eco, "Apocalyptic and Integrated Intellectuals: Mass Communications and Theories of Mass Culture," trans. Jenny Condie. In *Apocalypse Postponed: Essays by Umberto Eco*, ed. Robert Lumley (Bloomington: Indiana University Press, 1994), 17.

13. Ibid., 27.

14. Jacques Derrida, "No Apocalypse, Not Now (full speed away, seven missiles, seven missives)," *Diacritics* 14, no. 2 (1984): 20–31.

15. Frank Kermode, *The Sense of an Ending: Studies in the Theory of Fiction* (Oxford: Oxford University Press, 2000).

16. Peter Brooks, *Reading for the Plot: Design and Intention in Narrative* (New York: Alfred A. Knopf, 1984), examines the literary drive to an end from a Freudian perspective.

17. Chuck Barris, *Confessions of a Dangerous Mind: An Unauthorized Autobiography* (New York: Hyperion, 2002).

18. Umberto Eco, "The Phantom of Neo-TV: The Debate on Fellini's *Ginger and Fred*," trans. Jenny Condie, in *Apocalypse Postponed: Essays by Umberto Eco*, ed. Robert Lumley (Bloomington: Indiana University Press, 1994), 110.

19. The couch potato is simply a new version of the bookworm, a figure that Mitchell Stephens discusses in *The Rise of the Image, The Fall of the Word* (Oxford: Oxford University Press, 1998). The greatest extensions of this figure are the vestigial figure at the end of Paul Virilio, "The Last Vehicle," trans. David Antal, in *Looking Back on the End of the World*, ed. Dietmar Kamper and Christoph Wulf, 106–19 (New York: Semiotext(e), 1989), or the empaths or precogs in Steven Spielberg's *Minority Report* (2002). Max Headroom's blipvert victim watches television, but he might just as well be reading novels.

20. This is the preferred designation of a European—particularly French—politics.

21. Thomas Pynchon, *Gravity's Rainbow* (New York: Penguin Books, 1987). There has never been a film of a Pynchon novel, but there has been a television mini-series of his *V: A Novel* (Philadelphia: Lippencott, 1963). It is not that Pynchon is unable to be visualized, but his work seems counter to cinematic logic.

22. Lyotard, "Answering the Question: What Is Postmodernism?" trans. Régis Durand, in *The Postmodern Condition: A Report on Knowledge*, trans. Geoff Bennington and Brian Massumi.

23. André Bazin, "An Aesthetic of Reality: Neorealism: Cinematic Realism and the Italian School of the Liberation)," in *What Is Cinema?* vol. 2, trans. Hugh Gray (Berkeley and Los Angeles: University of California Press, 1971), 21.

24. In *Dutch: A Memoir of Ronald Reagan* (New York: HarperCollins, 2000), author Edmund Morris has to resort to creating a fictional character to tell the biographic story of Ronald Reagan. For Morris, it became a search for a man who wasn't there.

25. In John Badham's *WarGames* (1983), the computer responds to the question of whether the game of thermonuclear war is real or simulated with: What difference does it make? In David Fincher's *The Game* (1997) and David Cronenberg's *eXistenZ* (1999), characters are never sure when the game they are playing is over.

26. Jean Baudrillard, *Seduction*, trans. Brian Singer (New York: St. Martin's Press, 1991).

27. While most characters refuse an opportunity to leave the text behind, the characters in the wildly popular Christian novels of Tim LaHaye and Jerry Jenkins's *Left Behind* series struggle to do just that. The series begins as all the "saved" instantly vanish in the Rapture, leaving little textual residue. The main characters are those "left behind" who seek, to varying degrees, to join their former loved ones in being removed from the text (the archive of human history).

28. Slavoj Žižek, *The Sublime Object of Ideology* (London: Verso, 1989).

Chapter 7

1. Mary Ann Doane, "Information, Crisis, Catastrophe," in *Logics of Television*, ed. Patricia Mellencamp (Bloomington: Indiana University Press, 1990), 222–39. Patricia Mellenkamp, "TV, Time and Catastrophe, or Beyond the Pleasure Principle of Television," in Mellencamp, ed., *Logics of Television*, 240–66.

2. Woody Allen's auteurist oeuvre often replays the cultural antagonism between New York and Los Angeles, frequently layering that
   geographical difference onto the difference between serious film-
   making and other lesser forms of cultural production. Allen plays a
   successful television writer who longs to be a real, serious writer in
   Manhattan (1979). In *Crimes and Misdemeanors* (1989), Alan Alda
   plays Lester, a sold-out television comic turned television producer.
   His success and self-satisfaction figure as a constant rebuke to Allen character's (Clifford Stern), a documentary filmmaker. To his
   great frustration, Clifford is coerced into directing a filmed profile of
   Lester, the man who represents everything he repudiates. *Annie Hall*
   (1977) famously articulates Allen's vision of an artistically legitimate
   New York and a debased Los Angeles, the latter nevertheless managing to casually seduce the object of Allen's affections.

3. Alex McNeil, *Total Television: A Comprehensive Guide to Programming from 1948–1980* (New York: Penguin Books, 1980), 127, lists a
   first telecast of August 10, 1948. The Internet Movie Database shows
   a last iteration of the show in 1989–1990 (*http://www.imdb.com/title/
   tt1007204/.* Accessed January 19, 2008).

4. For a feminist critique of *Queen for a Day*, see Susan Douglas, *Where
   the Girls Are: Growing Up Female with the Mass Media* (New York:
   Three Rivers Press, 1995), 32–33.

5. Both Charles Barr, '"They Think It's All Over': The Dramatic Legacy
   of Live Television," in *Big Picture, Small Screen: The Relations between
   Film and Television*, ed. John Hill and Martin McLoone (Bloomington:
   Indiana University Press, 2003), 47–75, and Jane Feuer, "The Concept
   of Live Television: Ontology as Ideology," in *Regarding Television:
   Critical Approaches—An Anthology*, ed. Ann Kaplan (Los Angeles:
   University Publications of America/American Film Institute, 1983),
   112–22, comment on Bazin.

6. André Bazin, *What Is Cinema?* vol. 1, trans. Hugh Gray (Berkeley:
   University of California Press, 1967), 29.

7. Jean Renoir, quoted in Barr, '"They Think It's All Over,'" 49.

8. Barr, '"They Think It's All Over,'" 50.

9. Feuer, "The Concept of Live Television," 15; hereafter, page numbers
   cited parenthetically in the text.

10. Williams, Mark, "real-time fairy tales: Cinema Prefiguring Digital
    Anxiety," in *New Media: Theories and Practices of Digitextuality*, ed.

Anna Everett and John T. Caldwell (New York: Routledge, 2003), 163.

11. Sean Cubitt, *Timeshift: On Video Culture* (New York: Routledge, 1991), 30–31.

12. Feuer had already critiqued this type of technological determinism when it was voiced by Herbert Zettl: '"While in film each frame is actually a static image, the television image is continually moving, very much in the manner of the Bergsonian *durée*. The scanning beam is constantly trying to complete an always incomplete image. Even if the image on the screen seems at rest, it is structurally in motion. Each television frame is always in a state of becoming'" (Zettl, quoted in Feuer, "The Concept of Live Television," 13).

13. Martin Heidegger's "The Question Concerning Technology, in *The Question Concerning Technology, and Other Essays*, trans. William Lovitt (New York: Harper and Row, 1977), 3–35, argues that the technology responsible for the destruction of a humanist metaphysics inevitably strives to become metaphysical itself.

14. Nick Browne, "The Political Economy of the Television (Super) Text," *Quarterly Review of Film Studies* 9, no. 3 (1984): 174–82.

15. See *http://www.jumptheshark.com*. Some of the more common categories include: when a character gives birth, hits puberty, gets married, moves to a new city, or dies; when a new actor plays an established character; or whenever Ted McGinley joins the cast.

16. Barr, '"They Think It's All Over,'" 58.

17. Feuer, "The Concept of Live Television," discusses liveness used to create a family. See also Lynn Spigel, *Make Room for TV: Television and the Family Ideal in Postwar America* (Chicago: University of Chicago Press, 1992).

18. Fredric Jameson, *Postmodernism or, The Cultural Logic of Late Capitalism* (Durham, NC: Duke University Press, 1991), 16; hereafter, page numbers cited parenthetically in the text.

19. Jean Baudrillard, "The Ecstasy of Communication," trans. John Johnson, in *The Anti-Aesthetic: Essays on Postmodern Culture*, ed. Hal Foster (Port Townsend, WA: Bay Press, 1983), 126–34, describes television as the perfect embodiment of postmodernism, a medium that obscenely disables the imaginary from producing a self through or as a mirror. "But today the scene and mirror no longer exist," he notes; "instead, there is a screen and [a] network" (126). Meaghan

Morris, "Banality in Cultural Studies," in Mellencamp, ed., *Logics of Television*, 14–43, critiques Baudrillard's *De la seduction* and *Les strategies fatales* and expands this sense of fatal disability, of a viral overload of images and information in an "all-pervasive present" to include nostalgia:

> On the other hand, and even though there is strictly no past and no future in Baudrillard's system, he uses "fatality" as both a nostalgic and a futuristic term for invoking a classical critical value, *discrimination* (redefined as a senseless but still rule-governed principle of selectiveness). "Fatality" is nostalgic in the sense that it invokes in the text, for the present, an "aristocratic" ideal of maintaining an elite, arbitrary, and avowedly artificial order. It is futuristic because Baudrillard suggests that in an age of overload, rampant banality, and catastrophe (which have become at this stage equivalents of each other), the last Pascalian wager may be to bet on the return, in the present, of what can only be a simulacrum of the past (19–20).

20. Mellencamp, "TV, Time and Catastrophe," 240.
21. *Your Show of Shows* featured Carl Reiner, who himself would adopt a role not unlike that of Stanley "King" Kaiser on *The Dick Van Dyke Show* sitcom as the elusive and neurotic star of the fictional *Alan Brady Show*.
22. Similar attitudes can be found in Robert Zemeckis's *Back to the Future* (1985) and Francis Ford Coppola's *Peggy Sue Got Married* (1986).
23. Karl Marx, "On Greek Art in Its Time from a Contribution to the Critique of Political Economy," trans. Nahum Issac Stone, in *The Critical Tradition*, 2nd ed., ed. David H. Richter (Boston: Bedford Books, 1998), 393.
24. Ibid.

Chapter 8

1. Hélène Cixous, "The Laugh of the Medusa," trans. Keith and Paula Cowan, in *Critical Theory since 1965*, ed. Hazard Adams and Leroy Searle (Tallahassee: Florida State University Press, 1986), 309–20.
2. Andreas Huyssen, *After the Great Divide: Modernism, Mass Culture, Postmodernism* (Bloomington: Indiana University Press, 1986), 53.

3. Jeffrey Sconce, *Haunted Media: Electronic Presence from Telegraphy to Television* (Durham, NC: Duke University Press), 14–18, 58.

4. Ibid., 170.

5. Spike Lee's *Bamboozled* (2000) substantially replays *Network*, with race approximating the use of gender in the earlier film. In Lee's film, audiences are similarly impressionable, to the point of showing up for tapings in blackface, demanding fried chicken and chanting racially charged slogans on cue. See also the depictions of Lonesome Larry Rhodes's audience in Elia Kazan's *A Face in the Crowd* (1957).

6. E. Ann Kaplan's "Feminist Criticism and Television," in *Channels of Discourse, Reassembled*, 2nd ed., ed. Robert C. Allen (Chapel Hill: University of North Carolina Press, 1987), 211–53, gathers a sense of the feminine model and how it has pervaded television and the problem resulting from television's defusion throughout the culture at large. As her categorization and discussion of types of traditional feminist criticism of television—bourgeois, Marxist, radical—show, however, this defusion has not proved to be a radical challenge to traditional male power structures.

7. Sigmund Freud, "Femininity," trans. James Strachy, in *New Introductory Lectures*, ed. James Strachey (New York: W. W. Norton, 1964), 119.

8. Laura Mulvey, "Visual Pleasure and Narrative Cinema," in *Visual and Other Pleasures* (London: Macmillan, 1989), 14–26.

9. The famous network executive Brandon Tartikoff once said that after seeing *Network*, "I knew exactly what I wanted to be when I grew up—which was, of course, to be a woman"; *In-Between*, TNT Network, October 19, 1993.

10. Philip Levine, "Animals Are Passing from Our Lives," in *Selected Poems* (New York: Atheneum, 1984), 36.

11. Tania Modleski, "The Search for Tomorrow in Today's Soap Operas," in *Loving with a Vengeance: Mass-Produced Fantasies for Women* (New York: Methuen, 1982), 102; hereafter, page numbers cited parentheticaly in the text.

12. British cultural theorists who discuss this issue include John Ellis, John Fiske, and Stuart Hall.

13. Hal Hartley's notion of bardic television and Henry Jenkins's consideration of fan-based cultures attempt in different ways to redeem this style of reading.

14. Robert C. Allen, "Reader-Oriented Criticism and Television," in Allen, ed., *Channels of Discourse*, 112.
15. Robert C. Allen, "The Guiding Light: Soap Opera as Economic Product and Cultural Document," in *Television: The Critical View*, 4th ed., ed. Horace Newcomb (New York: Oxford University Press, 1987), 141–63.
16. To take Modleski's observation further, one could say that camp and its relationship to gay culture is in the vanguard of not just programming such as *Will and Grace* and *Queer Eye for the Straight Guy*, but of all popular culture in the twenty-first century.
17. A dominant trope of much reality programming, for instance, is a pandering to class aspirations. Contestants on programs like *The Apprentice* or *The Bachelor* may ostensibly seek a job or a mate, but the programs spend the most energy on displaying real estate, cars, luxury suites, Jacuzzi tubs, jewelry, evening gowns, and clichéd floral arrangements. You don't have to be a woman to want those.
18. Eve Sedgwick, *Epistemology of the Closet* (Berkeley and Los Angeles: University of California Press, 1990) addresses "heterosexual panic."
19. Modleski herself is aware of the bland ironies of a feminist co-opted by the feminized man. The appropriation of feminist studies by men who identify themselves as feminist does not necessarily imply a progressive diffusion of the field, but a leveling of issues into the hands of those who have always governed discourse. See Tania Modeski, *Feminism without Women: Culture and Criticism in a "Postfeminist" Age* (New York: Routledge, 1991).
20. Robin Wood, "Ideology, Genre, Auteur," in *Film Theory and Criticism: Introductory Readings* 5th ed., ed. Leo Braudy and Marshall Cohen (New York: Oxford University Press, 1999), 670.
21. Lynne Joyrich, "Critical and Textual Hypermasculinity," in *Logics of Television*, ed. Patricia Mellencamp (Bloomington: Indiana University Press, 1990), 156–72.
22. Leo Bersani, *Homos: The Straight Mind and Other Essays* (Cambridge, MA: Harvard University Press, 1995), 41; hereafter, page numbers cited parenthetically in the text.
23. Tom Green perpetuated the genre of castration when he had a cancerous testicle removed on *The Tom Green Show*. Later in the episode, he carried the preserved gonad around in a bottle and showed

it to unsuspectingly friends and family. This may complete the logic of *Candid Camera*.

24. Another reporter/anchor wannabe is the title character in Annabel Jankel and Rocky Morton's *Max Headroom* (1985), and this goal is accomplished by his being a digital entity. When women get involved in television newsroom politics—in such films as *Network*, James L. Brooks's *Broadcast News* (1987), Gus Van Sant's *To Die For* (1995), Jon Avnet's *Up Close and Personal* (1996), and Frank Oz's *The Stepford Wives* (2004)—more serious consequences, such as childlessness and isolation, murder, death, and body-snatching, ensue.

25. Guy Debord, *Society of the Spectacle*, trans. Donald Nicholson-Smith (New York: Zone Books), 1995.

Chapter 9

1. Toni Morrison, "Clinton as the First Black President," *New Yorker*, October 5, 1998, 31.

2. Ibid., 31.

3. The rumor that Clinton had fathered an illegitimate interracial child seems almost inevitable, as does the assertion by his enemies that the problem wasn't that he had sex out of wedlock, or that he had sex with a black woman, but that he had failed to pay child support, in the manner of a stereotypical ghetto father. For the Republican presidential contender John McCain—attempting to appeal to a more conservative southern audience—the slur implied in a rumor that he had fathered a black child out-of-wedlock and that he and his wife had then "adopted" the child hinged entirely on the possibility that he had had sex with a black woman. In both cases, presidential politics became lurid melodrama.

4. See Laura Mulvey, *Visual and Other Pleasures* (London: Macmillan, 1989).

5. See Robert Bly, *Iron John: A Book about Men* (Reading, MA: Addison-Wesley, 1990); Leo Braudy, *From Chivalry to Terrorism: War and the Changing Nature of Masculinity* (New York: Vintage, 2005); Susan Jefford, *Hard Bodies: Hollywood Masculinity in the Reagan Era* (New Brunswick, NJ: Rutgers University Press, 1994); Lynne Joyrich, "Critical and Textual Hypermasculinity," in *Logics of Television*, ed. Patricia Mellencamp (Bloomington: Indiana University Press, 1990), 156–72; Eve Kosofsky Sedgwick, *Epistemology of*

the Closet (Berkeley and Los Angeles: University of California Press, 1990); Kaja Silverman, *Male Subjectivity at the Margins* (New York: Routledge, 1992).

6. See, among others, Walter Hill's *48 Hrs.* (1982); John Landis's *Trading Places* (1983); Richard Donner's four *Lethal Weapon* films (1987, 1988, 1989, 1992); Costa-Gavras's *Mad City* (1997); Jerry Zucker's *Ghost* (1990); John McTiernan's *Rollerball* (2002); and David Fincher's *Fight Club* (1999).

7. *Strange Days* is set in Los Angeles in 1999, the year of *Bulworth*'s release. The year is also a symbol of potentially apocalyptic millennial shifts. Angry, impoverished, disenfranchised African Americans are ready to burn the city as riot police patrol the streets. But Lenny Nero (Ralph Fiennes) could care less, concerned only with making sleezy deals in illegal "playback chips." These chips can replay raw human experience such as rape and snuff sequences recorded directly from the cerebral cortex. *Strange Days* plays as a millennial meditation on the nature of voyeurism and the narcotic that is apparently cinema itself. Angela Bassett's Mace is the moral lodestone of the movie, a black-belt single-mom cop who rescues Lenny from his impotent turpitude. He emerges, with her grace, as a creature of existential angst whose self-conscious despair promises eventual redemption.

8. Christine Gledhill, "Recent Developments in Feminist Film Criticism," in *Re-Vision: Essays in Feminist Film Criticism*, ed. Mary Ann Doane, Patricia Mellencamp and Linda Williams (Los Angeles: University Publications of America, 1984), 1–48.

9. See also Jean-Louis Comolli, "Technique and Ideology: Camera, Perspective, Depth of Field," in *Movies and Methods* vol. 2, ed. Bill Nichols (Berkeley and Los Angeles: University of California Press, 1985), 40–57.

10. bell hooks, "Revolutionary Black Women," In *Black Looks: Race and Representation*, 41–60 (Boston, MA: South End Press, 1992), 45, notes that "a particular brand of black feminist 'essentialism'" does not allow for difference:

   Any individual present who was seen as having inappropriate thoughts or lingering traces of politically incorrect ideas was the target for unmediated hostility. Not surprisingly, those who had the most to say about victimization were also the ones who judged others harshly, who silenced others. Individual black women who were not a part of that inner circle learned that if they did not know the "right" thing to say, it was best to be silent. To speak against the grain was to risk punishment. One's speech might be interrupted or one might be subjected to humiliation and verbal abuse.

11. Norman Mailer, *The White Negro: Superficial Reflections on the Hipster* (San Francisco: City Lights Books, 1957), 2; hereafter, page numbers cited parenthetically in the text.
12. Carl Hancock Rux, "Eminem: The New White Negro," in *Everything but the Burden: What White People Are Taking from Black Culture*, ed. Greg Tate (New York: Broadway Books, 2003), 18–19, offers this comment:

> The postmodern pop-culture icon of the outlaw is complete and ready to be carried into the new millennium: Eminem does not *seek* to know pagan lore—he was *born* into it, has always spoken the language of it, has always danced to the music of it, has always dressed himself in the latest pagan wear, has never used this language, this music, or this apparel to *disguise* his true identity or to disguise his race, and he has never tried to dissociate himself from the source of his performance, the black male outlaw or outcast of hip-hop fame. Rappers Big Boi and Dre may go by the moniker Outkast, but Eminem proves that a *real* outcast has got to do more than make *Miss Jackson's* daughter cry—you got to fuck the bitch, kill the bitch, dump the bitch's dead body in the river, and not apologize for any of it. . . . . so far, only Eminem gets away with *being* Eminem, perhaps because he uses his visors and disguises to disguise his split personality as undisguised—raising the questions, who is the real outcast, who is the real Slim Shady, what has he inherited from culture to achieve his bad-boy, outcast minstrel, rebel superstar status, and *exactly* what identity crisis is being performed?

13. Richard Dyer, *White* (London: Routledge, 1997).
14. Ibid., 205.
15. Linda Williams, *Playing the Race Card: Melodramas of Black and White from Uncle Tom to O. J. Simpson* (Princeton, NJ: Princeton University Press, 2001), 300.
16. Herman Gray, *Watching Race: Television and the Struggle for "Blackness"* (Minneapolis: University of Minnesota Press, 1995), 74; hereafter, page numbers cited parenthetically in the text.

17. Herman Gray, "Politics of Representation in Network Television," in *Watching Race*, 70–92.

18. Robert M. Entman and Andrew Rojecki, *The Black Image in the White Mind: Media and Race in America* (Chicago: University of Chicago Press, 2000), 160, point out the difference between early radio and television representations of comic black characters, with their comedy rooted in their servitude, and the present: "Current racial ideology, rooted as it is in individual effort, is a humorless project, doubly so, ironically, because of a tendency to restrict public discourse on issues of ethnicity and race to polite but ultimately disengaged exchanges that suppress true feelings."

19. See Michael Eric Dyson, *Is Bill Cosby Right? Or Has the Black Middle Class Lost Its Mind?* (New York: Basic Civitas Books, 2005). Dyson attacks Cosby's own infamous attack on the impoverished black sense of victimization in favor of a politics of self-help and Emersonian self-reliance. Dyson identifies this call as part of the ideological strategy of "blaming the victim" and appropriating its potential threat or difference by denying victimhood the vocabulary to express itself, a strategy, we might add, equivalent to making traditionally black victims into oracles. In both cases, discourse is denied.

20. Entman and Rojeki, in *The Black Image in the White Mind*, 224, see racial discrimination as bad for business, particularly for contemporary niche-marketing media business, so ultimately it should wither away:

    Beyond this is the interest mass media possess in racial comity itself. Social alienation threatens their long-term profitability. ... Conditions of high alienation and cynicism about society's collective ability to solve problems through democratic deliberation and political action reduce the size and attentiveness of news audiences.

    As for entertainment, a shrinking mass audience watching in an increasingly sour frame of mind will render commercial time less valuable to advertisers, many of them mass marketers ... who do not seek narrow-niche audiences. Alienation from the larger community may drive yet further cultural segmentation, diminishing profitability of those mass media productions and advertisers seeking the largest audiences. In any case, deteriorating social trust diminishes the overall financial wealth of society; this reduces the money consumers have to spend on HBO, movie tickets, cars—all products, media and nonmedia—as it lessens the profitability of advertising.

For a differing perspective on the issue of 1970s black television representation, see David Marc, *Bonfire of the Humanities: Television, Subliteracy, and Long-Term Memory Loss* (Syracuse, NY: Syracuse University Press, 1995).

21. An alternative method of categorization is that of Philip Brian Harper, who speaks of two kinds of realism. One is simulacral realism: the representation of progressive possibilities (Diahann Carol in *Julia*) will be valuable despite the fact that these opportunities don't already exist (Nichele Nichols as Lieutenant Uhura in *Star Trek*). This is in conflict with mimetic realism, a mode in which television reflects the social reality of African Americans rather than trying to present it in a progressive light. The conflict presents an interesting dilemma: the positive portrayal of blacks in middle- or upper-middle-class environments is deemed inauthentic. As Harper writes, "Paradoxically, therefore, the insistence that television faithfully represent a set of social conditions conceived [by African American media critic John Oliver Killens and others] as composing a singular and unitary phenomenon known as '*the* Black experience' runs smack up against a simultaneous demand that it both recognize and help constitute the diversity of African American society." Philip Brian Harper, "Extra-Special Effects: Tele-visual Representation and the Claims of 'the Black Experience,'" in *Living Color: Race and Television in the United States*, ed. Sasha Torres (Durham, NC: Duke University Press, 1998), 71.

22. In cinema, a woman shown relaxing socially in the company of a racial other is a hint—as is a woman driving a car with a male passenger—that something terrible is about to happen. This can be seen as early as D. W. Griffith's *Broken Blossoms* (1919)—where decadence is symbolized by white women smoking opium with Asian men—and as recently as Robert Zemeckis's *Forrest Gump* (1994), in which Robin Wright's character joins the pointedly multiethnic counterculture and ends up contracting AIDS. The domestic upheaval in Adrian Lyne's *Fatal Attraction* (1987) is first foreshadowed when wife (Anne Archer) drives husband (Michael Douglas) to the ferry. Both Lana Turner (Tay Garnett's *The Postman Always Rings Twice*, 1946) and Jessica Lange

(Bob Rafelson's *The Postman Always Rings Twice*, 1981) invite their own doom by taking the wheel after successfully beating a murder rap.

Chapter 10

1. See Tom Wolfe, *Radical Chic and Mau-Mauing the Flak Catchers* (New York: Farrar, Strauss and Giroux, 1970).
2. Jane Feuer, "Melodrama, Serial Form, and Television Today," in *Television: The Critical View* 5th ed., ed. Horace Newcomb (New York: Oxford University Press, 1994), 551–62; hereafter, page numbers cited parenthetically in the text.
3. John Caughie, "Playing at Being American: Games and Tactics," in *Logics of Television*, ed. Patricia Mellencamp (Bloomington: Indiana University Press, 1990), 44–58.
4. An extended discussion of television and melodrama, focusing on *Dallas*, is Ien Ang *Watching Dallas: Soap Opera and the Melodramatic Imagination*, trans. Della Couling (London: Methuen, 1985).
5. See Christine Gledhill, ed., *Home Is Where the Heart Is: Studies in Melodrama and the Woman's Film* (London: BFI Publishing), especially Thomas Elsaesser, "Tales of Sound and Fury: Observations on the Family Melodrama," 43–69, and Laura Mulvey, "Notes on Sirk and Melodrama," 75–79.
6. This observation may be less true today than it was in 1990 when this article was published, but it is still relevant in many parts of the world.
7. Margaret Morse, "An Ontology of Everyday Distraction: The Freeway, the Mall, and Television," in *Logics of Television*, ed. Patricia Mellencamp (Bloomington: Indiana University Press, 1990), 193, notes, "Freeways, malls and television are the locus of an attenuated fiction effect, that is, a partial loss of touch with the here and now, dubbed here as distraction. This semi-fiction effect is akin to, but not identical with split belief—knowing a representation is not real, but nevertheless momentarily closing off the here and now and sinking into another world."

Chapter 11

1. Beverle Houston, "*King of Comedy*: A Crisis of Substitution," *Framework* 24, 1 (1984): 74; hereafter, page numbers cited parenthetically in the text.

2. G. W. F. Hegel, "The Preface to the Phenomenology," in *Hegel: Texts and Commentary; Hegel's Preface to His System in a New Translation; with Commentary on Facing Pages and "Who Thinks Abstractly?"* trans. and ed. Walter Kaufmann (Garden City, NY: Anchor Books, 1966), 28.

3. It is also distinct, for that matter, from science fiction. Here's Philip K. Dick's definition of what could be Hegel's TV: "VALIS (acronym of Vast Active Living Intellegience System from an American film): A perturbation in the reality field in which a spontaneous self-monitoring negentropic vortex is formed, tending progressively to subsume and incorporate its environment into arrangements of information. Characterized by quasi-consciousness, purpose, intelligence, growth and an armillary coherence." Philip K. Dick, *VALIS* (New York: Vintage Books, 1991), 7.

4. Janet Staiger, "Fans and Fan Behaviors," in *Media Reception Studies* (New York: New York University Press, 2005), 95–114, charts attempts by theorists—most notably Henry Jenkins—to rescue fans from their image as brainless, feminized, and pathologized by positing active engagements with the texts, producers, and/or other fans. Jenkins, "Reception Theory and Audience Research: The Mystery of the Vampire's Kiss," in *Reinventing Film Studies*, ed. Christine Gledhill and Linda Williams (London: Oxford University Press, 2000), 165–182, notes that

> new modes of critical writing are more and more drawing upon traditions of fan discourse, making the way for more openly appropriative, playful, autobiographical, and inventive genres of critical analysis. Such changes will not come easily, since they go against many of the rules of conventional critical discourse. Yet, these new genres of criticism may bring us closer to understanding the affective power of popular cinema. Soon, it may be possible for us, as students and academic critics, to imagine alternative endings of *Thelma and Louise* in our papers, even those that turn them into bats flying off to Mexico.

5. Murial Cantor, "Audience Control," in *Television: The Critical View*, 3rd ed. (New York: Oxford, 1982), 311–34.

6. See Raymond Williams, *Television: Technology and Cultural Form* (New York: Schocken Books, 1975).

7. Richard Hoggart, *The Uses of Literacy: Aspects of Working-Class Life* (London: Chatto and Windus, 1967).

8. John Ellis, *Visible Fictions: Cinema Television Video* (London: Routledge, 1982).

9. Stuart Hall, "Encoding/Decoding," in *Media Studies: A Reader*, 2nd ed., ed. Paul Marris and Sue Thornham (New York: New York University Press, 2000), 51–61.

10. John Fiske and John Hartley, *Reading Television* (London: Methuen, 1978).

11. Charlotte Brunsdon, "Television: Aesthetics and Audiences," in *Logics of Television*, ed. Patricia Mellencamp (Bloomington: Indiana University Press, 1990), 59–72.

12. The celebrity fantasies played out in the basement of the fictional *Wayne's World* cable show skit on *Saturday Night Live* and in Kramer's apartment on *Seinfeld* are just as delusional but less repulsive because they are now far more familiar and, furthermore, initially presented on television.

13. See Mary Ann Doane, "Film and Masquerade: Theorizing the Female Spectator," in *Femmes Fatales: Feminism, Film Theory, Psychoanalysis* (London: Routledge, 1991), 17–32, and Tania Modleski, "The Search for Tomorrow in Today's Soap Operas," in *Loving with a Vengeance: Mass-Produced Fantasies for Women* (New York: Methuen, 1982), 85–109.

14. René Girard, *Deceit, Desire, and the Novel: Self and Other in Literary Structure*, trans. Yvonne Freccero (Baltimore: Johns Hopkins University Press 1965).

15. Jerry Lewis and James Kaplan, *Dean and Me (A Love Story)* (New York: Broadway Books, 2006), 12.

16. The ballet of abasement between De Niro and Lewis enacts a Hollywood cosmology in which the greatest afflictions (paralysis, mental retardation, alcoholism, nerve disease) lead to the greatest critical acclaim.

17. Beverle Houston, "Viewing Television: The Metapsychology of Endless Consumption," *QRFV* 9, no. 3 (1984): 194.

18. See Michael Sofair's review of *Signs*, *Film Quarterly* 57, no. 3 (2004): 56–63.

Filmography

Ace in the Hole (1951, Billy Wilder; aka *The Big Carnival*)
The Adjuster (1991, Atom Egoyan)
Alien (1979, Ridley Scott)
Alien Nation (1988, Graham Baker)
Alien: Resurrection (1997, Jean-Pierre Jeunet)
All That Heaven Allows (1956, Douglas Sirk)
Annie Hall (1977, Woody Allen)
The Apartment (1960, Billy Wilder)
Artists and Models (1955, Frank Tashlin)
Auto Focus (2002, Paul Schrader)
Avalon (1990, Barry Levinson)
Back to the Future (1985, Robert Zemeckis)
Bamboozled (2000, Spike Lee)
The Beast with Five Fingers (1946, Robert Florey)
Being There (1979, Hal Ashby)
The Beverly Hillbillies (1993, Penelope Spheeris)
The Big Chill (1983, Lawrence Kasdan)
Bill and Ted's Excellent Adventure (1989, Stephen Herek)
Blade (1998, Stephen Norrington)
Blade Runner (1982, Ridley Scott)
The Blues Brothers (1980, John Landis)
Body Bags (1993, John Carpenter, Tobe Hooper, TV)
Bonnie and Clyde (1967, Arthur Penn)
Boogie Nights (1997, Paul Thomas Anderson)
Born in Flames (1983, Lizzie Borden)
The Brady Bunch Movie (1995, Betty Thomas)

Broadcast News (1987, James L. Brooks)
Broken Blossoms (1919, D. W. Griffith)
Bruce Almighty (2003, Tom Shadyac)
Bulworth (1998, Warren Beatty)
The Cable Guy (1996, Ben Stiller)
Caché (2005, Michael Haneke)
The Candidate (1972, Michael Ritchie)
Capricorn One (1978, Peter Hyams)
C'est arrivé près de chez vous [Man Bites Dog] (1991, Benoit Poelvoorde)
Chinatown (1974, Roman Polanski)
Cinderfella (1960, Frank Tashlin)
Cinema Paradiso (1988, Giuseppe Tornatone)
Urga [Close to Eden] (1990, Nikita Mikhalkov)
Confessions of a Dangerous Mind (2002, George Clooney)
Crimes and Misdemeanors (1989, Woody Allen)
Crooklyn (1994, Spike Lee)
The Day the Earth Stood Still (1951, Robert Wise)
Dead Ringers (1988, David Croneberg)
Death Race 2000 (1975, Paul Bartel)
Death to Smoochy (2002, Danny Devito)
La Decima Vittima [The Tenth Victim] (1965, Elio Petri)
The Deep End (2001, Scott McGehee and David Siegel)
Delirious (1991, Tom Mankiewicz)
Desk Set (1957, Walter Lang)
2 ou 3 choses que je sais d'elle [Two or Three Things I Know about Her]
     (1967, Jean-Luc Godard)
Dog Day Afternoon (1975, Sidney Lumet)
Donnie Darko (2001, Richard Kelly)
Duel in the Sun (1946, King Vidor)
Earth Girls Are Easy (1988, Julien Temple)
EDtv (1999, Ron Howard)
Eyes Without a Face (aka *Les yeux san visage*, 1959, Georges Franju)
eXistenZ (1999, David Cronenberg)
Explorers (1985, Joe Dante)
A Face in the Crowd (1957, Elia Kazan)
Fahrenheit 451 (1966, François Truffaut)
Family Viewing (1987, Atom Egoyan)
Fatal Attraction (1987, Adrian Lyne)

Father of the Bride (1950, Vincente Minelli)
Fight Club (1999, David Fincher)
Forest Gump (1994, Robert Zemeckis)
48 Hrs. (1982, Walter Hill)
Frankenstein (1931, James Whale)
Funny Games (1997, 2008, Michael Haneke)
Le Gai Savoir (1969, Jean-Luc Godard)
Galaxy Quest (1999, Dean Parisot)
The Game (1997, David Fincher)
Gattaca (1997, Andrew Niccol)
Geisha Boy (1958, Frank Tashlin)
Ghost (1990, Jerry Zucker)
Girl 6 (1996, Spike Lee)
Ginger e Fred (1986, Federico Fellini)
The Godfather, Part II (1975, Francis Ford Copolla)
The Groove Tube (1972, Ken Shipiro)
Grosse Point Blank (1997, George Armitage)
The Hand (1981, Oliver Stone)
The Hands of Orloc (aka *Orlacs Hände*, 1925, Robert Weine)
Henry, Portrait of a Serial Killer (1990, John McNaughton)
Henry: Portrait of a Serial Killer 2: Mask of Sanity (1996, Chuck Parello)
Hero (1992, Stephen Frears)
Holy Man (1998, Stephen Herek)
How to Get Ahead in Advertising (1989, Bruce Robinson)
I Was a Male War Bride (1949, Howard Hawks)
In and Out (1997, Frank Oz)
In the Bedroom (2001, Todd Field)
L'Inhumaine [The Inhuman Woman](1924, Marcel Herbier)
The Insider (1999, Michael Mann)
International House (1933, A. Edward Sutherland)
Invasion of the Body Snatchers (1956, Donald Siegel)
Invasion of the Body Snatchers (1978, Philip Kaufman)
It Should Happen to You (1954, George Cukor)
It's Always Fair Weather (1955, Stanley Donan)
La Jetée (1962, Chris Marker)
Johnny Mnemonic (1995, Robert Longo)
Jurassic Park (1993, Steven Speilberg)
Kentucky Fried Movie (1977, John Landis)

The King of Comedy (1982, Martin Scorsese)

Ladri di Saponette [The Icicle Thief] (1989, Maurizio Nichetti) Italian

The Last Hurrah (1958, John Huston)

The Last Movie (1971, Dennis Hopper)

The Last Picture Show (1971, Peter Bogdanovich)

The Last Wave (1977, Peter Weir)

The Late Shift (1996, Betty Thomas)

Lawnmower Man (1992, Brett Leonard)

Lawnmower Man 2: Beyond Cyberspace (1995, Farhad Mann; aka *Jobe's War*)

Lethal Weapon (1987, Richard Donner)

Lethal Weapon 2 (1988, Richard Donner)

Lethal Weapon 3 (1989, Richard Donner)

Lethal Weapon 4 (1992, Richard Donner)

Louis 19th, le roi des ondes [King of the Airwaves] (1994, Michel Poulette)

Mad City (1997, Costa-Gavras)

Magnificent Obsession (1954, Douglas Sirk)

Man on the Moon (1999, Milos Forman)

The Man Who Fell to Earth (1976, Nicolas Roeg)

The Manchurian Candidate (1962, John Frankenheimer)

Manhattan (1979, Woody Allen)

The Mask (1994, Chuck Russell)

The Matrix (1999, Andy and Larry Wachowski)

The Matrix Reloaded (2003, Andy and Larry Wachowski)

The Matrix Revolutions (2003, Andy and Larry Wachowski)

Max Headroom (1985, Annabel Jankel, Rocky Morton)

Minority Report (2002, Steven Spielberg)

Monster's Ball (2001, Marc Forster)

La Mort en direct [Death Watch] (1980, Bertrand Tavernier)

Mr. Mom (1983, Stan Dragoti)

Murder by Television (1935, Clifford Sanforth; aka *The Houghland Murder Case*)

My Favorite Year (1982, Richard Benjamin)

Naked Lunch (1991, David Croneberg)

Natural Born Killers (1994, Oliver Stone)

The Net (1995, Irwin Winkler)

Network (1976, Sidney Lumet)

Night of the Living Dead (1968, George A. Romero)

1984 (1984, Michael Radford)

Nothing Sacred (1937, William Wellman)

Nurse Betty (2000, Neil LaBute)

The Nutty Professor (1962, Jerry Lewis)

The Osterman Weekend (1983, Sam Peckinpah)

The Others (2001, Alejandro Amjenábar)

Panic Button (1962, George Sherman)

Professione: Reporter [The Passenger] (1975, Michelangelo Antonioni)

Peggy Sue Got Married (1986, Francis Ford Coppola)

Permanent Midnight (1998, David Veloz)

Pleasantville (1998, Gary Ross)

Poltergeist (1982, Tobe Hooper)

The Postman Always Rings Twice (1946, Tay Garnett)

The Postman Always Rings Twice (1981, Bob Rafelson)

Power (1986, Sidney Lumet)

The Positively True Adventures of the Alleged Texas Cheerleader-Murdering Mom (1993, Michael Ritchie)

Queen of the Dammed (2002, Michael Rymer)

Quiz Show (1994, Robert Redford)

Raging Bull (1981, Martin Scorcese)

Rain Man (1988, Barry Levinson)

Real Life (1979, Albert Brooks)

Return to Paradise (1998, Joseph Rubin; aka *All for One*)

The Ring (2002, Gore Verbinski)

Robocop (1987, Paul Verhoeven)

Robot Jox (1990, Stuart Gordon)

Rollerball (1975, Norman Jewison)

Rollerball (2002, John McTiernan)

The Running Man (1987, Paul Michael Glaser)

The Sands of Iwo Jima (1949, Allan Dwan)

Scream (1996, Wes Craven)

The Secret Cinema (1969, Paul Bartel)

The Searchers (1956, John Ford)

Serial Mom (1994, John Waters)

Series 7: The Contenders (2001, Daniel Minahan)

The Seven Year Itch (1955, Billy Wilder)

Sex, Lies and Videotape (1989, Steven Soderbergh)

Shane (1953, George Stevens)
Shocker (1989, Wes Craven)
Showtime (2002, Tom Dey)
The Sixth Sense (1999, M. Night Shyamalan)
Sleeper (1973, Woody Allen)
Sleeping with the Enemy (1991, Joseph Ruben)
Sliver (1993, Phillip Noyce)
Soapdish (1991, Michael Hoffman)
Soylent Green (1973, Richard Fleischer)
Splash (1984, Ron Howard)
Der Stand der Dinge [The State of Things] (1982, Wim Wenders)
Starman (1984, John Carpenter)
Star Time (1992, Alexander Cassini)
Stay Tuned (1992, Peter Hyams)
The Stepford Wives (2004, Frank Oz)
The Stooge (1952, Norman Taurog)
Strange Days (1995, Kathryn Bigelow)
Switching Channels (1988, Ted Kotcheff)
Tanner '88 (1988, Robert Altman; aka *Tanner: A Political Fable*)
The Terminator (1984, James Cameron)
Terminator II (1989, Bruno Mattei)
Tetsuo [Tetsuo, The Iron Man] (1992, Shinya Tsukamoto)
Thelma and Louise (1991, Ridley Scott)
There's Something about Mary (1998, Bobby and Peter Farrelly)
The Thrill of It All (1963, Norman Jewison)
Time Bandits (1981, Terry Gilliam)
To Die For (1995, Gus Van Sant)
Tommy (1975, Kurt Russell)
Tootsie (1982, Sydney Pollack)
Trading Places (1983, John Landis)
Tron (1982, Steven Lisberger)
The Truman Show (1998, Peter Weir)
12 Monkeys (1995, Terry Gilliam)
28 Days Later ... (2002, Danny Boyle)
Twin Peaks: Fire Walk with Me (1992, David Lynch)
200 Motels (1971, Tony Palmer, Frank Zappa)
2001: A Space Odyssey (1969, Stanley Kubrick)
The TV Set (2006, Jake Kasdan)

UHF (1989, Jay Levey)

Until the End of the World (1991, Wim Wenders)

Up Close and Personal (1996, Jon Avnet)

A Very Brady Sequel (1996, Arlene Sanford)

Videodrome (1983, David Cronenberg)

Virtuosity (1995, Brett Leonard)

Wag the Dog (1997, Barry Levinson)

War of the Worlds (2005, Steven Spieberg)

WarGames (1983, John Badham)

Wax, or the Discovery of Television among the Bees (1993, David Blair)

Wayne's World (1992, Penelope Spheeris)

Wayne's World 2 (1993, Stephen Surjik)

Le Week-end [Weekend] (1967, Jean-Luc Godard)

What Lies Beneath (2000, Robert Zemeckis)

What's Eating Gilbert Grape? (1993, Lasse Hallstrom)

Where the Green Ants Roam (1984, Werner Herzog)

Will Success Spoil Rock Hunter? (1957, Frank Tashlin)

Willy Wonka and the Chocolate Factory (1971, Mel Stuart)

Winchester '73 (1950, Anthony Mann)

Witness to the Execution (1994, Tommy Lee Wallace)

Written on the Wind (1956, Douglas Sirk)

Wrong Is Right (1982, Richard Brooks)

X: The Man with X-Ray Eyes (1963, Roger Corman)

Les yeux sana Visage [Eyes without a Face] (1959, Georges Franju)

Zabriskie Point (1970, Michelangelo Antonioni)

Zelig (1983, Woody Allen)

Zoolander (2001, Ben Stiller)

Bibliography

Allen, Robert C. "Introduction to the Second Edition: More Talk about TV." In *Channels of Discourse, Reassembled*, 2nd ed., edited by Robert C. Allen, 1–30. Chapel Hill: University of North Carolina Press, 1987.

————. "The Guiding Light: Soap Opera as Economic Product and Cultural Document." In *Television: The Critical View*, 4th ed., edited by Horace Newcomb, 141–63. New York: Oxford University Press, 1987.

————. "Reader-Oriented Criticism and Television." In *Channels of Discourse, Reassembled*, 2nd ed., edited by Robert C. Allen, 74–112. Chapel Hill: University of North Carolina Press, 1987.

Althusser, Louis. "Ideology and Ideological State Apparatuses (Notes Towards an Investigation)." In *Lenin and Philosophy and Other Essays*, translated by Ben Brewster, 127–86. New York: Monthly Review Press, 1971.

American Association of Pediatrics website (*http://www.aap.org/ healthtopics/mediause.cfm*, accessed Jan 9, 2008. Published online: 4/07). Source: *Television and the Family* (Copyright © 2007 American Academy of Pediatrics, Updated 2/07).

Ang, Ien. *Watching Dallas: Soap Opera and the Melodramatic Imagination*. Translated by Della Couling. London: Methun, 1985.

Arlen, Michael J. *Thirty Seconds*. Harmondsworth, England: Penguin, 1979.

Bakhtin. M. M. *The Dialogic Imagination*. Edited by Michael Holquist. Translated by Caryl Emerson and Michael Holquist. Austin: University of Texas Press, 1981.

Baker, William F., and George Dessart. *Down the Tube: An Inside Account of the Failure of American Television*. New York: Basic Books, 1999.

Barr, Charles. ' "They Think It's All Over': The Dramatic Legacy of Live Television." In *Big Picture, Small Screen: The Relations Between Film and Television*, edited by John Hill and Martin McLoone, 47–75. Bloomington: Indiana University Press, 2003.

Barris, Chuck. *Confessions of a Dangerous Mind: An Unauthorized Autobiography*. New York: Hyperion, 2002.

Barthes, Roland. *Camera Lucida: Reflections on Photography*. Translated by Richard Howard. New York: Hill and Wang, 1981.

———. *Writing Degree Zero*. Translated by Annette Lavers and Colin Smith. New York: Hill and Wang, 1977.

Baudrillard, Jean. "The Ecstasy of Communication," translated by John Johnson. In *The Anti-Aesthetic: Essays on Postmodern Culture*, edited by Hal Foster, 126–34. Port Townsend, WA: Bay Press, 1983.

———. *The Spirit of Terrorism: And Requiem for the Twin Towers*. Translated by Chris Turner. London; New York: Verso, 2000.

———. "Requiem for the Media." In *Video Culture: A Critical Examination*, edited by John G. Hanhardt, 124–43. Layton, UT: Peregrine Smith Books / Visual Studies Workshop Press, 1986.

———. *Seduction*. Translated by Brian Singer. New York: St. Martin's Press, 1991.

Bazin, André. *What Is Cinema?* vol. 1. Translated by Hugh Gray. Berkeley and Los Angeles: University of California Press, 1967.

Bergson, Henri. *Laughter: An Essay on the Meaning of the Comic*. Translated by Cloudesley Brereton and Fred Rothwell. New York: Macmillion, 1911.

Bersani, Leo. *Homos: The Straight Mind and Other Essays*. Cambridge, MA: Harvard University Press, 1995.

Bianculli, David. *Teleliteracy: Taking Television Seriously*. New York: Continuum Books, 1992.

Blanchot, Maurice. *The Writing of the Disaster*. Translated by Ann Smock. Lincoln: University of Nebraska Press, 1986.

Bly, Robert. *Iron John: A Book about Men*. Reading, MA: Addison-Wesley, 1990.

Bordwell, David, and Noel Carroll, eds. *Post-Theory: Reconstructing Film Studies*. Madison: University of Wisconsin Press, 1996.

Borges, Jorge Luis. "Of Exactitude in Science." In *A Universal History of Infamy*, 131. Harmondsworth, Middlesex, England: Penguin Books, 1973.

Borradori, Giovanna, *Philosophy in a Time of Terror: Dialogues with Jürgen Habermas and Jacques Derrida*. Chicago: University of Chicago Press, 2004

Bourdieu, Pierre. *On Television*. Translated by Priscilla Parkhurst Ferguson. New York: The New Press, 1998.

Boyd, Todd. *Am I Black Enough for You? Popular Culture from the 'Hood and Beyond*. Bloomington: Indiana University Press, 1997.

Braudy, Leo. *The Frenzy of Renown: Fame and Its History*. New York: Oxford University Press, 1986.

———. *From Chivalry to Terrorism: War and the Changing Nature of Masculinity*. New York: Vintage Books, 2005.

Brinkley, Joel. *Defining Vision: How Broadcasters Lured the Government into Inciting a Revolution in Television*. San Diego: Harcourt Brace, 1997.

Brooks, Peter. *Reading for the Plot: Design and Intention in Narrative*. New York: Alfred A. Knopf, 1984.

Brooks, Tim, and Earle Marsh. *The Complete Directory to Prime Time Network and Cable TV Shows: 1946–Present*. 6th ed. New York: Ballantine Books, 1995.

Browne, Nick. "The Political Economy of the Television (Super) Text," *Quarterly Review of Film Studies* 9, no. 3 (1984): 174–82.

Brunsdon, Charlotte. "Television: Aesthetics and Audiences." In *Logics of Television*, edited by Patricia Mellencamp, 59–72. Bloomington: Indiana University Press, 1990.

Brunsdon, Charlotte, Julie D'Acci, and Lynn Spigel, eds. *Feminist Television Criticism: A Reader*. Oxford: Clarendon Press, 1997.

Burnham, John. "Art and Technology: The Panacea that Failed." In *Video Culture: A Critical Examination*, edited by John G. Hanhardt, 232–48. Layton, UT: Peregrine Smith Books/Visual Studies Workshop Press, 1986.

Burton, Graeme. *Talking Television: An Introduction to the Study of Television*. London: Edward Arnold, 2000.

Butler, Jeremy. *Television: Critical Methods and Applications*, 3rd ed. Mahway, NJ: Lawrence Erlbaum Associates, Publishers, 2007.

Caldwell, John Thornton. "Boutique: Designer Television/Auteurist Spin Doctoring." In *Televisuality: Style, Crisis, and Authority in American*

Television, 105–33. New Brunswick, NJ: Rutgers University Press, 1995.

Cantor, Murial. "Audience Control." In *Television: The Critical View*, 3rd ed., edited by Horace Newcomb, 311–34. New York: Oxford University Press, 1982.

Cantor, Paul A. *Gilligan Unbound: Pop Culture in the Age of Globalization.* Lanham, MD: Rowman and Littlefield, 2001.

Caughie, John. "Playing at Being American: Games and Tactics." In *Logics of Television*, edited by Patricia Mellencamp, 44–58. Bloomington: Indiana University Press, 1990.

Cavell, Stanley. "The Fact of Television." In *Video Culture: A Critical Examination*, edited by John G. Hanhardt, 192–218. Layton, UT: Peregrine Smith Books/Visual Studies Workshop Press, 1986.

Cixous, Hélène. "The Laugh of the Medusa." In *Critical Theory Since 1965*, edited by Hazard Adams and Leroy Searle, 309–20. Tallahassee: Florida State University Press, 1986.

Clough, Patricia Ticeneto. *Autoaffection: Unconscious Thought in the Age of Teletechnology.* Minneapolis: University of Minnesota Press, 2000.

Collins, Jim. "Television and Postmodernism." In *Media Studies: A Reader*, 2nd ed., edited by Paul Marris and Sue Thornham, 375–84. New York: New York University Press, 2000.

Comolli, Jean-Louis. "Technique and Ideology: Camera, Perspective, Depth of Field." In *Movies and Methods*, vol. 2, edited by Bill Nichols, 40–57. Berkeley and Los Angeles: University of California Press, 1985.

Connor, Steven. *Postmodernist Culture: An Introduction to Theories of the Contemporary.* 2nd ed. London: Blackwell, 1997.

Coupland, Douglas. *Generation X: Tales for an Accelerated Culture.* New York: St. Martin's Press, 1991.

———. *Girlfriend in a Coma.* New York: ReganBooks, 1998.

Creed, Barbara. *The Monstrous-Feminine: Film, Feminism, Psychoanalysis.* London: Routledge, 1993.

Cubitt, Sean. *Timeshift: On Video Culture.* New York: Routledge, 1991.

Dates, Jannette L., and William Barlow, eds. *Split Image: African Americans in the Mass Media.* Washington, DC: Howard University Press, 1993.

Dayan, Daniel, and Elihu Katz. "Electronic Ceremonies: Television Performs a Royal Wedding." In *On Signs*, edited by Marshall Blonsky, 16–32. Baltimore: Johns Hopkins University Press, 1985.

Debord, Guy. *Society of the Spectacle*. Translated by Donald Nicholson-Smith. New York: Zone Books, 1995. [Originally published in France as *La société du spectacle* in 1967.]

Deleuze, Gilles, and Leopold von Sacher-Masoch. *Masochism: Coldness and Cruelty and Venus in Furs*. Translated by Jean McNeil. New York: Zone Books, 1991.

DeLillo, Don. *White Noise*. New York: Viking, 1985.

Derrida, Jacques. "Linguistics and Grammatology." In *Of Grammatology*, translated by Gayatri Chakravorty Spivak, 101–40. Baltimore: Johns Hopkins University Press, 1979.

———. "No Apocalypse, Not Now (full speed ahead, seven missiles, seven missives)." *Diacritics* 14, no. 2 (1984): 20–31.

Derrida, Jacques and Bernard Stiegler. *Echographies of Television: Filmed Interviews*. Translated by Jennifer Bajorek. Malden, MA: Blackwell Publishers Ltd., 2002.

Dick, Philip K. *Flow My Tears, the Policeman Said*. London: Grafton Books, 1976.

———. *VALIS*. New York: Vintage Books, 1991.

Dienst, Richard. *Still Life in Real Time: Theory after Television (Post-Contemporary Interventions)*. Durham, NC: Duke University Press, 1994.

Doane, Mary Ann. "Film and Masquerade: Theorizing the Female Spectator." In *Femmes Fatales: Feminism, Film Theory, Psychoanalysis*, 17–32. London: Routledge, 1991.

———. "Information, Crisis, Catastrophe." In *Logics of Television*, edited by Patricia Mellencamp, 222–39. Bloomington: Indiana University Press, 1990.

Douglas, Susan. *Where the Girls Are: Growing Up Female with the Mass Media*. New York: Three Rivers Press, 1995.

Dumm, Thomas L. "Telefear: Watching War News." In *The Politics of Everyday Fear*, edited by Brian Massumi, 307–21. Minneapolis: University of Minnesota Press, 1993.

Dunkley, Christopher. *Television Today and Tomorrow: Wall-to-Wall Dallas?* Harmondsworth, England: Penguin, 1985.

Dyer, Richard. *Stars*. London: British Film Institute, 1986.

———. *White*. London: Routledge, 1997.

Dyson, Michael Eric. *Is Bill Cosby Right? Or Has the Black Middle Class Lost Its Mind?* New York: Basic Civitas Books, 2005.

Eagleton, Terry. *The Function of Criticism*. London: Verso: 2005.

Ebert, Roger. Review of *Cinema Paradiso*. *Chicago Sun-Times*, March 16, 1996.

Eco, Umberto. "Apocalyptic and Integrated Intellectuals: Mass Communications and Theories of Mass Culture." In *Apocalypse Postponed: Essays by Umberto Eco*, edited by Robert Lumley, 17–35. Bloomington: Indiana University Press, 1994.

––––––. "A Guide to the Neo-Television of the 1980s." *Framework* 25 (1984): 18–25.

––––––. "The Phantom of Neo-TV: The Debate on Fellini's *Ginger and Fred*." In *Apocalypse Postponed: Essays by Umberto Eco*, edited by Robert Lumley, 108–11. Bloomington: Indiana University Press, 1994.

––––––. *Travels in Hyperreality*. Translated by William Weaver. San Diego: Harcourt Brace Jovanovich, 1986.

Ellis, John. *Visible Fictions: Cinema Television Video*. London: Routledge, 1982.

Ellison, Harlan. *The Glass Teat: Essays of Opinion on the Subject of Television*. New York: Ace Books, 1983.

Entman, Robert M., and Andrew Rojecki. *The Black Image in the White Mind: Media and Race in America*. Chicago: University of Chicago Press, 2000.

Enzensberger, Hans Magnus. "Constituents of a Theory of the Media." In *Video Culture: A Critical Examination*, edited by John G. Hanhardt, 96–123. Layton, UT: Peregrine Smith Books/Visual Studies Workshop Press, 1986.

Everett, Anna, and John T. Caldwell, eds. *New Media: Theories and Practices of Digitextuality*. New York: Routledge, 2003.

Feuer, Jane, "The Concept of Live Television: Ontology as Ideology." In *Regarding Television: Critical Approaches; An Anthology*, edited by Ann Kaplan, 12–22. Frederick, MD: University Publications of America/American Film Institute, 1983.

––––––. "Melodrama, Serial Form, and Television Today." In *Television: The Critical View*, 5th ed., edited by Horace Newcomb, 551–62. New York: Oxford University Press, 1994.

Feuer, Jane, Paul Kerr, and Tise Vahimagi, eds. *MTM "Quality Television."* London: British Film Institute, 1984.

Fisher, David E., and Marshall Jon Fisher. *Tube: The Invention of Television*. Washington, DC: Counterpoint, 1996.

Fiske, John. "British Cultural Studies and Television." In *Channels of Discourse, Reassembled*. 2nd ed., edited by Robert C. Allen, 284–326. Chapel Hill: University of North Carolina Press, 1987.

————. *Television Culture*. New York: Methuen, 1987.

Fiske, John, and John Hartley. *Reading Television*. London: Methuen, 1978.

Fitzpatrick, Kathleen. *The Anxiety of Obsolescence: The American Nvel in the Age of Television*. Nashville, TN: Vanderbilt University Press, 2006.

Flitterman-Lewis, Sandy. "Psychoanalysis, Film, and Television." In *Channels of Discourse, Reassembled*, 2nd ed., edited by Robert C. Allen, 172–210. Chapel Hill: University of North Carolina Press, 1987.

Foucault, Michel. *The History of Sexuality*. Vol. 1. Translated by Robert Hurley. New York: Vintage Books, 1980.

Freud, Sigmund. *The Ego and the Id*. Translated by James Stachey. New York: W. W. Norton, 1960.

————. "Femininity." In Sigmund Freud, *New Introductory Lectures*, edited by James Strachey, 99–119. New York: W. W. Norton, 1964.

Fukuyama, Francis. *The End of History and the Last Man*. New York: Free Press, 1992.

Girard, René. *Deceit, Desire and the Novel: Self and Other in Literary Structure*. Translated by Yvonne Freccero. Baltimore: Johns Hopkins University Press, 1965.

Gitlin, Todd. *Media Unlimited: How the Torrent of Images and Sounds Overwhelms Our Lives*. New York: Henry Holt, 2001.

————. "Prime Time Ideology: The Hegemonic Process in Television Entertainment." In *Television: The Critical View*, 5th ed., edited by Horace Newcomb, 516–36. New York: Oxford University Press, 1994.

————. ed. *Watching Television: A Pantheon Guide to Popular Culture*. New York: Pantheon, 1986.

Gledhill, Christine. *Home Is Where the Heart Is: Studies in Melodrama and the Woman's Film*. London: British Film Institute, 1987.

————. "Recent Developments in Feminist Film Criticism." In *Re-Vision: Essays in Feminist Film Criticism*, edited by Mary Ann Doane, Patricia Mellencamp, and Linda Williams, 1–48. Los Angeles: University Publications of America, 1984.

Gramsci, Antonio. *Selections from the Prison Notebooks*. Translated by Geoffrey N. Smith and Quintin Hoare. London: Lawrence and Wishart, 1971.

Gray, Herman. *Watching Race: Television and the Struggle for "Blackness."* Minneapolis: University of Minnesota Press, 2004.

Grossberg, Lawrence. "The In-Difference of TV," *Screen* 28, no. 2 (1987): 28–45.

Grossberg, Lawrence, Ellen Wartella, and D. Charles Whitney. *Media Making: Mass Media in a Popular Culture*. New York: Sage, 1998.

Hall, Stuart. "Encoding/Decoding." In *Media Studies: A Reader*, 2nd ed., edited by Paul Marris and Sue Thornham, 51–61. New York: New York University Press, 2000.

———. "The Whites of Their Eyes: Racist Ideologies and the Media." In *Modernism, Gender and Culture: A Cultural Studies Approach*, edited by Lisa Rado and William Cain, 18–21. Wellesley Studies in Critical Theory, Literary History, and Culture. London: Garland, 1997.

Harper, Phillip Brian. "Extra-Special Effects: Televisual Representation and the Claims of 'the Black Experience.'" In *Living Color: Race and Television in the United States*, edited by Sasha Torres, 62–81. Durham, NC: Duke University Press, 1998.

Harries, Dan. *The New Media Book*. London: British Film Institute, 2002.

Hartley, John. *Uses of Television*. London: Routledge, 1999.

Hegel, G. W. F. *Texts and Commentary; Hegel's Preface to His System in a New Translation; with Commentary on Facing Pages and "Who Thinks Abstractly?"* Translated and edited by Walter Kaufmann. Garden City, NY: Anchor, 1966.

Heidegger, Martin. *The Question Concerning Technology, and Other Essays*. Translated by William Lovitt. New York: Harper and Row, 1977.

Hill, John, and Martin McLoone, eds. *Big Picture, Small Screen: The Relations Between Film and Television*. Bloomington: Indiana University Press, 2003.

Hilmes, Michele. *Only Connect: A Cultural History of Broadcasting in the United States*. Belmont, CA: Thomson Wadsworth, 2007.

Hoggart, Richard. *The Uses of Literacy: Aspects of Working-Class Life*. London: Chatto and Windus, 1967.

hooks, bell. "Revolutionary Black Women." In *Black Looks: Race and Representation*, 41–60. Boston: South End Press, 1992.

Houston, Beverle. "*King of Comedy*: A Crisis of Substitution," *Framework* 24 (1984): 74–92.

———. "Viewing Television: The Metapsychology of Endless Consumption," *QRFV* 9, no. 3 (1984): 183–95.

Hubbell, Richard W. *Four Thousand Years of Television: The Story of Seeing at a Distance*. New York: G. P. Putnam's Sons, 1942.

Huxley, Aldous. *Aldous Huxley, The Perennial Philosophy*. New York: Harper and Brothers, 1945.

Huyssen, Andreas. *After the Great Divide: Modernism, Mass Culture, Postmodernism*. Bloomington: Indiana University Press, 1986.

Jacoby, Russell. *The Last Intellectuals: American Culture in the Age of Academe*. New York, Basic Books, 1987.

Jameson, Fredric. *Postmodernism or, The Cultural Logic of Late Capitalism*. Durham, NC: Duke University Press, 1991.

Jeffords, Susan. *Hard Bodies: Hollywood Masculinity in the Reagan Era*. New Brunswick, NJ: Rutgers University Press, 1994.

Jenkins, Henry III. "Star Trek Rerun, Reread, Rewritten: Fan Writing as Textual Poaching." In *Television: The Critical View*, 5th ed., edited by Horace Newcomb, 448–73. New York: Oxford University Press, 1994.

Johnson, Stephen. *Everything Bad Is Good for You*. New York: Riverhead Books, 2005.

Johnston, Claire. "Towards a Feminist Film Practice: Some Theses." In *Movies and Methods*, vol. 2, edited by Bill Nichols, 315–27. Berkeley and Los Angeles: University of California Press, 1985.

Joyce, Ed. *Prime Times, Bad Times*. New York: Anchor, 1989.

Joyrich, Lynne. "Critical and Textual Hypermasculinity." In *Logics of Television*, edited by Patricia Mellencamp, 156–72. Bloomington: Indiana University Press, 1990.

Kaplan, E. Ann. "Feminist Criticism and Television." In *Channels of Discourse, Reassembled*, 2nd ed., edited by Robert C. Allen, 211–53. Chapel Hill: University of North Carolina Press, 1987.

———. *Rocking Around the Clock: Music Television, Postmodernism, and Consumer Culture*. New York: Methuen, 1987.

Kermode, Frank. *The Sense of an Ending: Studies in the Theory of Fiction*. Oxford: Oxford University Press, 2000.

Kinder, Marsha. *Playing with Power in Movies, Television, and Video Games*. Berkeley and Los Angeles: University of California Press, 1991.

Kittler, Friedrich A. *Gramophone, Film, Typewriter.* Translated by Geoffrey Winthrop Young and Michael Wutz. Stanford, CA: Stanford University Press, 1999.

Kosinski, Jerzy. "A Nation of Videots." Interview by David Sohn. In *Television: The Critical View*, 2nd ed., edited by Horace Newcomb, 334–49. New York: Oxford University Press, 1979.

———. *Being There.* New York: Bantam Books, 1972.

Kristeva, Julia. *Powers of Horror: An Essay on Abjection.* New York: Columbia University Press, 1982.

Kroker, Arthur, and Marilouise Kroker. "Panic Sex in America." In *Body Invaders: Panic Sex in America*, 10–19. New York: St. Martin's Press, 1987.

Lacan, Jacques. "The Mirror Stage as Formative of the Function of the I." In *Écrits, A Selection*, translated by Alan Sheridan, 1–7. New York: W.W. Norton, 1977.

Lardner, James. *Fast Forward: Hollywood, the Japanese, and the Onslaught of the VCR.* New York: W. W. Norton, 1987.

Leonard, John. *Smoke and Mirrors: Violence, Television, and Other American Cultures.* New York: New Press, 1997.

Levine, Philip. "Animals Are Passing from Our Lives." In *Selected Poems.* New York: Atheneum, 1984, 36.

Lewis, Jerry, and James Kaplan. *Dean and Me (A Love Story).* New York: Broadway Books, 2006.

Lyotard, Jean-François. "Answering the Question: What Is Postmodernism?" In *The Postmodern Condition: A Report on Knowledge*, translated by Geoff Bennington and Brian Massumi, 71–82. Manchester, England: Manchester University Press, 1984.

MacCabe, Colin. *Godard: Images, Sounds, Politics.* London: Macmillan, 1980.

———. ed. *High Theory, Low Culture.* Manchester, England: Manchester University Press, 1987.

Mailer, Norman. *The White Negro: Superficial Reflections on the Hipster.* San Francisco: City Lights Books, 1957.

Mander, Jerry. *Four Arguments for the Elimination of Television.* New York: Quill, 1978.

Marc, David. *Bonfire of the Humanities: Television, Subliteracy, and Long-Term Memory Loss.* Syracuse, NY: Syracuse University Press, 1995.

———. *Demographic Vistas: Television in American Culture*. Philadelphia: University of Pennsylvania Press, 1984.

Marcuse, Herbert. *One-Dimentional Man: Studies in the Ideology of Advanced Industrial Society*. London: Routledge, 2006.

Marx, Karl. "On Greek Art in Its Time from a Contribution to the Critique of Political Economy." Translated by Nahum Issac Stone. In *The Critical Tradition*, 2nd ed., edited by David H. Richter, 392–93. Boston: Bedford Books, 1998.

Massumi, Brian. "Everywhere You Want to Be: Introduction to Fear." In *The Politics of Everyday Fear*, 3–57. Minneapolis: University of Minnesota Press, 1993.

Maynard, Joyce. *At Home in the World: A Memoir*. New York: Picador, 1998.

McCarthy, Anna. *Ambient Television: Visual Culture and Public Space*. Durham, NC: Duke University Press, 2001.

McLemee, Scott. "After the Last Intellectual." *Bookforum*, 14, no. 3 (2007): 15–17, 59.

McPherson, Tara. "Self, Other and Electronic Media." In *The New Media Book*, edited by Dan Harries, 183–94. London: British Film Institute, 2002.

McRobbie, Angela. "Feminism, Postmodernism and the 'Real Me.'" In *Media and Cultural Studies Keyworks*, edited by Meenakshi Gigi Durham and Douglas M. Kellner, 598–610. Malden, MA: Blackwell, 2001.

Meehan, Eileen R. "Why We Don't Count: The Commodity Audience." In *Logics of Television*, edited by Patricia Mellencamp, 117–37. Bloomington: Indiana University Press, 1990.

Mellencamp, Patricia. "TV, Time and Catastrophe, or Beyond the Pleasure Principle of Television." In *Logics of Television*, edited by Patricia Mellencamp, 240–66. Bloomington: Indiana University Press, 1990.

Miller, Mark Crispin. "Deride and Conquer." In *Watching Television: A Pantheon Guide to Popular Culture*, edited by Todd Gitlin, 183–28. New York: Pantheon, 1986.

Miller, Toby. "Turn Off TV Studies!" *Cinema Journal* 45, no. 1 (2005): 98–101.

———. ed. *Television Studies*. New York: British Film Institute, 2002.

Modleski, Tania. *Feminism without Women: Culture and Criticism in a "Postfeminist" Age*. New York: Routledge, 1991.

————. "The Search for Tomorrow in Today's Soap Operas." In *Loving with a Vengeance: Mass-Produced Fantasies for Women*, 85–109. New York: Methuen, 1982.

Morley, David. *The "Nationwide" Audience*. London: British Film Institute, 1980.

Morris, Edmund. *Dutch: A Memoir of Ronald Reagan*. New York: HarperCollins, 2000.

Morris, Meaghan. "Banality in Cultural Studies." In *Logics of Television*, edited by Patricia Mellencamp, 14–43. Bloomington: Indiana University Press, 1990.

Morrison, Toni. "Clinton as the First Black President." *New Yorker*, October 5, 1998, pp. 31–34.

Morse, Margaret. "An Ontology of Everyday Distraction: The Freeway, the Mall, and Television." In Logics of Television, edited by Patricia Mellencamp, 193–221. Bloomington: Indiana University Press, 1990.

Mulvey, Laura. *Visual and Other Pleasures*. London: Macmillan, 1989.

Ngai, Sianne. *Ugly Feelings*. Cambridge: Harvard University Press, 2005.

Pinsky, Robert. "To Television." *New Yorker*, August 10, 1998, p. 34.

Pomerance, Murray, ed. *Enfant Terrible! Jerry Lewis in American Film*. New York: New York University Press, 2002.

Postman, Neil. *Amusing Ourselves to Death: Public Discourse in the Age of Show Business*. New York: Penguin, 1986.

Pynchon, Thomas. *Gravity's Rainbow*. New York: Penguin Books, 1987, c1973.

————. *V., A Novel*. Philadelphia: Lippencott, 1963.

Real, Michael R. *Mass-Mediated Culture*. Englewood Cliffs, NJ: Prentice-Hall, 1977.

Rickels, Laurence A. *The Case of California*. Baltimore: Johns Hopkins University Press, 1991.

Rimbaud, Arthur. "Letter to Paul Demeny." In *Rimbaud Complete*. Translated and edited by Wyatt Mason. New York: The Modern Library, 2002, 366–70.

Ritzer, George. *The Globalization of Nothing*. Thousand Oaks, CA: Sage, 2003.

————. *The McDonaldization of Society*. Thousand Oaks, CA: Sage 2003.

Robson, David. "Frye, Derrida, Pynchon, and the Apocalyptic Space of Postmodern Fiction." In *Postmodern Apocalypse: Theory and Cultural Practice at the End*, edited by Richard Dellamora, 61–78. Philadelphia: University of Pennsylvannia Press, 1995.

Ross, Andrew. "Three Lives in a Day of *Max Headroom*." In *Logics of Television*, edited by Patricia Mellencamp, 138–55. Bloomington: Indiana University Press, 1990.

Rux, Carl Hancock. "Eminem: The New White Negro." In *Everything but the Burden; What White People Are Taking from Black Culture*, edited by Greg Tate, 15–38. New York: Broadway Books, 2003.

Schickel, Richard. "Rerunning Film Noir." *Wilson Quarterly* 31, no. 3 (2007): 36–43.

Schrader, Paul. "Notes on Film Noir." *Film Comment* (1972): 8.

Schulberg, Budd. *What Makes Sammy Run?* New York: Random House, 1941.

Sconce, Jeffrey. *Haunted Media: Electronic Presence from Telegraphy to Television*. Durham, NC: Duke University Press.

Scott-Clark, Cathy, and Adrian Levy. "Fast Forward into Trouble." *Guardian Weekend*, June 14, 2003, pp. 14–20.

Sedgwick, Eve Kosofsky. *Between Men: English Literature and Male Homosocial Desire*. New York: Columbia University Press, 1985.

_____. *Epistemology of the Closet*. Berkeley and Los Angeles: University of California Press, 1990.

Shlain, Leonard. *The Alphabet Versus the Goddess: The Conflict Between Word and Image*. New York: Viking, 1998.

Silverman, Kaja. *Male Subjectivity at the Margins*. New York: Routledge, 1992.

Smith, Anthony, ed. *Television: An International History*. 2nd ed. Oxford: Oxford University Press, 1998.

Smith, Valerie, ed. *Representing Blackness: Issues in Film and Video*. London: Athlone Press, 1997.

Sontag, Susan. "A Century of Cinema." In *Where the Stress Falls*, 117–22. New York: Picador, 2002.

Spigel, Lynn. *Make Room for TV: Television and the Family Ideal in Postwar America*. Chicago: University of Chicago Press, 1992.

_____. "The Making of a TV Literate Elite." In *The Television Studies Book*, edited by Christine Geraghty and David Lusted, 63–85. London: Arnold, 1998.

_____. "TV's Next Season?" *Cinema Journal* 45, no. 1 (2005): 83–90.

Staiger, Janet. *Media Reception Studies*. New York: New York University Press, 2005.

Stark, Steven D. *Glued to the Set*. New York: Free Press, 1997.

Stephens, Mitchell. *Rise of the Image, Fall of the Word*. Oxford: Oxford University Press, 1998.

Stokes, Jane. *On Screen Rivals: Cinema and Television in the United States and Britain*. New York: St. Martin's Press, 2000.

Sturcken, Frank. *Live Television: The Golden Age of 1946–1958 in New York*. Jefferson, NC: McFarland, 1990.

Smythe, Dallas. "On the Audience Commodity and Its Work." In *Media and Cultural Studies: Keyworks*, edited by Meenakshi Gigi Durham and Douglas M. Kellner, 253–79. Oxford: Blackwell, 2001.

Telotte, J. P. "Jerry in the City: The Topology of *The King of Comedy*." In *Enfant Terrible! Jerry Lewis in American Film*, edited by Murray Pomerance, 167–79. New York: New York University Press, 2002.

Thompson, Robert. "Too Many Cooks Don't Always Spoil the Broth: An Authorship Study of *St. Elsewhere*." In *Critical Approaches to Television*, edited by Leah R. Vande Berg, Lawrence A. Wenner, and Bruce E. Gronbeck, 78–92. Boston: Houthton Mifflin, 1998.

Torres, Sasha, ed.. *Living Color: Race and Television in the United States*. Durham, NC: Duke University Press, 1998.

Trow, George W. S. *Within the Context of No Context*. New York: Atlantic Monthly Press, 1997.

Venturi, Robert, Denise Brown, and Steven Izenour. *Learning from Las Vegas*, Rev. ed. Cambridge, MA: MIT Press, 1998.

Vidal, Gore. *Live from Golgotha: The Gospel According to Gore Vidal*. New York: Penguin, 1992.

Virilio, Paul. *Aesthetics of Disappearance*. Translated by Philip Beitchman. New York: Semiotext(e), 1991.

———. *Ground Zero*. Translated by Chris Turner. London: Verso, 2002.

———. "The Last Vehicle." In *Looking Back on the End of the World*, edited by Dietmar Kamper and Christoph Wulf, 106–19. New York: Semiotext(e), 1989.

Vonnegut, Kurt. *Timequake*. New York: G. P. Putnam's Sons, 1997.

Wagner, Jon, and Tracy Biga MacLean. "Cereality." In *Concerned Anthropophagists for the Rejuvenation of the Environment* 4 (1997): 3, 13–37.

Wallace, David Foster. *Infinite Jest*. Boston: Little, Brown, 1996.

Wartella, Ellen, and D. Charles Whitney. *Mass Media in a Popular Culture*. Thousand Oaks, CA: Sage, 1998.

White, Mimi. "Ideological Analysis and Television." In *Channels of Discourse, Reassembled*, 2nd ed., edited by Robert C. Allen, 161–202. Chapel Hill: University of North Carolina Press, 1987.